Oroville

OKANOGAN

Omak

Republic

FERRY

Kettle
Falls

Colville

PEND
OREILLE

Cusick

Chewelah

Priest
Lake

STEVENS

Nespelem

CHIEF
JOSEPH
DAM

GRAND COULEE
DAM

Grand
Coulee

Roosevelt Lake

SPOKANE

ELAN

DOUGLAS

Columbia

DRY FALLS

LINCOLN

Davenport

Mead

Spokane

Four Lakes

Cheney

Ford

d'A

C

ROCKY
REACH DAM

Wenatchee

ROCK ISLAND
DAM

Ephrata

Odessa

Sprague

Rosalia

WHITMAN

STEPTOE
★ BUTTE

GRANT

Moses
Lake

Moses
Lake

Ritzville

TTITAS

Ellensburg

Vantage

Warden

Lind

ADAMS

PALOUSE HILLS

Colfax

★ KAMIAK
BUTTE ★

Potla

La Crosse

Pullman

PRIEST
RAPIDS
DAM

Palouse

River

Yakima

Moxee City

Zillah

FRANKLIN

BENTON

Richland

Prosser

Yakima R.

Kennewick

ICE
HARBOR
DAM

Pasco

Snake

Riparia

River

GARFIELD

COLUMBIA

Dayton

Waitsburg

Asotin

ASOTIN

WALLA WALLA

Wallula

Walla Walla

McNARY DAM

DAY DAM

River

R.

Grande

Ronde

Wallowa R.

Scale

0   20   30   40   50 miles

Government of Washington State

Government of

Washington State

REVISED EDITION

By Mary W. Avery

UNIVERSITY OF WASHINGTON PRESS

SEATTLE AND LONDON

Library of Congress Cataloging in Publication Data

Avery, Mary Williamson, 1907-
    Government of Washington State.

    Published in 1951, 1955, and 1957 under title:
Government of the State of Washington; published
in 1961 as the government section of History and
government of the State of Washington.
    Includes bibliographies.
    1. Washington (State)--Politics and government.
I. Title.
JK9225 1967.A95 1973 353.9'797   73-13937
ISBN 0-295-95256-3

To the Memory of Emmett L. Avery

Preface to the 1973 Edition

This revision is an attempt to bring up to date the descriptive analysis of the structure of the state and local government of the state of Washington as presented in the previous edition of this book. Since the last revision, made in 1966, the Washington State Legislature has made a number of shifts in the structure of the administrative agencies, in some instances reorganizing such units more than once during this period. Inasmuch as I try to record any change in the name or function of existing state agencies (and the main local ones), so that a reader can trace the evolution of the present departments or other units from their beginning to the present time, I have mentioned changes made by the legislature since 1966, which were then sometimes repealed at a later session. Many of these references have been placed in footnotes, so that the reader who is interested only in the general development of the present governmental structure may omit them.

In order to indicate something of the day-to-day activities of as many as possible of the state governmental departments, in their implementation of the functions assigned to them by law, I have quoted fairly extensively from the various recent reports made by such agencies. Some of this statistical information has also been placed in footnotes, so that it will not interrupt the account of the general responsibilities of a particular office.

In this connection, I want to express my appreciation to the staffs of the state departments, who have been extremely helpful in answering questions and sending reports to me. For local government, the Washington State Association of Counties and the State Soil and Water Conservation Committee have been more than generous in their assistance, and I am very grateful to the members of all of these agencies as well as to the staffs of the Spokane Public Library and of the State Library, who have given a great deal of time to finding documents that I could not locate elsewhere.

Mary W. Avery

Spokane, Washington
January 1973

Preface to the 1966 Edition

This volume is a revision of the government section of *History and Government of the State of Washington* (1961), used as a text for Washington history and government courses in both colleges and high schools. Public officials and private citizens also benefit from having a general descriptive treatment of the current organization of state and local governmental agencies in the state. This book, brought up to date through the 1965 session of the Washington State Legislature, attempts to fill the needs of these various groups.

The material is taken almost entirely from primary sources—laws passed by the Washington territorial and state legislatures, decisions of the state supreme court, reports of executives and administrative agencies, and pertinent federal documents. The aim is to present a readable account of the present structure of our state and local government, showing the powers and duties of each office and its relations with other agencies; the evolution of the offices with current suggestions for changes intended to effect streamlining or greater efficiency in their operation; and a statement of the main problems confronting our legislature and courts. I have tried to indicate the advantages and disadvantages of proposals for the short ballot, reapportionment commission, unicameral legislature, combined county-city government, and other devices under consideration for the improvement of the machinery of government. The role of the ordinary citizen in working effectively for good government is stressed.

Over the years, so many people have helped with the preparation of one or another of the versions of this book that it is impossible to name them all. However, I should like to express my appreciation to Professor Herman J. Deutsch, Mrs. Alta Grim, Mrs. Hazel Mills, Glenn Jones, Norman Braden, Professors Paul L. Beckett, Claudius O. Johnson, Thor Swanson, and Emmett L. Avery, and the Washington State University Library administration and staff.

Mary W. Avery

Pullman, Washington
September 1966

Contents

Illustrations

Maps

Government of Washington State

1. Government of Washington Territory

The inhabitants of Washington participated in three separate governmental jurisdictions before statehood: the provisional government of Oregon, a local government in existence from 1843 to 1848; the territory of Oregon, 1848-53; and the territory of Washington, 1853-89. In this discussion, there will be no description of the Oregon provisional government, but it is necessary to consider the differences between the governmental system of a territory of the United States and that of a state in order to understand the transition from the territories of Oregon and Washington to statehood for Washington. As background, it is desirable to discuss briefly the way in which territories came into being and their basic characteristics.

UNITED STATES TERRITORIAL SYSTEM

In 1787 the United States Constitution had not yet been ratified, and the thirteen states which made up the United States at that time were still operating under the Articles of Confederation drawn up by them during the American Revolution. The states turned over to their new federal government the land outside their settled boundaries, running to the Mississippi on the west and to the Ohio River on the south, which they had held as British colonies. This area was known as the Northwest Territory.

Congress recognized that, as its population increased, the Northwest Territory would undoubtedly be divided into states. Until there were enough settlers to undertake the responsibilities of statehood, however, some form of government had to be provided. This would amount to a kind of probationary period. During this time, the settlers would have the protection of the United States government and basic rights of United States citizens, but they would not have the amount of self-government granted to actual states. The Ordinance of 1787, sometimes called the Northwest Ordinance, was drafted by Congress to provide a scheme of government in this prestate period for regions which were to be known as *territories*.

Later, the United States acquired other lands by purchase (Louisiana, for example), by treaty (Oregon), and as a result of war (the Philippines). As long as the territories made from these acquisitions were in North America, there was no doubt that they could some day be states. The various islands in the Atlantic and Pacific, however, presented a different problem. Before the days of the airplane, they were considered to be too far away to take part in our government as states. Moreover, in many of these islands, the residents were almost completely Asiatics who had a type of government then so different from ours that people doubted if they could ever adapt themselves sufficiently to our form to apply for statehood.

The question then arose as to whether the United States Constitution guaranteed to the residents of the islands the individual rights which it had, in practice, granted to those in the territories of the continental United States that would eventually be states. The United States Supreme Court, in various cases on this question, formulated the principle that all of the civil rights specified in the Constitution applied to the residents of those territories that were preparing for statehood. These were given the name *incorporated territories*. The Court ruled, however, that, as far as individual rights were concerned, only the fundamental parts of the United States Constitution applied to residents of the territories that, presumably, would never be states. These were called *unincorporated territories*.

The Supreme Court did not try to list all of the fundamental clauses in the United States Constitution—that is, clauses which protected individual rights so important and so universal that they should never be denied to anyone within the jurisdiction of the United States government. The Supreme Court decided in each case brought to it whether such a right had been violated.

It is interesting to note examples of constitutional requirements which have been held by the Court to apply to both kinds of territories. Congress may not pass a *bill of attainder* or an *ex post facto* law in either type of territory, for example, just as it may not for any state. A bill of attainder is a law taking away from a person his rights under the law, called his *civil rights*. An ex post facto law makes a crime of an act already committed, even though it was legal at the time it was done.

The United States Constitution specifies, too, that a state may not put a tariff on goods coming into it from another state, and the question arose as to whether this applied also to goods coming into the United States from an unincorporated territory, as Puerto Rico was at that time. The Court ruled that it did not. As long as Puerto Rico was not an incorporated territory, customs duties could be levied as though it were a foreign power. In a case in Hawaii where a man appealed a death sentence on the grounds that he had not had a jury trial, the Court ruled that the right of trial by jury is not a fundamental right, but one of procedure, called a *formal right*. The reasoning behind this ruling is that trial by jury is essentially a characteristic of the Anglo-Saxon legal system and that it might not achieve justice at all in a country whose judicial tradition was based on some other means of determining guilt.

Anything which is merely a *means* of arriving at justice and fundamental liberties for an individual is held not to be binding for an unincorporated territory, since some other means might achieve the result more efficiently. However, once a territory has been held by Congress to be an incorporated one and in preparation for statehood, all sections of the United States Constitution pertaining to individual rights apply, whether they are of a fundamental or of a procedural nature.

Organic Act

As Congress created each new territory, it wrote an *organic act* to give the outline of government for the territory. The details varied, depending on whether the territory was regarded as incorporated or unincorporated, how many inhabitants it had, how well it could support a government, and so on. However, each organic act was based largely on the Ordinance of 1787.

Appointment of Territorial Officials

Because territories are regarded as not yet prepared to govern themselves as states do, it would be expected that they would have less choice in the selection of their territorial officials. This proved to be the case. Instead of electing a governor and other territorial officials from among their own residents, the people had these officers appointed for them by the president of the United States. The Organic Act for Washington, enacted by Congress in 1853, stated that the territorial officials were to be governor, marshal, chief justice, two associate justices, territorial attorney, and secretary. The United States Senate was allowed to approve their appointment.

Not being able to elect these officials was a sore point with the residents of Washington Territory. They particularly resented having easterners sent out to govern them. In 1859 and many times thereafter, the territorial legislature sent memorials to Congress asking that the American citizens in United States territories be allowed to choose their own governors and judges. One concern was that appointed officials were frequently absent from the territory for such long periods that the people were inconvenienced. An 1866 memorial said that in 1865 two of the three judges were gone for so many months that no supreme court session was held, nor were some of the district court sessions. The legislators complained, in addition, that the problems of a distant region would be less familiar, and therefore more difficult to solve, for easterners than for local people.

In 1875 the Washington territorial residents were even more disgruntled because Congress had passed a law allowing the governor in a territory to appoint the auditor, the treasurer, and the superintendent of schools, instead of allowing the territorial legislature to appoint them or the voters to elect them. The legislature again sent a memorial to Congress protesting against this law. The petition made the point that since the salaries of these officials were paid from territorial funds, they should be chosen by the territory, as they had been since 1853. As a result, Congress repealed the law and allowed the voters again to elect their own auditor, treasurer, and school superintendent, but the president of the United States continued to appoint the governor, marshal, three justices, attorney and secretary.

Territorial Legislature

The Ordinance of 1787 prescribed two stages of territorial government. In the first, the territory had no legislative body, and its laws were passed by Congress. In the second stage, after the number of free white males in the territory had reached five thousand, it was granted a territorial legislature. Before 1853 when Congress adopted the Organic Act establishing Washington Territory, the national government had ceased to create territories of the first stage; consequently, although the entire population of Washington had not reached five thousand in 1853, Congress allowed the new territory of Washington to have a legislature, called a legislative assembly, from the beginning.

The territorial legislative assembly created by the Organic Act consisted of two houses: the upper house, called the council, and the lower house, called the house of representatives. At first, the people of the territory were allowed to elect nine members to the council and eighteen to the house of representatives. As the population increased, the Organic Act provided that the legislature could raise the number of members of the house of representatives to a maximum of thirty.

At the first session of the territorial legislature in 1854, the members raised the number in the house of representatives to twenty-two, and by 1877 the number in the house had been increased to thirty. The council continued to consist of nine members until 1879 when Congress allowed the legislature to raise its size to twelve, but required that the number in the house be reduced to twenty-four. In 1879 the legislature petitioned Congress to set the number for the council by dividing the population by eighteen, and to have at least one member in the house for each two thousand people in the territory.

The population at that time was 57,784.

At the beginning of the territorial period, the legislature met every year, but in 1865 the legislators sent a memorial to Congress, stating that there was not enough legislative business to warrant the legislators' leaving their farms and businesses every year. Besides, they said, printing costs were so high and the territory so large that copies of the *Session Laws* often did not reach people for a year. This meant that the legislators frequently changed a law without really knowing how it had worked, since the people had not yet had a chance to try it out. Congress granted their request, and the sessions were made biennial with the 1869 session, the next one being held in 1871.

Congress evidently thought that if our territorial legislators did not need to meet each year, they did not require sixty days for a session (the length of time allowed by the Organic Act); consequently, Congress cut the session to forty days. The legislators found, however, that this period was too short, and in 1877 they petitioned Congress to allow them sixty days every other year. They explained that the great size of the territory plus the variety of climate and occupational interests—such as mining, lumbering, shipping, fishing, grazing, and shipbuilding—required that they give more than forty days to the discussion of the territory's affairs. Congress allowed them to return to the sixty-day period in 1883.

The large area and small population made it necessary for the county and city governments to act much more on their own responsibility than they do today. In one instance, a board of county commissioners decided to annul a law passed by the legislature because the commissioners did not approve of it. In 1875, while Spokane and Stevens counties were joined, the legislature changed the county seat from Colville to Spokane and ordered the county commissioners, who lived in Colville, to move the county records to Spokane by 1 May 1876. W. P. Winans, a pioneer, reports that in the *Journal of the Stevens County Commissioners* for 26 April 1876 the commissioners recorded their decision that the law regarding the county seat change was void. It had been passed as an amendment to a law which had been repealed in the meantime, and the commissioners stated that it was impossible to amend a law after it had been repealed. The county seat for Stevens County remained at Colville. Now, of course, a law passed by the state legislature could be declared void only by the courts.

Congressional Supervision of the Territorial Legislature

As stated in the Organic Act, the territorial legislature was allowed to pass laws on any subject on which Congress had not forbidden it to legislate. In practice, this meant that the legislature, meeting in Olympia, could take care of all local matters—type of county organization, procedure for elections, local taxation, road building and maintenance, schools, public welfare, and similar matters. Copies of all laws passed by the legislature had to be sent to Congress, however, and Congress could veto any law it disapproved. Congress vetoed one law, passed by the territorial legislature in 1865, to divide Skamania County between Clark and Klickitat counties and abolish the Skamania County government. The support for the territorial law had come from people in Skamania County and elsewhere who were trying to break the Oregon Steam Navigation Company's monopoly on transportation on the Columbia River. The company owned not only the commercial ships on sections of the river above Portland, but also the portage railroad around the Cascades, which had been built on the Oregon side of the Columbia. The Washington Territory Transportation Company was formed to build a rival portage railroad on the north side of the river, but the Skamania County officials were so closely associated with the Oregon Steam Navigation Company that they managed to block the granting of rights-of-way across the older company's land. Consequently, the Washington Territorial Legislature abolished the county so that the Washington company could secure the needed permission from Clark and Klickitat counties, which were not under the control of the Oregon Steam Navigation Company. That company, however, sent a lobbyist to Washington, D.C., who was able to persuade Congress to veto the territorial law abolishing Skamania County, and the Oregon Steam Navigation Company was thus able to maintain its monopoly for a number of years afterward.

A second law vetoed by Congress was an arrangement of the districts for holding territorial district courts in 1868. The president of the United States had appointed Christopher C. Hewitt as chief justice of the territorial supreme court for Washington Territory. As a supreme court judge, he was also judge of one of the district courts in the territory. So many people disliked Justice Hewitt that the legislature changed the boundaries of the court districts in such a way that Stevens County constituted a single district. Justice Hewitt was assigned to this district and was required to live there. This would obviously hinder him greatly in presiding over the meetings of the territorial supreme court in Olympia, and Congress vetoed this law as an arbitrary one. Ordinarily, however, Congress interfered with few territorial laws.

One can easily see that Congress had much more control over a territorial legislature than it does over a state legislature, since Congress cannot veto a law passed by a state legislature.

Territorial Representatives in Congress

In addition to electing the members of the territorial legislature, the people of Washington Territory also were allowed by the Organic Act to elect a delegate to the United States House of Representatives in Washington, D.C. Unlike the representatives in Congress from our states, however, the territorial delegate could not vote. His only privilege was that of introducing and speaking on bills being considered by the House, called the *privilege of debate.*

Territorial Taxation

Because Congress levied taxes on the new territory and because the Washington territorial delegate to Congress had no vote, those taxes were actually "taxation without representation," a principle which had caused much agitation at the time of the American Revolution. In fact, the territorial legislature referred to this parallel situation in a memorial sent to Congress in 1883. The usual justification for this practice was that the federal government contributed so much money to the support of the territory that the receipts overbalanced the amount paid in taxes. The legislators in Washington Territory, however, did not agree. In the 1883 memorial, they stated that the congressional appropriation for the territory was a "trifling contribution" and that the territory bore the brunt of the costs of government. They mentioned that the territorial government spent over sixty thousand dollars each year just to support an insane asylum, a penitentiary, and a university, and that the taxpayers in the territory would gladly pay the salaries of the governor and secretary in order to have the privilege of electing them. One newspaper editor did prefer territorial government to that of a state because of the money contributed by Congress to a territory. An article in the *Olympia Overland Press* quoted sums—such as $222,600 for mail service, $330,000 for military roads, and so on—reaching a figure of over $100 for each person in the territory. He was in a decided minority, however.

In the Organic Act for Washington Territory, Congress had appropriated $10,000 for capitol buildings, plus sections 16 and 36 in each township for the support of public schools. In addition, annual salaries were specified for the appointive territorial officials and members of the territorial legislature. For example, the governor was to receive $1,500 plus $1,500 for acting as superintendent of Indian affairs; the three justices $2,000 each; the secretary $1,500; and the members of the legislature $3.00 per diem and a travel allowance.

Territorial Court System

In the Organic Act for Washington Territory, Congress stipulated that the court system was to consist of a supreme court, district courts, probate courts, and courts of justices of the peace. The federal government would appoint three judges, who would, as a group, be the supreme court for the territory and, individually, act as the judges for the district courts. The territory was left free to choose the probate court judges and the justices of the peace in whatever way the legislature wished.

At the beginning of the territorial period, the legislature divided the territory into three judicial districts, one for each of the three judges. Each judge was required to hold a session of the district court twice a year in each county of his district, except for the smallest counties, which were combined for judicial purposes. The district courts tried all criminal cases except petty ones, which were assigned to courts of justices of the peace, and all civil suits in which the amount claimed was over $100, except for probate cases, which were heard in the separate probate courts.

Inasmuch as these same three judges also met as the supreme court to hear cases appealed from the district courts, one of the supreme court judges would have presided at the original trial in the lower court. Because the purpose in an appellate hearing is to have a second look at a case, the whole principle of an objective review is spoiled when the first judge is allowed to participate in the analysis by the second court.

The people in Washington Territory evidently resented this situation because in 1883 the legislature asked Congress to establish a fourth judicial district in the territory. Then the district judge who had presided at a trial in the district court would not act as a member of the supreme court when that particular case was being heard. Congress agreed to the request, and four districts were set up in 1886.

The legislature, at its first session, decided to allow the voters to elect a probate judge for each county for a three-year term. In all cases involving probate of wills and testaments, the probate courts had *exclusive jurisdiction*, that is, they were the only courts allowed to hear such cases.

The territorial probate courts could appoint persons to act as administrators or executors in settling an estate; they could appoint and dismiss guardians for orphans or insane persons, or for apprentices; they could hear disputes over wills or the actions of a guardian; and they could examine and approve or disapprove the claims for payment made by any of these appointees or claims made against the guardians or administrators by anyone else in connection with their official duties.

Twice during the territorial period, the legislature tried having the probate courts hear criminal cases and some civil suits besides probate cases, but this additional jurisdiction was not maintained long in either instance. In 1857 the probate courts were given a criminal term each month during which the probate judge plus one justice of the peace (or two if there was more than one justice in the county) made up a court to hear criminal cases punishable by a term in the county jail instead of the penitentiary. The county auditor was made the clerk for these criminal sessions. Civil cases in which the amount in controversy was less than $500 could also be heard by the probate courts, in addition to the district courts; but for the civil cases, the probate judge was to act without the justices of the peace. Two years later the criminal and civil jurisdiction was taken away from the probate courts, and they were confined to hearing estate matters only.

Then in 1863 probate courts were again given *concurrent jurisdiction* with the district courts in the types of criminal and civil cases mentioned in the preceding paragraph. When two different types of courts are given concurrent jurisdiction for certain cases, either court may hear them. The second time, the probate courts had the additional power for only one year, and it may be that the 1863 law represented one of the kind mentioned earlier, where the law was repealed before some of the court officials in the territory knew that it had been passed. At that time neither the probate court judges nor the justices of the peace were required to have a law degree, and people probably did not like having them decide civil and criminal cases in which knowledge of the law might make a difference.

The territorial inhabitants were conscious, however, of their need for some kind of local courts with jurisdiction over cases which lay between those handled by courts of justices of the peace and those heard in the district courts. In 1865 the legislature sent a memorial to Congress urging that it raise the civil jurisdiction of courts of justices of the peace to cases involving $200 because of the long distances to be traveled from some isolated areas to the nearest district court. Eighteen years later Congress responded by doing even more than had been requested. In 1883 it raised the amount to $300 for justice of the peace courts, but in 1891 the figure was returned to the original $100.

With this exception, the jurisdiction of the courts of justices of the peace remained almost the same during the territorial period. Samples of the civil cases involving not more than $100 are: an action that someone might take to make another fulfill a contract; a suit for damages to one's person or his property; a claim against someone who had defaulted on a bond; a suit to foreclose a mortgage or a lien on personal property; an action to recover money from someone who had made use of a mining claim to which he did not have the legal right. In any such cases, however, if the title to real property was involved, the case would have to be tried by a district court rather than by a court of a justice of the peace, and the same requirement was made if the action involved claims for damages for false imprisonment, slander, or seduction. Also, as we have seen in connection with probate courts, if someone brought a complaint against a person because of his actions as an administrator or executor of an estate, he would have to bring suit in the probate court rather than in a court of a justice of the peace.

As far as criminal cases were concerned, in 1854 the justices of the peace could try those for which the fine would be $30.00 or less. In 1860 the amount was raised to $100. Samples of such crimes as given in the territorial laws are: assault and battery; violation of estray laws in regard to keeping livestock from running at large or seizing stray animals unlawfully; obstruction of highways and bridges; forcible entry; malicious trespass; petty larceny; public nuisance.

If a case was appealed from a court of a justice of the peace, it went to the district court, and from there appeals went to the supreme court of the territory. We shall consider court matters in more detail when we study our state judicial system in chapter 5.

Public Schools

From the beginning of its territorial period, Washington has been fortunate in having specific money for the support of public schools. In the Organic Act creating the territory of Washington, it was stated that sections 16 and 36 in each township in the new territory were to be used for the common schools of the territory. These lands could be sold or leased, and the money thus received was to be used only for school expenses.

Territorial Capital

In the Organic Act, the first governor was ordered to set the time and place for the election to choose the congressional delegate and the members of the first legislature. He was also to name the temporary capital for the territory until the people could select the permanent one at an election. Governor Isaac Stevens reached Olympia in late November 1853, named that town the temporary capital, and set 30 January 1854 as the day for the election.

First Territorial Legislature

The first legislature of any government unit has to act as a kind of additional constitutional convention by completing the framework of the new government outlined in the document creating it—in this case, the Organic Act drawn up by Congress. The first Washington legislature had to create offices and to specify the procedure to be followed by the various governmental agencies. It had to establish a salary scale for local officials and to provide a system of taxation to finance the government. It had to regulate the activities of the officials in each department so that roads, schools, county buildings, court proceedings, property-title registration, and all of the other governmental functions might be provided. We shall include these topics in the history of our state and county agencies which were later responsible for these activities.

The first legislature for the territory of Washington was composed of ten farmers, seven lawyers, four mechanics, two merchants, two lumbermen, one civil engineer, and one surveyor. This group, which represented the various interests of the people fairly well, accepted Governor Stevens' suggestion that a commission or committee from the legislature be appointed to draw up the first code of laws. When the commission made its report after several weeks, it was accepted almost without change, and this code of laws remained the foundation of the government of the territory until it was made a state in 1889.

ENABLING ACT

When Congress admitted Washington as a state, it brought into the union at that same time Montana, North Dakota, and South Dakota. The bill granting statehood to Washington, Montana, and Dakota territories was called an *omnibus bill* because it covered all of them in one document. The sections in the bill pertaining to the organization of the state of Washington are referred to as our *Enabling Act* because their purpose was to "enable" the territory of Washington to become the state of Washington.

The Enabling Act listed the steps the territory must take before Congress would declare it a state. Inasmuch as the United States Supreme Court has ruled that Congress has sole control over the admission of states, a territory has to comply with the requirements of its Enabling Act or remain a territory. Once a territory has been admitted as a state, however, Congress has much less control over it. There is then no way for Congress to keep a new state from amending its constitution if it wishes to change some clause put in only because the Enabling Act required it.

If a state, whether new or old, amends its constitution or passes a law contrary to the Constitution of the United States or its laws or treaties, the state law will in due time be declared void by a federal court, but Congress has no power to veto a state constitution or law.

In several cases, the United States Supreme Court has ruled on whether or not a state is bound by requirements in its Enabling Act, and it has followed the principle that Congress may require of a new state only what it may demand of an older state, or what is in the nature of a contract between Congress and the new state. If the federal government and a new state were to agree that for a period of years the state would impose no tax on state land sold by the federal government, the agreement would be binding on the state because it is definitely in the form of a contract—it would relate to the value of land in contracts made by individuals.

For example, in the proposed state constitution for Arizona, there was a clause permitting the voters of the new state to remove a judge by popular vote, a method of ousting an elected official known as the *recall*. Congress passed a resolution to admit Arizona under its proposed state constitution, but President William Howard Taft vetoed this resolution because the proposed Arizona Constitution contained the provision for the recall of judges. The territory of Arizona removed that provision and was then admitted as a state; but Arizona soon amended its constitution, restoring the recall of judges. The Supreme Court then ruled that this state had a right to make such an amendment because the matter of the recall was a political one over which Congress had no control.

Representative Form of Government

In establishing the requirements for Washington Territory to become a state, Congress directed the people of the territory to elect seventy-five delegates to a constitutional convention to be held in Olympia. There were many specific statements as to what this constitution had to contain. For example, the Enabling Act instructed the convention delegates to provide a republican form of government in the new state. We think of the term *republican* as applying only to a political party of that name, but, in this usage, with a lower-case *r*, it refers to a government by representatives elected by the people in the area concerned. Thus, the Washington constitutional delegates had to provide that the laws governing the residents of the new state would be passed by a group of legislators elected for that purpose by the voters of the state.

The federal Constitution requires each state to have a republican (representative) government; however, the Constitution does not say which branch of the federal government is to enforce this requirement. Therefore, the Supreme Court has ruled that guaranteeing to a state a representative form of government is a matter belonging to the political branches of the federal government—Congress and the president. If Congress seats the senators and representatives sent to it from any state, it does, by that act, admit that the state has a form of government sufficiently representative of its people to qualify. Because it is a political matter, the Court will not make specifications saying that a certain percentage of the citizens must be allowed to vote in order for the state to have a republican form of government.

We shall learn in a later chapter that the Fifteenth Amendment to the United States Constitution says that no state shall forbid a person to vote because of his race or color, and that the Nineteenth Amendment states that a person's sex may not be used as a basis for preventing him or her from voting; but a state can make any other qualifications for voting that it wishes. The Fourteenth Amendment, passed after the Civil War, contained an attempt to force the southern states to allow Negroes to vote by providing that the number of a state's representatives in Congress should be cut in proportion to the number of male citizens above the age of twenty-one in that state who were not allowed to vote. No attempt has been made to enforce this provision.

At the present time, however, Congress is using other means to try to force states to allow Negroes, primarily in the deep-South states, to vote. In 1965 it passed a law permitting federal registrars of voters to be sent to states in which persons could demonstrate that they were not included in the regular state registration machinery because of their color or race. Agitation for this protection increased greatly after the 1954 and later decisions of the United States Supreme Court that segregation of races in public institutions or in private agencies providing public accommodations is unconstitutional. Courts were then able to consider individual complaints of discrimination in various phases of life, and Congress has now written such decisions into law.

The United States Supreme Court is now also willing to consider another aspect of voting rights, that of apportionment, which means the number of persons represented by a state legislator or national congressman. We will discuss apportionment in the chapter on the electorate, and in that chapter we shall also treat the recent requirement by Congress that age be taken into account, too, in qualifications for voting for the president and vice-president of the United States—that the states must allow persons eighteen years old to vote for those offices.

Civil Rights

The Enabling Act ordered delegates to the Washington constitutional convention to be certain that the people were protected in a number of specific rights. For example, everyone was to have religious freedom, and no one was to have any civil or political right taken away from him because of his race or color. These are also requirements of the United States Constitution. The federal Bill of Rights, which consists of the first ten amendments to the national Constitution, forbids *Congress* to interfere with freedom of religion, of speech, and of the press, and the many other civil rights taken for granted now. The Bill of Rights, though, does not control any state government in this respect. If the Bill of Rights were the only safeguard of individual rights in the United States Constitution, there would be nothing in it to prevent a state government from establishing a state church or suppressing many personal rights. The Fourteenth Amendment to the United

States Constitution does, however, prohibit a state government from passing any law which removes any privileges that its residents have as United States citizens. The amendment adds that no state shall "deprive any person of life, liberty, or property, without due process of law; nor deny to any person within its jurisdiction the equal protection of the laws." In the United States Constitution, therefore, it is the Fourteenth Amendment, rather than the Bill of Rights, that protects the civil rights of an individual from acts of state government.

Strictly speaking, therefore, it would be unnecessary in a state constitution to prohibit a state from violating personal rights. In practice, however, people like to have such clauses repeated in their state constitutions as a kind of double protection.

Land Grants for Schools

We saw that in the Organic Act, Congress set aside part of the public lands for territorial uses. The grant of two sections in each township for schools was particularly important. In the Enabling Act for the state of Washington, this grant of school lands was confirmed, and the significant clause was added that these lands could not be sold for less than $10.00 an acre (at that time, this represented a much higher value on land than it does today). This restriction was included to prevent a state official from accepting a bribe to sell the school lands for practically nothing.

In the Enabling Act, it was also stipulated that money received from the sale of these lands was to go into a *permanent school fund* and that only the interest on this money could be spent. The fund itself, called the principal, would thus never get smaller, and a continuing source of money would always be available for our public schools. The Enabling Act gave other sources of income to the schools, such as 5 percent of the money received from the sale of all other state lands. Later, the state legislature added tax levies and other means of producing money for the schools, and these will be discussed in chapters 2 and 7.

In the Enabling Act, large grants of land were also made for the use and support of state normal schools, state capitol buildings, and state charitable and reforming institutions. Title to all lands not transferred to the new state or claimed already by individuals was to remain in the hands of the federal government for its disposal.

Method for Ratifying the State Constitution

The Enabling Act specified that after the state constitution was written by the elected delegates to the constitutional convention, the voters of the territory were to vote on whether they wished to accept it as the basis for their state government. If they accepted (*ratified*) it, the constitution would be submitted to the president of the United States for approval before the state of Washington could be declared in existence.

WASHINGTON STATE'S CONSTITUTION

Constitutional Convention, 1889

The seventy-five delegates to the constitutional convention included three delegates from each of the territory's twenty-five legislative districts. In order to give some representation to the minority party, which at that time was the Democratic party, Congress included a provision that each voter in a district could vote for only two delegates. The territorial central committee of each party recommended candidates, but the campaigning was done largely by the political groups in each district; as a result, the platform of the same party differed in various parts of the state. In fact, both the Republicans and the Democrats in many areas of the territory adopted the same principles—restricting the legislature in the state constitution, protecting the rights of individuals, and regulating corporations. Many of the candidates made speeches promising that, if elected, they would work to keep the railroad companies under strict control. The convention delegates were chosen at an election on 14 May 1889, and they met in Olympia on 4 July. The delegation consisted of forty-three Republicans, twenty-nine Democrats, and three independents. They came from all sections of the United States, and there were a number from foreign countries: five from Scotland, three from Germany, two from Ireland, and two from Canada. Only one had been born in the territory of Washington. There were twenty-one lawyers, thirteen farmers, six merchants, six doctors, five bankers, four cattlemen, three teachers, two real-estate dealers, two editors, two hop-growers, two loggers, two lumbermen, one minister, one surveyor, one fisherman, and one mining engineer. The variety of interests present probably contributed to the well-rounded constitution produced by the group.

Models for Our State Constitution

The convention employed court reporters to record in shorthand all of the speeches and debate in the assembly, but unfortunately Congress had not appropriated sufficient funds to pay for transcribing the proceedings, and they were destroyed later. A summary of the proceedings was made, in addition, and the secretary of state retained this in its original form until 1962, when it was published as *The Journal of the Washington State*

State Capitol, Olympia. In 1889-90, the voters chose Olympia to be the permanent capital. The capitol building was completed in 1928 and cost more than $7,380,000. (Photo by Washington State Department of Commerce and Economic Development)

Constitutional Convention.[1]

The delegates were naturally influenced by constitutions of other states with which they were familiar. The constitutions of Oregon, California (particularly for the court system), and Wisconsin seem to have been used most often, although altogether provisions from twenty-three state constitutions were included. W. L. Hill had published a proposed constitution in the *Portland Oregonian,* and the delegates approved of it sufficiently to use it as their basis. They also considered a proposed constitution drawn up by the Walla Walla Constitutional Convention of 1878, which the people had approved at that time, but which had not been acted upon by Congress. In addition, the delegates received resolutions from civic groups, cities, territorial officials, and individual lobbyists. When all these various sources had been analyzed and the constitution brought together, the delegates had to be certain that it contained nothing contrary to any provision of the United States Constitution or of the Enabling Act.

Characteristics of Our State Constitution

As a result of this blending of many suggestions to fit individual needs, our state constitution has several striking features. One is the large number of restrictions on the powers of the state legislature. The debate on the powers of the legislature began with its size. Some delegates favored a large legislature on the grounds that it would be too expensive for corporations and other special interests to corrupt a large body, but that they could bribe or otherwise influence a small group. Other delegates maintained just the opposite stand—that a large legislature was too expensive for the people to support and that if the leaders of either a small or large group were corrupted, the rest would follow. The final vote favored a maximum of 99 members in the house, and not more than half of that in the senate.

One aspect of the size was the question of whether the legislature should consist of one or two houses (a house of representatives and senate). The fact that they considered a *unicameral* (one-house) legislature is surprising, inasmuch as a *bicameral* (two-house) legislature was maintained by all states at that time, and a unicameral legislative body had not been seriously considered since the Illinois convention of 1870. In 1934 the voters in Nebraska adopted a unicameral legislature, but even now it is the only state that does not have a bicameral legislature. Many of the delegates to our 1889 constitutional convention thought that it would be interesting and probably

1. Ed. Beverly Paulik Rosenow (Seattle: Book Publishing Company, 1962). The editor has included in an appendix as much of the delegates' opinions and remarks as she could locate in newspaper accounts of the time and later reminiscent statements, research articles, and doctoral dissertations.

more efficient to have a one-house legislature, but they were evidently uneasy about such a drastic experiment. On 23 July 1889, the *Seattle Post-Intelligencer* expressed the hope that some other state would try it out.

Once the bicameral legislature was chosen, the delegates set about defining its powers, which were limited in many ways: the legislature could meet only for a specific time—sixty days every other year; it could raise neither its own salaries nor those of the executive officials above a certain point; it could not pass special laws (those for one person or group) on a large number of subjects; and it could have very little leeway in establishing types of courts. It was even proposed that a clause be included in the constitution requiring each legislator to take an oath that he would not accept a bribe. This was defeated because the majority of the delegates realized that the legislature itself would have to set its standards for the ethical conduct of its members if those standards were to be effective. The fear of an overly powerful or corrupt legislature was so great that a delegate was quoted in a Tacoma newspaper as saying that if a foreigner were suddenly dropped into the convention, he would think that the delegates were fighting a great enemy—the legislature.

The delegates seemed to be less afraid of the executive officials than of a legislature, and, as a result, gave more powers to our governor than the chief executive of many states has. This trust in the executive did not extend to all of the delegates, however. Some argued for allowing the legislature to override the governor's veto by a simple majority, and a few wanted him to have no veto power whatever. Delegates who were familiar with constitutional theory and practice in other states were able to demonstrate that a governor has to have some means of curbing unwise legislation. As a result, the convention gave our governor a more complete veto power than the governor of any other state has—the Washington governor can not only veto a complete bill, but also any item in any bill. The usual two-thirds majority of members present in a legislative session is required to override his veto.

A petition sent to the constitutional convention showed that the people wanted a long list of elective officials. They felt that they would be safer if they had great elective power. The delegates granted their requests by creating eight elective executive offices, to which the legislature later added a ninth.

Statutory Material

If constitutional delegates try to limit the power of the legislators or other public officials by placing many specific restrictions on their actions, the resulting constitution will contain matters of detail as well as fundamental principles. The former often cause trouble because detailed procedures ordinarily need to be altered from time to time, and it is difficult to change a state constitution. In our case, any constitutional amendment must have the approval of the members of each house of the state legislature before it can be submitted to the voters at an election, and then it must be approved by a majority of those voting before it can go into effect.

A law passed by the state legislature, however, may be changed or repealed simply by a majority vote of the legislators. Matters of detail in a constitution are thus called *statutory* material—provisions that are better handled by laws *(statutes)* than by clauses in the constitution. Without statutory items, a constitution deals only with matters of principle or fundamental policies, and these change as people's ideas change in regard to what functions they expect from a government. Ordinarily, such developments are very slow, and there is time for constitutional amendments to take care of them.

Maximum Salary Regulations

One statutory item in our state constitution that needed to be revised for a long time was the matter of maximum salaries. In 1889 the maximum salary of $6,000 set for the governor seemed large enough to be adequate at any time in the future, but by the 1920s, such a salary was absurdly low for a person having desirable qualifications for the governorship. Our governors then had to be men who either had private means or were willing to make a real financial sacrifice in taking the office. Such a necessity naturally limited the number of qualified people from whom candidates could be secured, not only for governor, but also for the other executive positions, which were under similar salary restrictions, except for the commissioner of public lands. In 1948 the voters approved a constitutional amendment removing these maximum figures, and the legislators may now fix their own and the other salaries at whatever figures they think wise.

Other examples of statutory material in our state constitution will be discussed in later chapters, which deal with the appropriate subjects.

Regulations Regarding Corporations

The large number of farmers among the convention delegates represented a group that was afraid of the growth of corporations, particularly railroads. Many of the delegates agreed that such corporations were profiting from land holdings which the people of Washington Territory could otherwise have had. As a result, the members of the constitutional convention wrote into the state constitution many regulations in regard to corporations, and to railroads in particular. For example, railroads were declared to be common carriers and thus under legislative control; and they were not to share earnings or make discriminating charges between groups of people in Washington or between Washington and other states.

The farmers in the constitutional convention would have liked to go even further in restricting corporations. Proposals were made that the constitution provide for an elective railroad commission, which would have the power to regulate rates charged within the state, and that each corporation doing business for profit in the state would have to maintain an office where its books would be open for inspection. The constitutional delegates received many protests in letters, telegrams, and editorials in newspapers against these clauses. The opponents argued that the new state could not develop without good transportation and that anything that would inhibit railroad construction in the state would be injurious to its economic progress. Consequently, neither of these requirements was put into the state constitution, but, as a compromise, in Article XII, Section 18, the statement was made that the legislature was to pass laws fixing maximum passenger and freight rates and that it might, if it wished, create a "railroad commission" whose powers and duties would be defined by the legislature. In chapter 3, we shall trace the history of the legislature's actions in this matter.

Land Titles (Private and Public)

The emphasis on the right to hold land can be seen, too, in Article XIX of the state constitution, which orders the legislature to exempt part of a person's property from being sold for debts. The legislature provided that, it a person owns a home, he may register it as his homestead, and a part of it cannot be seized for most types of debts. Certain exemptions were also made for personal property. This idea of land for individuals as against land for big business organizations was later a part of the platform of the People's party, which was influential in the state of Washington during the 1890s. The clause prohibiting aliens from owning land in the state was the result of anti-Chinese feeling that remained after the bitterness of the earlier anti-Chinese riots. The clause preventing ownership of land in the state by persons not United States citizens was not removed until 1966 when the voters approved a constitutional amendment repealing that clause.

The question of public lands also caused one of the most heated debates during the convention. Tide and harbor lands would come under the control of the new state, as well as the lands granted to the state by the federal government for schools. Shipping companies and other industrial concerns were eager to buy the shore area of Puget Sound, particularly at the points where the water was deep enough for good harbors. The presence of oil and other minerals along the shore out to the low-tide line made the entire coast potentially very valuable, and the timber and minerals as well as their agricultural capacity made the school lands a great prize, too.

Some people lobbied to have the convention give the cities concerned title to the harbor and tide lands, because they felt certain that the city councils would then sell the land to them. Delegates from east of the Cascades and some of those from the west believed strongly that the state would lose a tremendous amount of money if these lands were sold. Judge George Turner, a Spokane delegate, led the fight to keep the ownership of these lands for the state. The pressure to sell tide lands became so strong that the convention divided the question into harbor lands and tide lands. Permanent ownership of harbor lands was left to the state under the control of a harbor line commission, and a clause was added forbidding any lease of such lands for longer than thirty-five years. For the tide lands, the most that the advocates of state control could get was the statement that these lands belonged to the state. This left the legislature free to allow them to be sold, retained, or leased. With the present increased demand for recreational use of water and beaches along salt- and fresh-water shores in the state, the question of the right of an owner of such property to prevent public use of the beach is still vehemently debated.

At first, nearly all of the delegates favored retention of school lands by the state. But when they realized that if all of this land had to be leased indefinitely the state would become involved to an unwieldy extent in running farms, lumber operations, and industries, they changed their minds. The constitution therefore does not forbid the sale of school lands, but it does include reasonable safeguards for their disposal. These will be discussed in connection with the financing of our schools.

Questions of Prohibition and Woman Suffrage

On two questions, the convention delegates could not make up their minds—woman suffrage and prohibition of the sale of alcoholic beverages. In 1883 the territorial legislature had allowed women to vote, but in 1887 the territorial supreme court declared woman suffrage unconstitutional on the basis of the Organic Act. Since a state constitution was being written, such a provision could be included, and then there would be no doubt as to its legality. There was still so much argument about the matter, though, that the delegates hesitated to commit themselves, as they did also about the problem of liquor sales. Although there was considerable sentiment in favor of prohibition, this again was a question on which opinion was divided.

Because the constitution had to be presented to the people for ratification at an election, the delegates decided to let them vote at the same time on the questions of woman suffrage and prohibition as separate items. Both pro- posals were defeated in the election, woman suffrage by about two to one and prohibition by a smaller margin. In 1910 the state's voters adopted a constitutional amendment allowing women to vote from 1912 on, eight years before the national woman suffrage amendment. This will be discussed in more detail in chapter 6.

RATIFICATION OF OUR STATE CONSTITUTION

The people voted to accept the constitution by a ratio of almost four to one. The vote was 40,152 to 11,879. The counties that voted against ratifying the constitution—Asotin, Walla Walla, Franklin, Columbia, and Garfield—were angry because the convention had refused to provide in the state constitution that a county might subsidize a railroad. The issue had arisen in 1887 when G. W. Hunt, president of the Oregon and Washington Territorial Railroad Company, had offered to build a railroad line to connect Walla Walla with the Northern Pacific line for a subsidy of $100,000. This amount was almost completely subscribed by 1889 when Hunt said that he would extend the line to Dayton, Waitsburg, and the Grande Ronde valleys and release part of the subscription demanded if bonds were issued instead by the counties. The Oregon Railroad and Navigation Company did not want this competition and lobbied against the subsidy. Some delegates, too, were afraid that county officials could not withstand pressure for issuing bonds in larger amounts than was wise and so voted against this proposal. In retaliation, many of the voters in the counties affected voted against accepting the state constitution. Their number was too small to prevent ratification, however.

President Benjamin Harrison, upon receiving word of the ratification of the constitution, examined it and was satisfied that it contained all of the requirements specified in the Enabling Act. On 11 November 1889 he declared that the state of Washington was admitted to the union. Since 11 November later became the date for celebrating the armistice for the First World War, until recently we observed both occasions on the same date under the title Veterans' Day. The 1969 legislature, however, changed Veterans' Day to the fourth Monday in October.

FIRST STATE LEGISLATURE

Even with the statutory items mentioned above, our state constitution is fairly well limited to general principles of state government. Consequently, the first state legislature had to act somewhat as a supplementary constitutional convention in order to complete the organization of our new state government. For example, it had to define the duties of each state official required by the constitution and to set the salary for each within constitutional limits, if there were such. The legislature found it necessary, also, to add to the offices established by the constitution. Examples of the offices created in the 1889-90 session or continued by it from territorial days are: insurance commissioner, state geologist, state printer, fish commissioner, game warden, state librarian, State Library Commission, State Medical Examining Board, national guard officers, Mining Bureau, State School Land Commission, and state sealer of weights and measures. The titles for many of these offices have been changed by succeeding legislatures, and their present forms will be noted in later chapters on the subjects to which the offices pertain.

In the first session of the state legislature, too, laws had to be passed, or territorial laws adapted, to cover taxation and public finance, roads, elections, education, types of county and city government, railroads and other public utilities, insurance, public and private lands, irrigation, systems of courts, and court practices to be followed in civil and criminal cases. This was a difficult task, but the legislature succeeded in producing a workable system of state and local government, which has gradually evolved into its present form.

The 1889-90 legislature ordered the voters to decide whether the state capital should remain at Olympia or be moved to North Yakima or Ellensburg, and the vote left it at Olympia.

State Symbols

A state ordinarily has certain objects as its symbols, usually products identified with the state's flora and fauna plus a flag. Our state legislature has recognized a flag, tree, flower, bird, fish, and song as official symbols of the state of Washington.

The state flag must be of dark green silk or bunting with a reproduction of the state seal in the center. If a fringe is used, it is to be of the same gold or yellow color as the seal. The state tree is the western hemlock, *Tsuga heterophylla,* the state flower is the *Rhododendron macrophyllum,* the state bird is the willow goldfinch, and the fish is the steelhead trout, *Salmo gairdnerii.* The last was not added until 1969.

In 1969 the legislature revised the list of legal holidays in the state as follows: Sundays; New Year's Day; February 12, Abraham Lincoln's birthday; the third Monday of February, celebrated as George Washington's birthday; the last Monday of May for Memorial Day; July 4th; the first Monday in September, Labor Day; the second Monday of October, Columbus Day; the fourth Monday of October, Veterans' Day; the fourth Thursday in November, Thanksgiving; December 25, Christmas; general election day; any day proclaimed by the governor as a legal holiday.

SUGGESTED READINGS

The chief primary sources for a study of the territorial government of Washington and the creation of our state are the *Session Laws of Washington Territory;* the Organic Act; *The Journal of the Washington State Constitutional Convention, 1889,* ed. Beverly Paulik Rosenow (Seattle: Book Publishing Company, 1962), and the state constitution, including the Enabling Act. A copy of the state constitution may be secured from the secretary of state, Olympia, whenever he has funds for an adequate supply. The *Legislative Manual* is the most useful document containing the state constitution, inasmuch as it also includes the United States Constitution, rules of the state house of representatives, rules of the state senate, lists of senators and representatives, and other helpful information. The other source material is ordinarily difficult for students to obtain unless such sets of official documents are available in the county courthouse, a college or university library, a large city library, or the private library of an attorney or judge.

Accounts of the organization and functioning of the Washington territorial government may be found in older standard histories of the state and in a few recent books on various aspects of territorial politics. These works also contain numerous bibliographical references to articles in periodicals.

Bancroft, H.H. *History of Washington, Idaho and Montana.* (Vol. 31 of his *Works.*) San Francisco, Calif.: History Company, 1890.

Beckett, Paul. *From Wilderness to Enabling Act: The Evolution of the State of Washington.* Pullman: Washington State University Press, 1968.

Fuller, George W. *A History of the Pacific Northwest.* 2nd ed., rev.; New York: Alfred A. Knopf, 1941.

Johannsen, Robert W. *Frontier Politics on the Eve of the Civil War.* Seattle: University Washington Press, 1955.

Johansen, Dorothy O. *Empire of the Columbia: A History of the Pacific Northwest.* New York: Harper and Brothers, 1965.

Meany, Edmond S. *History of Washington.* New York: Macmillan Company, 1924.

Snowden, Clinton A. *History of Washington.* New York: Century History Company, 1909. 4 vols.

2. State Executive Departments

The functions of our state government are usually classified as executive, legislative, and judicial. The legislative branch makes the laws for the state; the executive branch sees that these laws are put into effect; and the judicial branch interprets the laws. In so doing, the judiciary has to decide not only what the laws mean and whether or not they are constitutional, but also when and how they are broken. This last phase includes the working of our entire state court system.

Recently, students of government have thought that two additional branches should be recognized: the administrative branch and the electorate. The assistants to the executive branch make up the administrative group, which performs the work of our many state agencies, such as the state Department of Ecology, the Department of Social and Health Services, and so on. The electorate consists of all eligible voters within the state. It is actually the most important branch of our government since, in a democracy, the people decide what kind of government they want and which persons they want to administer the business of government.

In this state, the electorate also has powers that the voters of many states do not have. In 1912 the initiative, referendum, and recall amendments to our state constitution were adopted, giving the voters themselves the right, by petitions and elections, to pass laws, to repeal those passed by the legislature, and to remove from office all elective officials except superior and supreme court judges. These procedures and the other branches of our state government will be discussed in chapters 3, 4, and 5.

MEMBERS OF EXECUTIVE DEPARTMENT

The executive department in this state is composed of nine elective officials: governor, lieutenant governor, secretary of state, treasurer, auditor, attorney general, commissioner of public lands, superintendent of public instruction, and insurance commissioner. All of these except the insurance commissioner were established by the constitution, and the state legislature added that office. For the term of office, salary, and other statistical details concerning these officials, see Table 1 at the end of this chapter. They are responsible separately to the voters and do not form an executive committee or "cabinet" under the direction of the governor. Because the executive function is distributed among these various officials rather than being concentrated in the governor alone, ours is called a *divided executive.*

DIVIDED EXECUTIVE

There are arguments made for and against this type of executive control. The main disadvantage of a divided executive is that to vote intelligently, a voter must spend a great deal of time checking the history of the many candidates. Very few people are willing to do this, and even those who try have trouble finding out what the various candidates believe on current questions, what their training and experience have been, and what kind of work they can be expected to do.

If the ordinary person asks himself the name of our present commissioner of public lands, for example, or that of the insurance commissioner, or state treasurer, state auditor, or any other of these nine executive officials (except those of governor and, possibly, lieutenant governor), the chances are that he will not know. Yet each voter is called upon to vote for all of these officials every four years.

If we voted for the governor alone, he would then have to appoint the heads of these departments. Students of government who favor such a procedure believe that it would make for more efficient government than does our present system. As it is now, the governor may belong to one political party and half or more of the remaining eight executives may belong to another party. In fact, in our state in 1948, a Republican was elected governor; the office of superintendent of schools is nonpartisan; and the remaining seven executive officials elected that year were Democrats. In 1952 five Republicans, including the governor, three Democrats, and one nonpartisan candidate were elected. In 1960 all eight partisan elected officials were Democrats. In 1964, two were Republicans, including the governor, and six were Democrats. In 1972, three were Republicans, including the governor, and five were Democrats.

Because the views on government policy of the two parties sometimes differ decidedly, an executive branch that is divided politically can mean a deadlock or confusion when some departments may be trying to put one policy into effect and others a conflicting one. They are controlled by state laws pertaining to their departments, but these are general enough that the departmental heads have considerable leeway within the law. Because the governor cannot dismiss the other elective officials who disagree with him, he is sometimes unable to effect his own policies. Yet, since in the people's minds he represents all of the executive departments, they often hold him responsible for the entire administration.

Even in 1889, the writers of our constitution evidently questioned the necessity for electing a large group of executives, because they specified that the legislature may abolish the offices of lieutenant governor, state auditor, and commissioner of public lands if it wishes. In fact, in the constitutional convention, there was much feeling against allowing the office of lieutenant governor to be created.

The people who do not favor the short ballot—that is, the system of electing a governor and allowing him to appoint and dismiss the other executives—are afraid that it would give the governor too much power, that he would build up a political machine and the voters would lose control of their government. Certainly if ordinary citizens pay no attention to their state government and fail to vote, it is possible for an unscrupulous individual to gain political power. It is argued, though, that if the voters are conscientious about studying the policies and actions of their state officials and vote intelligently, the people can get rid of a governor, if they wish, more easily than they can oust nine different officials.

Many persons who are afraid of giving our governor the power to appoint six or seven additional officials often are not conscious of the number of people whom he appoints now to other state offices—over 350. If the head of a state department is appointed rather than elected, the agency is called an administrative department. For a list of this large group in our state, see the tables at the end of chapter 3. When one realizes the present extent of the governor's appointive powers, he is probably less inclined to think that adding another half-dozen appointees would make much difference.

Some students of government who favor a short ballot would still have at least the state auditor and the attorney general chosen in some other way. In the case of the auditor, part of his function is to audit the account books of the other executive officials; therefore, if he were appointed by the governor, he would have to audit the books of the person to whom he owed his position.[1] A similar difficulty would confront the attorney general, too,

---

1. In his biennial report for 1968-70, the state auditor gives his views in regard to the complicated problem of the agency to whom, ideally, the state auditor should be responsible. He feels that the auditor needs to be free from pressures by the legislature as well as by the executive branch, and he believes that the auditor can function best if he is elected by the voters and is thus answerable to them. State of Washington, *Forty-First Biennial Report of the State Auditor* (1971). For further information on this subject, see the section on the Legislative Budget Committee, pp. 44-46.

inasmuch as he is the legal adviser of the state officials; in addition, if one of them violates a law in connection with his official duties, the attorney general has the responsibility for bringing suit against him. He might then have to investigate or prosecute another appointee of the governor. Theoretically, he would be required to bring suit against the governor himself if he found that the chief executive was breaking the law. In practice, however, there have been very few attempts to bring a governor to trial unless he is first removed from office by the legislature through impeachment proceedings or legislative removal, or by the voters through the recall system. The reason is that even if a governor is convicted of a crime, he may pardon himself if he is still governor. Isaac I. Stevens, the first governor of Washington Territory, is said to have pardoned himself for a fine for contempt of court, but the documents concerning the case were destroyed in a fire a number of years later.

Even if, under a short-ballot system, two or more of the present executive officials were not appointed by the governor, they would still not have to be elected by the voters. In Alaska, for example, the people elect only the governor and the secretary of state. The governor then appoints eighteen of the twenty-eight additional executive and administrative officials, and the others are chosen by boards or departmental heads authorized by the legislature to do so, some with the approval of the governor. In New Hampshire the voters elect only the governor, who appoints five of the seven main department heads, and the legislature chooses the other two. Louisiana and South Carolina now have the largest number of elective heads of agencies—fourteen, each.

GOVERNOR'S POWERS AND DUTIES

For the sake of convenient organization, we may divide the powers and duties of our governor into those relating to his position as chief executive and those concerning the legislature.

Position as Chief Executive

As chief executive, the governor is required by the state constitution or the state legislature to supervise the conduct of all executive officers and to see that the laws are put into force faithfully.

We have noted earlier that because the governor does not appoint the remaining executive officials, it is difficult for him to supervise the operation of their offices as far as matters of policy are concerned. If they are not fulfilling the duties required of them by law, however, the governor does have a degree of control over them, through the clause in the constitution that says, "The governor may require information in writing from the officers of the state upon any subject relating to the duties of their respective offices . . ." (Article II, Section 5). In some states, the governor does not have this power, and it is clear that an official would hesitate to admit in writing that he was doing something contrary to law or to make false statements for fear his report would give a basis for actual prosecution.

If our governor has reason to believe that a state official is breaking a law in connection with his official duties, he may ask the attorney general to investigate the matter and bring suit if the evidence warrants it. The governor has the same power, too, in regard to county or other local officials, except that he asks the county prosecuting attorney to make the investigation in that case. If the prosecuting attorney is involved, however, or for some reason does not follow up the request, the governor may ask the attorney general to act in place of the prosecuting attorney. If the governor feels that a situation has arisen that is harmful to the public interest, but which he does not have the power to remedy by law, he may report the matter to the next session of the legislature. The legislators may then pass a law that will, presumably, take care of the problem in the future.

The state budget, which is prepared in the governor's office by the director of program planning and fiscal management[2] and approved by the governor, also gives the governor a means of influencing policies in the offices of the other executive officials. If he feels, for example, that a particular project should be undertaken by a state official, he can provide for it in the budget. If he disapproves of a plan proposed by one of the state officials (unless it is one required by law), he may refuse to include money for it in the budget. The legislature has the power to change any budget item presented to it by the governor, but usually it will not do so except by increasing or decreasing the amount requested for each major item. One reason for this is that the legislature has given the governor the responsibility for the budget. A more compelling reason is that preparing the budget is such a long and difficult task that, in their sixty-day sessions, the legislators do not have the time for the study necessary to make up the budget from the beginning.

The 1959 legislature gave to the budget director the additional responsibility of approving or disapproving claims made for services rendered or materials sold to state agencies. This function was previously assigned to the state auditor. Checking vouchers presented for payment to see if they are legitimate claims against the proper fund is the task of a comptroller, and many students of political science and business administration have maintained for some time that the governor, through the person responsible for compiling the preliminary budget, should act as comptroller for the state, rather than the state auditor. Their argument is that, since the governor's office is authorized by the state constitution to see that the laws passed by

2. Called the budget director until 1967.

the legislature are put into effect, he should be in charge of supervising the expenditures allowed by the legislature in appropriation bills, which are based largely on the budget approved by the governor. For a summary of the various ways in which state expenditures have been handled in the past, see the section on the state treasurer and state auditor in this chapter.

Although the state constitution does not consider the matter of the political influence of the governor over the other executive officials, it is an important lever, at least for the ones who belong to his own party. Since he is expected to be the leader of his party in the state, his policies are ordinarily regarded as those of his party. Therefore, unless he loses control of his state political organization to such an extent that his views are disregarded, his policies will be followed to a considerable degree by the officials who are members of his party.

As part of his function as head of the state, the governor also has very great appointive powers. We have mentioned that he appoints over 350 heads and members of departments, boards, or committees which make up the administrative branch of our state government. Most of these will be discussed in chapter 3. Besides these specific appointments, the governor has the power to fill vacancies occurring in any of the other executive offices or among the United States senators or representatives, superior or supreme court judges, and in certain county offices. This means that if an official dies, or for any reason cannot continue in the position, the governor chooses someone to take his place until the end of the term for which he was elected, or until the next general election.

Since the main function of a chief executive is to see that the laws are faithfully executed, the governor must be able to use force of some kind if the regular police force cannot cope with the situation. The commonest causes of such an emergency are fires, floods, earthquakes, or other catastrophes that destroy lives and property to such an extent that the courts cannot function normally. Then looting and violence may occur. Mob action also can cause damage to life and property. In recent years fights have broken out between groups protesting some action by an agency of the federal, state, or local government (such as the war in Vietnam, disputes over racial discrimination, and other social problems). In some instances the resulting riots have led to deaths and destruction of property. In the category of such occurrences in which executive action may be taken our *Session Laws* list riots, unlawful strikes, or an unlawful assembly of more than ten persons who are attempting to commit a serious crime or are endangering anyone's property or life.

Public feeling has run high between those who feel that local and state police brand anyone protesting a government action or advocating social reform a dangerous rioter and those who feel that police should have much greater authority to disperse demonstrations by force and greater freedom to use force in protecting property from possible mob action. Because of the intensity of emotion on the part of both groups, the 1969 legislature in its first special session considered the question of what were necessary police powers in times of local crisis and tried to define the kind of emergency that would require special action and what it should be.

The 1969 law gives to the governor the power to decide when a state of emergency shall be proclaimed. His order must be in writing and filed with the secretary of state, and he is required to give as much public notice through the various news media as is practical. As soon as order is restored in the area where violence has occurred, the governor must issue a proclamation of termination. While the order is in effect, the governor may enforce any of the following prohibitions: individuals must stay off the public streets or out of any other public place during the hours listed; no group of persons can assemble on the streets or in any other open place, whether it is public or private; an individual cannot manufacture, possess, or transport a molotov cocktail or similar explosive device; he cannot possess firearms outside his own residence or place of business; he cannot sell, purchase, or dispense alcoholic beverages, or other properties that the governor believes should be prohibited to help preserve life, health, property, or the public peace, and such other prohibitions as he deems necessary. Actions harmful to an individual or ones creating a nuisance may be raised to misdemeanors or felonies during the state of emergency, and anybody sixteen years or older will be prosecuted as an adult. The governor may order out the state militia to help the local police.

Even before this 1969 law, the state constitution has always given the governor the right to call out the militia (state military reserve forces, which are usually known as the national guard) to act under his direction as commander-in-chief in restoring order if enough people are uncontrollable that they prevent our civil courts from operating normally. However, the 1969 law attempts to state in more specific terms what suspension of free assemblage or possession of firearms or alcoholic beverages the police, either with or without the assistance of the national guard, may enforce if the governor believes that destruction of property or physical violence has reached an emergency status.

If the situation continues to be uncontrollable to the degree that our civil courts cannot operate normally, the state constitution gives our governor the right to go even further and declare that a state of martial law exists. In that case, military courts, called courts-martial, take the place of our regular courts, and such civil protections as the right to a writ of habeas corpus do not operate. An explanation of the principle of a writ of habeas corpus will be given in chapter 5 in connection with the discussion of our court system, and the organization of the state militia will be treated in chapter 3.

There are other ways in which the governor's actions relate to the actions of our courts. He has the power to remit fines and to pardon or commute the sentence of anyone convicted of a crime by any of the state courts. The constitution specifies that the legislature may make whatever regulations it wishes concerning the pardoning power of the governor, and, at the present time, the Board of Prison Terms and Paroles[3] recommends to the governor the action which it thinks he should take in a given case. The theory is that if a person is convicted of a crime, a penalty of a fine or imprisonment, or both, is required by law unless the court suspends the sentence. Neither society nor the criminal may benefit, however, if the same penalty is automatically assigned to each convict, regardless of his age, mental and emotional condition, previous criminal record, degree of education or training of some kind, and other factors. Therefore, the law in this state covering the punishment for most of the serious crimes sets a maximum sentence to be served in the state penitentiary or reformatory and then allows the Board of Prison Terms and Paroles to fix the minimum sentence. For the membership of the board, which is appointed by the governor, see chapter 3.

Even though the law creating the board made it an advisory group to the governor, questions have arisen as to how far the governor is bound by the board's recommendations. Consequently, as part of the 1955 law on the board, the legislature stated specifically that the governor's pardoning power was not limited in any way by a decision of the Board of Prison Terms and Paroles. He may commute a sentence or grant a pardon to any convicted person regardless of the board's recommendation, and he may revoke any parole granted by the board. The constitution requires that the governor report to each legislature the reprieves, commutations, or pardons that he has granted since its last session and the amount of each fine canceled, with the name of the person for whom it was waived and the reason for the action.

Our governor also has the power to return a person to another state if he is wanted there for trial for a crime or if he has escaped after conviction for a crime. The term used for this power in our *Session Laws* is *extradition,* but political scientists prefer to call it *interstate rendition,* since the word *extradition* technically means international rendition, the surrender of a person by one country to another.

The United States Constitution gives the power of interstate rendition to the governors of our various states, so that our state laws simply have to establish machinery for putting it into effect. If a suspected criminal who is wanted in Illinois, for example, is found in the state of Washington, our

3. For further details of this board, see Table 3 at the end of chapter 3. Each board, commission, and committee is entered alphabetically under the italicized word in its title.

police may arrest him and hold him until the governor of Illinois can ask the governor of Washington to send him back to Illinois for trial.

Although the governors usually return the fugitives from justice to the states where they are wanted, the governor cannot be forced to do so. In our state the governor until 1967 asked the prosecuting attorney of the county where the alleged criminal was found to investigate the circumstances and to make a recommendation as to whether justice could be better served by sending him back or by leaving him here. In that year the law was changed to allow the governor to require the official making such a request to give sufficient evidence to justify the governor's asking for the return of a fugitive from another state. In 1971 the legislature went even further in this respect and permitted the governor to have such a fugitive arrested if he finds the evidence convincing. However, then the suspect must be taken before a magistrate for a hearing, and if a writ of habeas corpus is applied for, the prosecuting attorney must be given notice of the hearing.

If our state needs to recover a person from another state, the prosecuting attorney presents to the governor his written application for a requisition for his return. If the person has already been convicted in this state and has escaped from confinement, the prosecuting attorney, the Board of Prison Terms and Paroles, or the warden of a prison may present the application to the governor.

There have been instances where a man has lived as a respectable member of a community for a number of years and then has been identified as an escaped convict from another state. In this situation, a governor may feel that the man should not be returned to serve out his sentence in the state where he was convicted.

Congress has allowed Washington and neighboring states to make an interstate compact by which general regulations for the return of paroled convicts under certain circumstances are observed by all of the states concerned. The 1955 legislature added juvenile delinquents to this category and directed the governor to make a compact with any other state to return juvenile delinquents or runaway juveniles. If such an arrangement is made, the governor is to designate someone as compact administrator to attend to the details.

These regulations point up the fact that the governor is the only state official who may communicate officially with the government of another state or of the United States.

Deeds to state lands, commissions (certificates) stating that an individual is the holder of a state office, and certain state contracts have to be signed by the governor to be official. The records of the governor and of the legislature are regarded as sufficiently important to warrant having an elective secretary of state to preserve them.

The state constitution gives the governor three means of controlling or influencing the legislature: the veto, the calling of special sessions, and the sending of a message to each session of the legislature.

The veto power of a governor is one of the so-called *checks and balances* of the American system of government. The powers of the branches of our state and national governments are separated so that, in theory, the executive, the legislative, and the judicial departments do not encroach on each other's jurisdiction. However, to keep any one of them from acting in an arbitrary or irresponsible manner and to bring the three branches together to assure a workable government, some kind of connecting links must be provided.

When the Washington State legislature passes a bill, the governor is given the power to examine it to see if he thinks it will be a good law. If so, he signs it and it becomes law. If, however, he thinks the bill is not constitutional or that it is unnecessary or that it will waste the taxpayer's money or is undesirable for some other reason, he vetoes it. In that case, the bill cannot become law at that session unless two-thirds of the members present in both houses of the legislature pass it again over his veto.

In our state, the governor has to veto a bill to kill it. He cannot ignore it by "putting it in his pocket," as the president of the United States can, to accomplish a veto. If a state has *pocket veto,* the governor has to sign a bill to make it law. If he does not sign it, the bill is vetoed automatically. In our state, the reverse is true. A bill becomes law unless the governor actually vetoes it, giving his reasons for so doing. Political scientists find that our system has the advantage of forcing a governor to make public his reasons for vetoing a bill. He cannot let it die an inconspicuous death.

It was pointed out earlier that, ironically, after debating whether to give our governor any veto power at all, the constitutional delegates gave him an extremely wide veto power in that, in addition to the usual power of a governor to veto a whole bill, ours may also veto part of a bill—the right of *item veto.* Until recently, governors of states (except Washington) who had any type of item veto (thirty-nine of the forty-eight states then in existence) had this partial veto only in regard to appropriation bills. Those governors could remove an appropriation in the main budget bill passed at each session to allot funds to the various state agencies. Our state, however, was the only one in which the governor could veto any part of any bill. By 1972, however, a few other states had expanded the use of item veto by their governors. In Oregon the governor may use item veto in appropriations bills and also in new bills that declare the act an emergency; in South Carolina, Tennessee, and Wisconsin, as in Washington, the governor now has complete item veto, and, in addition, forty of the present fifty governors have the power of item veto of appropriations bills. North Carolina is the only state in which the governor has no veto power at all over bills passed by the legislature.

The advantages of the item veto are that undesirable points in a bill may be eliminated without destroying the whole bill and that riders may not be attached. A *rider* bill is one attached to another bill which deals with a different subject. The president of the United States, for example, does not have the power of item veto and must accept all or none of a bill. Therefore, Congress sometimes takes advantage of this fact and attaches to a bill that the president especially wants passed, a measure that he would veto by itself. Congress hopes then that the president will let the unwanted bill go through in order to avoid vetoing the one he favors.

In our state, however, riders are unconstitutional, even without the item veto. The constitution says, "No bill shall embrace more than one subject, and that shall be expressed in the title" (Article II, Section 19). The state supreme court is often called upon to rule as to whether a law includes more than one subject and is, therefore, unconstitutional. In 1951, for example, this provision caused the governor to call a second extra session of the legislature. He called a first special session because during the regular 1951 session the legislators could not agree on a tax measure to provide sufficient revenue to meet the appropriations. At the first special session, the legislature combined a tax bill with the appropriations bill. The law was contested in the Thurston County superior court and then appealed to the state supreme court, which agreed with the decision of the lower court that the law was unconstitutional because it dealt with more than one subject. (The court found it also unconstitutional because the tax levied on corporations, called an excise tax, was actually a kind of state income tax. On either count, however, the law would have been nullified.) The governor then called a second special session to levy a tax that would be constitutional and to re-enact the appropriations bill. At that session, they were enacted as separate laws.

In the interests of economy, in some states the governor has the power to reduce money allotments for specific items in the general appropriations bill, as well as the power to remove them completely. In Washington, however, the governor cannot reduce an appropriation. He has either to leave it as it is or take it out entirely. Except for appropriation bills, some people doubt that the item veto is effective because often a bill is worded in such a way that it is difficult to remove a part without making the remainder ambiguous or unworkable. It has been argued that some laws have been killed just as effectively by the removal of an item as if they had been vetoed as a whole. Then, if the legislature has adjourned and cannot pass the vetoed parts over the governor's nullification, the law, as changed, stays on the books at least until the next session of the legislature. Political scientists agree that it is bad public policy to have ineffective laws in force, and there has been more agitation recently for a proposal to the voters for the repeal of the complete item veto, at least, through a constitutional amendment. However, no resolution has yet been passed by the legislature to that effect.

In Washington, either a whole bill or a part of a bill which is vetoed after the adjournment of the legislature is presented to the legislators at the next session (two years later, unless a special session is called in the meantime) for reconsideration.

In Virginia, Alabama, and Massachusetts, the governor has an alternative to vetoing a bill. He may send it back to the legislature with recommendations for changes that would make the bill acceptable to him. If the legislature refuses to change it, the governor can still veto the bill if he wishes. Although in our state the constitution does not provide for the preveto reconsideration, our governor does sometimes indicate to legislative leaders or to the press that he objects to certain features of a bill, which the legislature can then change, if it wishes, before the bill goes to the governor.

In our state, the governor is the only person who can call the legislature into special session—or *extra sessions,* as it is called in the laws—a legislative meeting in addition to the regular biennial session. This term comes from the fact that the constitution says, "He may, on extraordinary occasions, convene the legislature . . . (Article III, Section 7). The session is, then, an extraordinary one. In some states, the governor has to ask the advice of an executive advisory council about calling a special session, and in others the legislators may themselves call a special session by vote or if a certain percentage of them (the size varies) petition for one. In Washington, however, no restrictions are put on the governor's power in this respect.

Our state constitution specifies that when the governor calls a special session of the legislature, he shall do so by issuing a proclamation "in which shall be stated the purposes for which the legislature is convened" (Article III, Section 7). Since the governor states the subjects to be considered by the legislature, the question has arisen as to whether the legislators are limited to those topics alone during the extra session or whether they may pass laws on other subjects, too, if they wish. A case was taken to our state supreme court on this matter, and the court ruled that even in a special session called by the governor to consider specific measures, the legislature is a sovereign body and may legislate on anything it chooses. In practice, the legislative leaders ordinarily meet with the governor at the beginning of a special session and agree with him as to what subjects they will consider, but they are not legally bound to restrict themselves to those topics.

At the present time, if one counts those states where the legislature may convene special sessions by its own vote plus those allowed by their constitutions to consider any subject they wish in a special session, thirty-three do not have to limit themselves to the problems specified in his proclamation by the governor, and seventeen are thus restricted.

The governor is also required by our constitution to recommend to the regular biennial legislative sessions the laws which he wants to have passed. These recommendations are called the "Governor's Message," corresponding to the "State of the Union Message" delivered to Congress by the president. The phrase "condition of the affairs of the state" is used in the state constitution to describe the theme of the governor's address.

The message has a strong influence on the legislature, particularly when both houses happen to have a majority from the governor's political party. Even when this is not the case, the prestige of the governor's office is such that his proposals are almost always introduced into the legislature as bills for consideration, and, if a majority of the legislators do not want to pass them into law, they try in the debate on the bills to make speeches which, when reported in the news media, will convince the voters that the bills are unsound. At the same time, the governor can communicate with the people through the press, radio, and television in support of his program, hoping that the voters will then urge their legislators to vote for it.

LIEUTENANT GOVERNOR

Our state constitution gives to the lieutenant governor the two usual functions of that office—to act as governor if the governor is unable to perform his duties and to be presiding officer (president) of the state senate. We have mentioned that the office of lieutenant governor is one which the legislature may abolish if it wishes, and some students of government feel that the office is unnecessary. The problem of an official to act as governor when the chief executive is absent or incapacitated is taken care of by Amendment VI to our state constitution, which provides that, if the governor is removed, resigns, or is incapable of performing his duties, the lieutenant governor shall act in his place; then if something happens to the lieutenant governor, the remaining executive officials (except for the insurance commissioner, whose office was not created by the state constitution) form a line of succession in the following order: secretary of state, state treasurer, state auditor, attorney general, superintendent of public instruction, and commissioner of public lands. Thus, if the office of lieutenant governor were abolished, the secretary of state or some other official could be named as the vice-governor to succeed the governor during a vacancy in his office. In eight of the ten states that do not have the office of lieutenant governor, the president of the senate serves as vice-governor, and in the remaining two the secretary of state has that function.

Our lieutenant governor's job as presiding officer of the senate is not an exclusive one since the constitution states that "Each house shall elect its own officers; and when the lieutenant governor shall not attend as president, or shall act as governor, the senate shall choose a temporary president" (Article II, Section 10). In practice, the majority party in the senate names one of its leaders as president pro tem, and he presides in the absence of the lieutenant governor.

In 1938 an interesting situation occurred in which there was a question as to whether Governor Clarence D. Martin or Lieutenant Governor Victor A. Meyers was actually governor at the moment. It happened that Governor Martin left for a conference in Washington, D.C., on 12 April 1938, at which time Lieutenant Governor Meyers was also out of the state. The latter returned to Olympia after five o'clock in the afternoon on April 19 with a notarized proclamation calling for a special session of the legislature; the proclamation had to be authenticated by the secretary of state to be official. Since the office of the secretary of state had closed at five o'clock, the lieutenant governor had to wait until eight o'clock the next morning to present his proclamation to the secretary of state, Mrs. Belle Reeves. She refused to sign it on the grounds that eight minutes earlier Governor Martin had called her from Spokane to say that he was back in the state. Therefore, Mrs. Reeves argued that Lieutenant Governor Meyers could not act as governor because Governor Martin was in the state at the time.

Lieutenant Governor Meyers then asked the state supreme court to compel Mrs. Reeves by a writ of mandamus to issue his proclamation calling for a special session of the legislature on the basis that the seal of the notary public was sufficient. The court ruled that it was not—that the state seal was necessary, and that before it could be obtained from the secretary of state, the actual governor had returned to the state, thereby nullifying the power of the lieutenant governor to act as governor.

Justice John S. Robinson concurred in the majority decision, but for different reasons. In his written opinion on the matter, he stated that he interpreted the amendment on the line of succession to the governorship to mean that if both the governor and lieutenant governor are out of the state (as they were), the secretary of state becomes the acting governor until the governor's return, so that Lieutenant Governor Meyers had no right, even when he returned to the state, to claim the powers of governor, which remained in the hands of Mrs. Reeves. Justice Robinson pointed out that one had to include "absence" in the meaning of "disability" as used in Amendment VI, since "removal, resignation, death, or disability" are the only contingencies provided for in the amendment, which presumably superseded earlier laws on that question. He likened the governor's return from an absence outside the state to that of a business executive coming back to his office and taking over his duties from an assistant who had attended to them while the former was gone.

SECRETARY OF STATE

As his title implies, the secretary of state acts as a "secretary" in recording official state papers, largely in connection with the governor's office and with the legislature. As we have seen in connection with a proclamation calling a special legislative session, an act of the governor, to be official, must be written out and stamped with the state seal, which is in the custody of the secretary of state. The state seal has a picture of George Washington in the center and around it the phrase, "The Seal of the State of Washington, 1889." Because it identifies a paper as an official document, the state seal is kept very carefully by the secretary of state.

Type of Documents Recorded

Whenever the governor issues a pardon, a deed to any state lands, a proclamation, or any other official document, the secretary of state stamps the paper with the state seal and copies or summarizes the document. The original paper is then sent to the proper person, and the record is kept in the office of the secretary of state.

In order to do business in this state, a corporation must pay a license fee to the secretary of state and present to him an official description called *articles of incorporation,* drawn up when the corporation is formed. The secretary of state is required by law to distribute free copies of the state laws relating to corporations, so that those interested may have accurate information. Trademarks also have to be registered in the secretary's office, as well as copyrighted songs. Charters for municipal corporations must also be on file in his office.

The secretary of state is required to keep a correct copy of the state laws, as passed by the legislature and signed or vetoed by the governor, and the legislative journals and memorials. Until 1969 he was responsible for seeing that they are correctly printed at the state printing plant and distributed according to law. Now this duty is performed by the Statute Law Committee. Copies of the laws go to certain officials and to libraries acting as depositories, and the remainder are sold to the public at prices authorized by the legislature. Four thousand copies are filed in the office of the secretary of state.

Most public officials have to take an oath of office and give a *bond.* Giving a bond consists in depositing a certain amount of money, or collateral, as guarantee that the official will not misuse the public funds that pass through his hands or violate his oath of office in some other way. If he is later convicted of doing so by a court, he loses the money deposited. The documents indicating that such money (whatever amount is required by law) has been placed on deposit are called official bonds, and these, plus the oaths of office for state officials, are kept by the secretary of state. Bonds for notaries public are also deposited in his office.

Duties in Connection with Elections

After the votes are counted in each election precinct by the local election officers, the statements of the number of votes received by each candidate are sent to the county auditor who, with the other members of the county election board, canvasses (adds) the total of the votes within the county. The county auditor then forwards to the secretary of state the total number of votes cast within his county for each state and national officer. After every general election, the secretary of state canvasses the votes from the counties and announces the names of the successful state and national candidates. He publishes an abstract of the votes, including a list of all state, local, and national officers elected in the state. Anyone may get a copy of the abstract from the secretary of state.

For any officer serving more than one county, the procedure for canvassing the votes after a primary election is similar, except that when the secretary of state receives the returns from the county auditors, he is required to call the state treasurer and state auditor to meet with him as the State *Canvassing* Board to add the votes. That board then certifies the list to the secretary of state, who must publish it in the legal newspaper at the state capital. In the primary election, which precedes the general election, a nominee for each political party is chosen to run for each partisan office, and two candidates are chosen for each nonpartisan office. (For judges of the supreme court, appeals courts, superior courts, justices of the peace, state superintendent of public instruction, and directors of first-class school districts, if one person has a majority of all votes cast for the position, only his name is printed on the general election ballot with a space for the writing in of a name by a voter. Except for school districts having an enrollment of 70,000 pupils or more, no primary is held for the office of superintendent of public instruction or first-class school district officers if, after the last day for withdrawal as candidates, no more than two candidates have filed for each position.)

The secretary of state is also required to issue a special ballot in years of presidential elections to allow persons to vote for the president and vice-president of the United States if they are eligible to vote in state elections except for residence requirements. He is responsible for seeing that *Voters' Pamphlets* and *Candidates' Pamphlets* are issued before general elections to give the voters information on issues involved in proposed initiatives, referenda, constitutional amendments, and statements by or on behalf of individual candidates. Specific procedures for these and other election regulations will be discussed in detail in chapter 6.

Voting machines are used to an increasing extent now, particularly in our cities, because they enable people to vote faster, and they save time in counting votes. The secretary of state, the superintendent of public instruction, and the state insurance commissioner make up the State *Voting* Machine Committee, which supervises the checking and operation of voting machines to make certain that they are accurate and are being used properly. The 1971 legislature elaborated the section on automated voting facilities by requiring the secretary of state to provide uniform regulations for maintaining electronic voter registration records or automatic data processing systems.

Bureau of Statistics

In addition to his work as a recorder and custodian of these various documents, the secretary of state is required by the constitution to maintain a Bureau of Statistics, Agriculture, and Immigration. As head of this bureau, he has been given by the legislature the title of ex officio commissioner of statistics. In this capacity, he gathers information concerning our state and publishes it for general use. The bureau has been particularly interested in preparing pamphlets on the resources of our state, and these are distributed upon request.

STATE TREASURER AND STATE AUDITOR

State Budget

As we noted earlier, the budget is the basis for allocation of funds to departments. At the present time, the director of program planning and fiscal management in the governor's office prepares the budget, but his office (under a different title) was not created by the legislature until 1947. Before that time, there were various procedures for giving the legislature an estimate of money needed and available for the state's expenses for the biennium. As early as 1866, while Washington was still a territory, the legislature passed a law requiring the territorial treasurer to submit to the house of representatives at each regular session an estimate of the probable expenditures of the territory for the next appropriations period. The first state legislature in 1889-90 transferred this job to the state auditor, who continued to make a biennial estimate of the state's receipts and expenditures until 1921, when the Department of Efficiency was created to take over this function as part of its duties. In 1935 the Department of Finance, Budget, and Business was established, with one division in charge of the preparation of an actual budget for the legislature to consider.

Inasmuch as the governor could not make efficient recommendations to the legislature for desirable appropriations laws without relating them to probable receipts and expenditures, it became obvious that he needed to have charge of the preparation of the budget. Consequently, in 1947 the legislature gave the governor the authority to appoint a director of the budget who worked under his direction. The 1969 legislature continued that system, but with a different title and somewhat different organization. It created the Office of Program Planning and Fiscal Management in the governor's office, which is now composed of the Central Budget Agency and the state planning, program management, and population and research divisions of an agency that had been called the Planning and Community Affairs Agency. Consequently, the person who is now in charge of preparing the preliminary state budget in the governor's office is called the director of program planning and fiscal management, and, in addition to being responsible for the work of budget director, he now is in charge of planning an efficient accounting system for the state and surveying the administrative and business methods and the physical needs and industrial activities of the various state agencies with the view of recommending to the governor and legislature any improvements possible and assisting the departments in their plans and operations.

The first step in the preparation of the budget is that each head of a department or other agency makes an itemized statement of the amount of money he will need for his office for the next two years and gives it to the director of program planning and fiscal management, who equalizes these requests as best he can and puts them together into a preliminary budget for the governor's approval. The estimates of expenses submitted by the legislature and by the supreme court are the only ones that may not be altered by the director or the governor.

The governor studies the preliminary budget and then holds hearings at which the heads of departments may appear and argue for the amount they have requested. The governor is required to ask the Legislative Budget Committee to name one or more persons to attend the hearings, and, in the year of an election for governor, the retiring governor must ask the governor-elect to be present at the hearings, also. After the hearings, the governor decides on the amount of money which he will request from the legislature for each state agency and puts this information into the form specified by the legislature for the final budget.[4] The governor is required to

4. In Part I, the governor explains the budget, outlines his proposed financial policy, and sets forth anticipated revenues by fund and source along with tabulations of

have the budget ready for the legislature by the fifth day of the session, unless it grants him an extension, and the legislature must adopt it not later than thirty days prior to the beginning of the next fiscal period.

The legislature is free to increase or decrease the amount asked by the governor for any item, and, since levying taxes to bring in sufficient revenue to meet even a minimum budget is the most difficult task for legislators, the general appropriations bill is usually slow in passage. In recent years, it has regularly taken one or more special sessions following the biennial meeting of the legislature to pass the law embodying the budget.

In order to have some of its own members work on the subject between sessions, the legislature in 1951 created the Legislative Budget Committee, and subsequent sessions have continued it. In 1967 the legislature made this committee consist of eight senators and eight representatives to be appointed by the president of the senate and the speaker of the house, respectively. Not more than four members from the same house may be from the same political party. The senate and house confirm the appointments from their own groups, and, if a vacancy arises on the committee between legislative sessions, the remaining members appoint someone from the same political party to take the absent member's place. The committee is empowered to appoint an executive official, called the legislative auditor, and to employ necessary research and clerical help.

The committee has the power to make postaudits of the financial transactions of any state agency, and it is required to make its official report to the legislature by 31 December of the year prior to the convening of a session. In this report, the committee gives its opinion of the degree to which state offices have made their expenditures according to the will of the legislature; makes recommendations for reducing the cost of government in various fields, for promoting "frugality and economy" in state agencies, and for an "improved level of fiscal management"; and indicates the efficiency and accuracy of the regular postaudits of the state government.

As part of its audit, the committee evaluates the quality of "performance" by state and local officials, using this as a partial measure of their success in managing the state's fiscal operations. The state auditor feels that this should be a part of his job,[5] but the 1969 legislature indicated its support of the committee in this respect by stating that the state auditor's funds should not be used "for performance audits of state and local agencies, but shall be limited to use for fiscal legal audits."

---

proposed expenditures classified by fund and purpose for each outlay. In Part II, he gives a detailed breakdown of expected income and disbursements for the operation of the various state departments, and in Part III, he lists similar information in regard to capital projects—that is, proposed buildings or other large undertakings.

5. *Forty-First Biennial Report, State Auditor.*

The 1971 legislature authorized the Legislative Budget Committee to order reductions in expenditures from general fund appropriations for elected public officials and public educational agencies, except those of higher learning, to equal the percentage of reduction ordered by the governor in departments whose heads are under his control if revenues prove insufficient during a biennium to meet the expenses of the various agencies.

Because automated devices are considered increasingly desirable for the ordering of state supplies, payment of claims, and other record-keeping connected with state and local governmental operations, recent legislatures have turned their attention to expanding the use of data-processing machines. The 1969 session created the Data Processing Advisory Committee, including among others the director of program planning and fiscal management, to advise the governor and director on the extent to which automation in these areas is desirable. The governor and director then have the authority to develop data-processing systems to serve statewide heads of state and local government agencies, and to delegate to any state agency the power to acquire the necessary equipment. The legislature regards this step as the beginning of a statewide system to secure and store information to fill the needs of the legislative, executive, and judicial branches.

Payment of Claims

After the legislature has passed the general appropriations bill so that each state agency knows the amount of money it will have for the next biennium, the governor asks the head of each state governmental unit to indicate to the director of program planning and fiscal management how much of his allotment he intends to spend during a particular month or quarter of the biennium. With the advice of the director, the governor may then change the rate of spending so that an office will not use up too large a proportion of its income early in the fiscal period. The governor cannot make changes, however, in the spending plan (called *breakdown*) for the agencies headed by an elective official, the legislature, the judiciary, the commodity commissions, or the state institutions of higher education.

When any state agency owes a person money, either for salary or for materials furnished, the head of the department or committee or board makes out a claim or voucher for each payment and sends the claims to the director of program planning and fiscal management, who checks to see if the expense appears to be a legitimate one, according to law, and if it is within the amount of money allotted for that particular month or payroll period. If the claim comes within these categories, the director forwards the voucher to the state treasurer who makes out a warrant to the claimant. Warrants can be cashed by the recipient at a bank as checks can. When banks return to the state treasurer canceled warrants that have been cashed, he redeems them; that is, he allots an equal amount of money from the state treasury to the banks that cashed them. The treasurer then gives to the state auditor a record of each expenditure, so that when the latter makes his audit of the financial accounts of all state agencies, including the office of the state treasurer, he will have the necessary records for such an examination.

Until 1959 the state auditor not only checked the books of state officials after funds were paid out to see that all of the money was spent according to law and that state funds were not misused, but he also made the preaudit of vouchers now handled by the director of program planning and fiscal management. Formerly, the auditor, as well as the director, checked each claim before it was paid to see that it represented a legitimate claim against state funds. Then at the close of the fiscal period, the auditor checked each agency's books to make certain that they balanced and that the money had actually been spent as authorized.

The auditor previously had both preauditing and postauditing functions. It is considered better accounting practice if the same person is not responsible for both phases of auditing, since his judgment in a postaudit would be somewhat influenced by what he had decided in his preaudit. Various reports were made to the legislature by the Legislative Council (a group whose composition and functions will be discussed in chapter 4) recommending that the state auditor be only a postauditor and that the preaudit or comptroller's function be allocated to another official. The legislature followed this recommendation in the 1959 session by giving the preaudit duties to a budget director.

In making the change, the legislature stated that it expected the governor, through the budget director, to work out a modern accounting system for each state agency so that the receipts and expenditures would be properly and systematically accounted for. Since 1969 the director of program planning and fiscal management has continued with this assignment and also makes a survey of the degree of efficiency in the various agencies and reports to the governor if he finds duplication of work or a lack of coordination between two or more state offices. He is to review the pay scale and job classification schedule of all agencies if they are not part of the state merit system (civil service).

In addition to being responsible for the postaudit of state agencies, the state auditor also has to supervise trained accountants to check the books of local officials (in counties, cities, and districts) after the money has been spent to ascertain if the accounts are accurate and show no evidence of fraud. There are now approximately 1,800 units of this kind in the state.

The 1959 legislature in summarizing the present function of the state treasurer said that he is to "receive, keep and disburse" all state funds not expressly assigned to some other custodian. He is to make payments from the state treasury only on the vouchers mentioned above, signed by the head of the agency authorizing the expenditure on forms approved by the director of program planning and fiscal management. The amount of money handled by the treasurer in this way is so large that he needs a big staff of bookkeepers and accountants to maintain correct and adequate records. The total amount of money spent by the state from 1 July 1969 to 30 June 1970 was over $1,137,000,000.

A discussion of the types of taxes and fees that produce the revenue from which these expenditures are made will be included in chapter 7, "County Government," for when the state constitution was written, the basis of our revenue system was the real property tax, which is levied by our county commissioners. Some mention is also made of taxation problems in the section on the Department of Revenue in chapter 3.

An ex officio fiscal agent for the state, the treasurer handles transfer of money between Washington and any other state or between our state and the federal government, in addition to acting as accountant for state funds spent within the state. The state treasurer and state auditor are also members of a large number of committees.

ATTORNEY GENERAL

State officials need a lawyer to advise them on legal matters, and the state constitution specifies that the attorney general is to act in this capacity. He is required to advise the members of the legislature, the governor and other state officials, and county prosecuting attorneys on questions of law which concern their duties. In preparation for drafting a law, a legislative committee may need to know whether a bill under consideration is constitutional. Such a group can ask the attorney general to give his opinion on this matter, and the members of the legislature themselves may ask him for advice on questions concerning their duties or an interpretation of the state constitution.

Opinions

In addition, many laws give state officials certain powers, and sometimes various interpretations can be made of the degree of power granted. A state official needs to be as certain as possible of his ground before he attempts to put a regulation in force. Again, it is the attorney general who interprets the law in question, and one or more attorneys are assigned to each major agency to attend to questions.[6] For example, the secretary of state needs opinions

6. State of Washington, *Fortieth Biennial Report and Opinions of the Attorney General* (1969-70).

on the interpretation of laws regarding elections, corporation requirements, and so on. The state treasurer, state auditor, superintendent of public instruction, insurance commissioner, and other executive officials need legal advice in their official work, and so do the administrative officials described in the following chapter—director of agriculture, State Highway Commission, director of ecology, and so forth. In 1969-70, the attorney general and his staff gave 53 formal and 319 informal opinions in answer to questions by state and local officials in addition to writing a large number of memoranda in response to such inquiries.

Samples of opinions given to state officials in 1969-70 are: the Water Pollution Control Commission has the authority to establish water quality standards for waters of the state, including drains and reservoirs of irrigation and drainage systems, and persons who propose to discharge industrial wastes into such water are required to obtain a permit to do so; the provisions that prohibit persons convicted of certain crimes from carrying a pistol do not apply to an individual whose charge has been dismissed by the court, but do apply to a convicted person who is on a parole discharge; federal rather than state requirements for equal opportunity employment for women apply to employers hiring for projects financed by federal funds; the director of fisheries may close a given area to commercial fishing, but allow sports fishing there if such action is taken for purposes of conservation and protection of the state's fisheries.

If a case involving an opinion of the attorney general is taken to the state supreme court, the court may decide that the attorney general was wrong and lay down a different interpretation, and, in such a case, the decision of the supreme court is final, rather than that of the attorney general. Because he is expected to know our state constitution and our laws thoroughly, however, and to be well acquainted with the previous decisions of our supreme court, his opinion in such matters carries a great deal of weight.

The attorney general and his staff also help state officials by preparing or approving the many contracts or agreements that are necessary for the disposal or use of state land or other resources, the construction of buildings, or the performance of other services.

State's Attorney

Besides acting in an advisory capacity, the attorney general is also an attorney for the state. If a lawsuit is brought against a state officer over any of his official actions, the attorney general acts as his lawyer and defends him in court. He does not act as his attorney, however, if the case concerns some nonofficial action of the state officer—that is, a suit brought against him as a private citizen. If a state official finds it necessary to bring legal action against anyone in order to perform his official duties, the attorney general prosecutes the case. If a lawsuit involving the state is taken to the state supreme court, the attorney general likewise acts as the state's lawyer there, whether the state is in the position of plaintiff or defendant. Samples of cases argued by the attorney general or one of his staff before the state supreme court from 1969 to 1970 are: *State v. Ponten,* in which the state supreme court overruled the decision of the Spokane County Superior Court and declared that if the state caused an individual to lose water from wells when excavations were made for highway purposes, the state was liable for the damage done; *Lackman, v. Department of Labor and Industries,* in which the supreme court held that motels may be included within the statutory term *hotel* if certain facilities and services are provided. The attorney general's division also joined with the corresponding Oregon department to argue in the United States district court for the district of Oregon against the proposed shipment of nerve gas by the United States Army across the state of Washington. Although the district court refused to grant an injunction, the secretary of defense canceled the shipment.

Powers as Investigator

We saw earlier that the governor has the power to ask the attorney general or any prosecuting attorney to investigate the affairs of any corporation doing business in the state; and his power of investigation is not limited to corporations, for, in any violation of criminal law, the governor may request the attorney general to investigate if the need arises. The attorney general can instruct a prosecuting attorney to take action. If the prosecuting attorney fails to do so, the attorney general may conduct a prosecution. Usually, if the attorney general or an assistant appears in a superior court, he is there at the request of the prosecuting attorney of the county. During 1969-70 the attorney general or an assistant participated in 9,637 cases in county superior courts; 313 cases before the state supreme court; 1,591 before the United States district courts; 22 before the United States circuit court of appeals; and 27 before the United States Supreme Court. At the end of 1970 the attorney general was employing 130 assistant attorneys general.

STATE SUPERINTENDENT OF PUBLIC INSTRUCTION

The state superintendent of public instruction has the task of supervising the public schools of the state. In order to maintain adequate standards in the schools, the state superintendent is allowed to hire trained educators as assistants, and he plus his staff make up the state Department of Education.

They are responsible for seeing that the standard of educational training in our public schools is as high as possible and that it is fairly uniform throughout the state. Schools must therefore bestandardized so that a student graduating from a particular type of school in one part of the state will have had similar training to that given in such a school in other parts of the state. The state Department of Education employs trained supervisors who inspect the schools in the state and report on their condition. Where help is needed, either in planning buildings or improving classroom teaching, the staff attempts to supply it.. The 1961 legislature created a new division within the Department of Education, the special education for students of superior capacity. Its purpose is to demonstrate to local school districts methods for providing courses for superior students. It does research and conducts pilot programs as part of its work on this phase of the department's responsibility. Details of the contacts between the staff of the state Department of Education and the various county and school district officials will be discussed in chapter 7.

Although the state Department of Education sees that each school meets a certain standard in the type of courses offered and that teachers have the amount of training required, the department does not set these standards itself. They are decided upon by another group, the State Board of Education.

State Board of Education

The State Board of *Education* was created by the state legislature to establish the course of study to be given in our public schools. The curriculum must be uniform throughout the various counties, although leeway is given for some courses to suit local needs. The state legislature requires that certain courses be given in the public schools. Once the framework of the curriculum is fixed by the legislature or the Board of Education, the Department of Education fills it in and tries to make certain that each individual school adheres to the requirements.

In 1947 the legislature changed the personnel of the State Board of Education. Formerly, it consisted of prominent educators in the state, such as the presidents of our state institutions of higher education, plus others who were appointed by the governor. Now, however, the State Board of Education consists of fourteen persons not connected with the public schools or our colleges, two from each of the congressional districts in the state. The members, who serve six-year terms, are chosen at a convention of delegates from the local school boards throughout the state, and conventions are held in only part of the congressional districts for each election so that the terms will be staggered. The only additional qualification for the office of state board member is that he be a resident of the congressional district from which he is elected.

The 1967 legislature added an electoral system for counting votes for members of the State Board of Education whereby each vote by a school director is given as many electoral points as there were enrolled students in his district on the last day for filing declarations of candidacy for the position. A majority of electoral points then determines the winning candidates. The state board appoints three persons to act with the state superintendent of public instruction as a canvassing board to count the votes.

In addition to determining the standards for our elementary and high schools, the State Board of Education has to approve the program given by the various colleges and universities in the state for prospective public school teachers. By this means, the board tries to make certain that our teachers will be well trained.

If schools in all of our counties are to meet uniform standards for education, money received for schools has to be apportioned or *equalized* so that poorer counties receive more than they are able to raise from local taxes. State funds are maintained by the legislature to be distributed in this manner. In chapter 1, we mentioned the permanent school fund, which was named in the Enabling Act to receive money from lands granted originally by the federal government to Washington territory for educational purposes. Certain taxes also go into the state's funds for proportionate allocation to school districts.

Tax sources used as the basis for determining the amount of state aid available are: local taxes, grants in lieu of taxes; the high school district fund; 1 percent of the real estate excise tax; public utility district excise tax; and funds paid to the state for its part in federal forest maintenance.

Special situations that also make a school district eligible for certain state funds are: large cost of pupil transportation; excess costs in handicapped children's program; education of children in state institutions; number of approved courses in adult education; and the degree of operation of approved vocational technical schools.

Each intermediate school district superintendent of schools sends a copy of the budget for the schools of his area to the State Board of Education, and, by comparing the budgets, the state board can tell which counties have the least money available for schools. It then instructs the state superintendent to allocate the proper amount (through the state treasurer) to individual county treasurers to be distributed locally by the intermediate school district superintendent. A county has to levy a local tax proportionate to the amount of its taxable property before it can receive these state funds. The 1969 legislature required that each school district must collect at least five-sixths of the maximum amount allowed by law or have its amount of state school funds reduced by an amount equaling the difference.

Since the invention of the automobile, school districts have been constantly increasing in size because it is easy to transport pupils longer distances. When the number of schools in two or more counties had thus become small enough that a county superintendent of schools was not needed for each county, proposals were discussed by educators and legislators as to means of reducing the number of comparable superintendents. The result was that the legislature proposed to the voters a constitutional amendment, which was adopted, that omitted the title of county superintendent of schools from the list of mandatory local officials. In 1965 the legislature instructed the State Board of Education to adopt a statewide plan for dividing the state into service areas, which may include several counties or be limited to one, and by 1971 this system was in effect. One intermediate school district superintendent would then be appointed by an elective intermediate school district board of education for each of these larger areas. For a detailed presentation of the procedures in choosing the local school officials and their duties, see chapter 7.

In addition to being concerned about problems of consolidation of districts, members of school superintendents' offices at the various levels, other educators, and public officials feel an urgency to make all phases of our school system sufficiently strong to meet the challenge of the "space age." They want to make the greatest possible effort to learn what type of occupation best suits each public school student and then give him or her excellent training along those and other lines.

If a child has an aptitude for scientific studies, he needs adequate training and stimulation in them. But, if our type of society is to grow stronger, he must also have sufficient background in the arts and social sciences to know how to use our technological advances for the good of society and the enrichment of individual lives. Recently, people in general have become acutely aware of the necessity of this type of broad education to make it possible to banish war, poverty, and waste of human and natural resources. For the same reasons, if a student has a bent for social sciences or humanities, he, in turn, needs to have a similar breadth of interests and, along with his major studies, learn enough scientific theory to have a clear view of the total problem and opportunity facing our culture.

Children who have been deprived of an early school background that makes such learning possible or even seem desirable need special help from staff members who understand their problems and attitudes. Such disadvantaged children often come from families in which racial discrimination in addition to poverty or family neglect have been factors for several generations. In our area, black people, Mexican-Americans, and Indians have been particularly subject to a lack of educational background because of the greater difficulties their parents faced in getting jobs. Because of the fact that Indians are still, for the most part, living together on reservations, securing an education that fits them for work off the reservation, if they want it, while still retaining facets of their ethnic culture presents a special problem. Consequently, the office of the state superintendent of schools has, in recent years, sponsored studies of means of achieving such a result and projects to implement them with aid from federal funds.

A booklet entitled *The Red Man in America* gives specific figures and case histories of Indians and their high rate of unemployment, disease, and poverty throughout the country. For the programs in this area, a publication called *Are You Listening Neighbor?* summarizes the attempts being made to encourage Indian participation in advising on curriculum changes and specific projects to provide motivation for Indian children to prepare for academic or vocational training and at the same time recapture as many of their traditional skills and interests as possible.[7]

COMMISSIONER OF PUBLIC LANDS

The state may buy and sell or lease land, and the commissioner of public lands has been the official during our statehood period who is primarily responsible for such transfers, except for those lands which specific state agencies—such as the State Parks and Recreation Commission, state Department of Fisheries, and state Department of Game—buy for recreational or other uses. (The legislature requires that certain transactions made by some of these departments be handled through the office of the commissioner of public lands acting in his various capacities.)

In the state constitution, the office of the commissioner of public lands is listed as one of the executive departments, but the legislature is allowed to define the commissioner's duties and to abolish his office if it wishes. As the value of state lands has increased with growth of population, industry, and demand for the use of public lands and waters, the legislature has gradually given boards, rather than a single official, much of the control over the state lands—tide lands, shore lands, oyster beds, school lands, capitol lands, forest lands, and land used for agricultural or other purposes. The commissioner of public lands, however, still arranges for surveys of these lands, which serve as the basis for determining the value so that a fair price can be set for their disposal or use. The commissioner also acts as the secretary of the Board of

7. *The Red Man in America* was published by the state superintendent's office in 1970, and reprints articles written for the *Seattle Post-Intelligencer. Are You Listening Neighbor?* (1969) is a report of Indian Affairs Task Force, which is a joint task force of the governor's Advisory Council on Urban Affairs and the governor's Indian Advisory Committee.

Natural Resources, the agency named by the legislature to supervise the sale or lease of state lands, and as executive head of the Department of Natural Resources, which carries out the decisions of the board.

BOARD OF NATURAL RESOURCES

The legislature has given the Board of Natural Resources the function of approving the value set on each piece of land and arranging for its sale or lease if such transfer seems in the state's interest. The board consists of five members: the governor, the superintendent of public instruction, the commissioner of public lands, the dean of the College of Forest Resources of the University of Washington, and the director of agricultural sciences of Washington State University.

The composition of the board demonstrates that the legislature wanted some member with a particular knowledge of each type of state land. For example, the superintendent of public instruction would know the problems of handling school lands; the dean of forestry could advise on the use and value of forest lands; the director of agricultural sciences on grazing and other agricultural lands, and so on. Until 1957 a separate board had to approve the disposal of each type of land, some of these agencies having been created by the state constitution and some by the legislature. When the management of state lands became such a tremendous job that it was extremely cumbersome to have a number of agencies involved in appraising them, the Legislative Council recommended that they be consolidated. The legislature in 1957 then substituted the Board of Natural Resources for all of the former groups. Those created by the legislature could be abolished. If those required by the state constitution had additional duties, the agencies were retained for those functions. If they did not, the Board of Natural Resources was defined by the legislature as fulfilling the constitutional requirement.

For example, the Board of State Land Commissioners, which had been required to appraise school lands, was abolished; the State Forest Board, which was to supervise the sale or lease of forest land, was abolished; the State Capitol Committee, which was created by the state constitution, remains in existence, but its duties in regard to appraisal of capitol lands and resources are now transferred to the Board of Natural Resources; and the latter is likewise to act as the board of harbor line commissioners, also required by the state constitution to determine the line dividing the state's tide and shore lands from those under private ownership. In addition, sustained yield committees, which regulated logging on state lands so as to retain the timber stands, were abolished, and the Division of Forestry was removed from the state Department of Conservation (then called the Department of Conservation and Development) and placed in the Department of Natural Resources.

Besides determining the value of all state lands, the Board of Natural Resources is required to establish policies to insure the acquisition, management, and use of the state's land according to sound principles. Once these are formulated, the Department of Natural Resources is responsible for administering the regulations of the board.

Department of Natural Resources

The Department of Natural Resources manages over 4,000,000 acres of forests, ranges, and agricultural lands, 700 miles of tide lands, 3,500 miles of shore lands along navigable rivers and lakes, 6,700 acres of harbor area, and from 1,800 to 2,000 miles of beds of navigable waters, all of these state owned.

According to the director, "The Department is an action-oriented organization. We fight fires, sell and harvest timber and wood products, lease lands for grazing, agricultural, mineral, oil and gas exploration and commercial and recreational purposes. We construct primitive recreation areas, participate in aquaculture development, supervise mined land rehabilitation, and a multitude of other activities. All of our activities deal with natural resources—land, trees, minerals and water; and we manage them to contribute to a better way of life for the citizens of our state, for now and for tomorrow."[8]

Inasmuch as timber has been the source of one of the state's leading industries, preservation of forests has been greatly stressed, and the legislature requires that loggers on state and, to a minimum extent, on private lands follow conservation techniques in logging. The Department of Natural Resources enforces state regulations on logging, reforestation of logged-over areas, or other uses of state forest land or timber. In addition, the department itself does a vast amount of reforestation on state lands.

The amount of timber seemed inexhaustible to the early settlers. In fact, on the coast they were more concerned with getting rid of enough trees to make a clearing for houses than with encouraging trees to grow. In 1862 the territorial legislature asked Congress in a memorial if it would pay the settlers to cut timber from federal lands, since the forests on Puget Sound were so dense that clearing them for agriculture was almost impossible "and at least, very unprofitable." The legislators added that the lumber mills had been expensive to build for that reason and that it would take the people a century or more "to materially change the forest that is very densely standing." The

8. *The Totem* (June, July, August, 1971). *The Totem* is published by the Department of Natural Resources. Unless otherwise noted, information and quotations in this section are from this issue of *The Totem*.

amazement of the memorialists would have been great had they been told that in the 1940s we would be importing Douglas fir, and even lumber from certain other types of evergreen trees, because our own supply was practically gone. Those who lived into the 1890s did begin to see that the forests were disappearing, because in 1895 the state legislature asked Congress to pass a law to protect our forest reserves.

During the territorial period, people on the east side of the Cascades were encouraged to plant trees. In 1873 the legislature allowed the boards of county commissioners in Stevens and Whitman counties to exempt property up to $300 per acre from all taxation except territorial if the owner would agree to plant and cultivate trees.

Even by 1877 forest fires had done enough damage that the territorial legislature authorized fines against anyone who started a forest fire from carelessness, and by 1903 the state legislature made the commissioner of public lands ex officio state forest fire warden. The boards of county commissioners were to act as local deputies to supervise fire fighting in forests. This arrangement, however, did not provide sufficiently good organization to combat forest fires successfully, and serious fires continued until it became evident that a more efficient system was necessary.

Most of us have seen mountainsides with only stumps of trees remaining, where there was obviously at one time a thick evergreen forest. When the timber is cut off, trees for future use are gone for several generations, ground water protection is lost, erosion sets in, farmland is ruined, and floods usually follow. Part or all of this cycle has meant real tragedy to many communities. Loggers and lumber mill employees are thrown out of work when the available supply of timber is gone in a lumbering region. This type of unemployment still makes a difficult situation in some of our towns today. Loss of timber stands can come from forest fires and also from wasteful cutting of trees. To fight against such destruction, the state legislature has passed laws for the protection of our forests and has given to the Department of Natural Resources the job of enforcing them.

Forest Practices Act

It was mentioned above that people may lease forest lands for cutting timber through the Department of Natural Resources. For many years, the legislature has required that when loggers lease such land, they leave a sufficient number of trees on the state land to provide for reforestation. In 1945 the legislature passed a law, called the Forest Practices Act, which requires that minimum conservation practices be followed in cutting timber even on private land if the stand in question consists of a certain number of board feet per acre (now two thousand). From 1945 to 1947, the supervisor of forestry within the Department of Conservation and Development enforced these regulations on both state and private land. Now the supervisor is a member of the Department of Natural Resources, appointed by the commissioner of public lands.

The Forest Practices Act was contested and a case brought in the superior court for Pend Oreille County in 1948 in which the defendant claimed that the law was an unconstitutional use of the state's police power. The superior court held that the law was, indeed, unconstitutional, and in 1949 the state appealed the case to the state supreme court, where the law was upheld as being sufficiently in the public interest to justify such reasonable regulation of the use of private property. The original defendants then made an appeal to the United States Supreme Court, which likewise upheld the law as a valid one. Consequently, it is now in effect, with the amendments added since 1945 by the legislature.

The present procedure is that the owner of a timber stand is required to notify the supervisor of natural resources that he intends to log a certain area, including maps for identification and a statement as to how he plans to observe the stipulation that the specified number and kind of trees be left uncut. (If an operator rather than the owner is making the arrangements, either the owner has to agree to be responsible for the operator's compliance with the law or the operator has to give bond.) If the supervisor is satisfied with the conservation proposals, he issues a permit for the area to be logged. Then if an inspector from the supervisor's office finds that the terms of the agreement are not being met, he can order logging operations halted until the logger gives a sufficient bond for restocking the area. If, after five years, he has not planted new trees, he forfeits his bond, and the supervisor uses the money to do the restocking.

Alternative methods of conservation are allowed under the Forest Practices Act. *Selective logging* may be followed, in which only trees of a certain size or age are cut, leaving a partial forest from which another crop of trees may be cut every few years. But it is difficult to bring heavy machinery into the woods and cut only certain trees, the expensive procedure necessary for selective logging. *Sustained-yield cutting* is less expensive because everything is cleared out of certain strips and everything left in others. For example, trees on the crown of a hill or on a ridge may be left to reseed the hillside so that a sustained yield of timber will be maintained. However, recently conservationists have become concerned over the erosion and resulting soil loss from this method, called *clear cutting* in neighboring states. Consequently, experimentation is continuing to take into account as many aspects as possible of both conservation and expense to the loggers.

From the 2,000,000 acres of state-owned forests, the timber sales division of the department sells 774,000,000 board feet of lumber annually (with a value in 1970 of over $40,000,000). However, ecological values are now considered very important, and protection of the land figures prominently in all special sales and contracts now being written.

Various techniques are following in these attempts to protect the land. In some areas operators cut small trees from virgin old-growth stands; these stunted trees can then be used instead of being broken into unusable chunks of wood during a regular harvesting operation. Also dense new stands are thinned to give sufficient light and space to the remaining trees. If the terrain will not suffer, caterpillar machinery is used in logging; however, if this will result in unjustified soil disturbance, skyline equipment is used.

During World War II, lumber companies realized that they would profit from the practice of conservation policies, since it was evident that without them the industry would be almost gone in a few years. Consequently, many lumber companies are doing even more in the way of conservation than the law requires. They are planting seedlings to build up new forests on land that was completely logged off before the Forest Practices Act went into effect and are working with state officials to get everyone to regard timber as a crop to be harvested each year or every few years as other crops are.

To aid in the program for improving timber culture on private land, the Forest Land Management Division of the department employs twelve farm foresters throughout the state to give assistance to timber owners and to see that the provisions of the Forest Practices Act are observed. The division maintains tree nurseries and drops seeds by plane on burned-over or logged land where that is feasible. Where it is not, the areas are hand-seeded. The division also conducts research on controlling insects or diseases that affect trees and does as much as is possible to eliminate attacks.

Fire Protection

Fire is another major threat to the existence of forests, and the Fire Control Division of the department is in charge of preventing and controlling forest fires. The work of the state fire fighters is very similar to that done by the United States Forest Service in our national parks and forests. Both use airplanes to spot fires. In 1970 seven helicopters and fourteen planes were under contract with the Department of Natural Resources for this purpose. In the past smoke jumpers and supplies were dropped from the planes where they were needed for fire fighting. In combating an extensive fire, the fighters still sometimes use parachutes in this fashion, but recently fire retardant chemicals have been successfully sprayed from an air tanker to extinguish many forest fires.

Before airplanes were available for fire scouting and fire fighting, *lookouts* were employed to spot the start of a forest fire. Now, fewer lookouts are

maintained, only 29 in 1970, fourteen in western Washington, twelve of which are largely used to collect weather data, and fifteen in eastern Washington. Usually, these men or women live on the top of a mountain and keep watch over the surrounding forests for a sign of fire. They report regularly to men at ranger stations, who go out to fight fires. The forest rangers also cut trails or do other work involved in serving the public in these areas.

Fires caused by trains are now decreasing because in 1970 the department required all nonturbocharged locomotives passing through forest lands in Washington to be equipped with approved spark arresters. This type of fire decreased, whereas all other man-caused fires increased in that year by 43 percent. The use of fire for cooking by campers presents another main source of forest fires, and in dry weather fire permits have been required on state land for many years. The 1971 legislature added the provision that the foresters issuing fire permits take into consideration air quality effects as well as fire safety aspects. Now the Fire Control Division, the Air Quality Section of the Washington State Department of Ecology, and the various air pollution control authorities are trying to design one permit that will regulate all outdoor burning.

Log Patrol Act

In logging activities, many logs are lost while floating downstream to a mill or trucking outlet, or in other ways, and in order for the owner to be able to prove that a particular log is his, it has to have some identifying mark called a log brand. Anyone wishing to use such a brand is required to apply to the law enforcement division of the Department of Natural Resources for a permit to do so by sending the impression of the brand burned in a piece of leather or a clear drawing, plus a written description of the mark. A staff member then checks to find if it differs from all others registered with the division, and, if it does, he records it as the brand of the owner, and no one else may use it.

In the Log Patrol Act the legislature requires that any person using a boat to push or pull log booms through the water secure a license from the law enforcement division, and if these log patrol boats pick up stray logs the law states that their operators must turn the logs over to the division, which manages their sale and sends a percentage of the sale price to the owner (if he can be located by the log brand), or to the state if the log is unbranded. Income to the state in 1970 from the sale of stray logs was $80,636.82.[9]

9. State of Washington, Department of Natural Resources, *The Seventh Biennial Report* (1969-70).

Fire fighter, Yakima County. Although great strides are being made in the use of airplanes and other modern techniques to fight forest fires, the "infantrymen" still must carry the brunt of the battle. (Photo by Washington State Department of Natural Resources)

State and Federal Cooperation

In many places state forests are adjacent to national forests, and it is necessary then for the state and federal foresters to arrange a cooperative program. If the state system for fighting fires is poor, a fire from a state forest may spread into a national forest, and, if the two crews do not work together, a tragic increase in the loss of timber results. To prevent this kind of waste and to aid individual states, Congress passed the Clark-McNary Act in 1924, establishing a system of federal aid for forest administration. The secretary of agriculture in Washington, D.C., examines the requests of states for funds and determines if the state is making an adequate effort to control forest fires. If the secretary of agriculture approves the plan submitted to him by a state, he may release funds to it.

Reforestation Acts

A similar arrangement was made possible in 1937 when Congress passed the Cooperate Farm Forestry Act. It provided that federal funds can be added to state money for the planting of new trees. Federal funds released to our state for these purposes are now administered by the Department of Natural Resources, which maintains tree nurseries where seedlings are raised for planting on state land and for sale to lumber companies or private individuals. The Board of Natural Resources may also buy or lease land that is logged over, or for other reasons is suitable for reforestation projects. When the board has acquired such land, it may be designated as state forest land, and the Department of Natural Resources can plant trees on it and hold the land until it is again ready for cutting.

State forest land cannot be sold, but it may be leased, and timber or other products from it may be sold. The sale of Christmas trees from such land is one specific action under the board's control. With its approval, the Department of Natural Resources makes agreements with dealers to take these trees, mainly from land where trees of commercial size will not grow or where thinning of second-growth trees is desirable. The legislature permits the same procedure for individuals who want to harvest huckleberry brush, salal, sword fern, cascara, and other minor forest products from state forest land.

Multiple Use of State Lands

The cultivation of timber is only one of the many uses of lands owned by the state. In fact, the Department of Natural Resources is now stressing the concept of multiple use of state lands, attempting to make them available also for agricultural, recreational, and mineral purposes, more than one at a time wherever possible. For example, the 1969-70 biennial report of the department gives statistics on the conversion of low-income dry state land into valuable agricultural land through joint projects between the department and the lessees to irrigate the land; on the leasing of dry land for grazing where irrigation is not feasible, sometimes simply by fencing in a spring to provide clean water for the livestock and produce game or game bird sanctuaries at the same time. With the present awareness of the importance of ecological considerations, more emphasis is placed on trying to find out what the maximum uses of any state land can be without destroying its potential for future use and enjoyment by people. The federal Soil Conservation Service and the Agricultural Extension Service give advice on the scientific management of land for agricultural and conservation purposes, and various educational and governmental agencies with specialists in biology, chemistry, and allied sciences aid in analyzing the effects of a particular land use on animal life, soil depletion, air pollution, and other aspects of environmental health.

Nearly all state land, except that under intensive agricultural development, has some possibilities of recreational use. Camping, fishing, hiking, and other outdoor activities are known to thousands of people visiting our state parks and forests, from which timber may also be sold where feasible. Tide and shore lands along lakes, Puget Sound, and the ocean itself are among the most treasured of such sites. The Interagency for Outdoor Recreation was established through an initiative to distribute state and federal recreation funds, and it has approved for the 1971-73 biennium an appropriation for the Department of Natural Resources to add primitive camp and picnic sites to those already on state-owned tide land. Three of these are oriented to the physically handicapped and mentally retarded and are located near Tacoma, Spokane and Vancouver. Other activities of the department related to tide lands consist in forming a project with the Lummi Indians to harvest seaweed from the waters of northern Puget Sound, called aquaculture; leasing tracts for commercial harvesting of geoduck clams; leasing tide and shore lands to oil and gas companies for exploratory drilling; and renting harbor areas. During the 1969-71 biennium, the income for the state from bids for oil and gas leases equaled $236,446 and from the department's water area program $1,492,398.

The detrimental effects of strip mining, if the stream beds and banks are left piled high with the sand and rocks removed, led the legislature in its 1969 session to require that operators of surface-mining projects restore the area to the point where it may be used for some subsequent purpose specifically spelled out beforehand, plus restoring stream channels and banks to a condition minimizing erosion, siltation, and other pollution. The Division of Mines and Geology is responsible for enforcing this law. The division also evaluates ore samples from mineral deposits. In addition, the Division of Mines and Geology is conducting research leading to a geologic map of the state for use by persons interested in mineral deposits and also by those who want such information for recreational purposes.

In an attempt to disseminate information on the need for concern for environmental quality, the department maintains a supervisor of environmental services and staff in the office of the state superintendent of schools. One of their projects is the Outdoor Education Laboratory on Whidbey Island and other smaller areas for outdoor education. During the 1969-71 biennium, 54,520 school children received environmental education training.

Honor Camps

The Department of Natural Resources cooperates with the Division of Institutions of the Department of Social and Health Services in establishing adult and youth forest camps where honor prisoners from the penitentiary and reformatory and juvenile institutions, respectively, do useful work in state-owned forests. Examples of accomplishments in these camps during 1970 are: adult camps, slash was disposed of on 529 acres, youth camps, 347 acres; adult camps, 189.3 miles of roads were maintained, youth camps, 371.7 miles; adult camps, 5,117 acres were planted to trees, youth camps, 581 acres. Many other types of projects are also undertaken.

State Capitol Committee

Although in accordance with the 1957 law, the Board of Natural Resources now appraises capitol lands, the State *Capitol* Committee is still responsible for making contracts for the construction of new capitol buildings or the repair of existing ones. It is assisted in this work by the engineers in the Department of General Administration, which supervises the construction and maintenance of capitol buildings.

The 1961 legislature authorized the State Capitol Committee to acquire additional property for expansion of the state capitol grounds and instructed the Department of General Administration to develop an over-all plan for capitol buildings and grounds, subject to the approval of the State Capitol Committee. No state agency may construct buildings in Thurston County except on state capitol grounds without the approval of the State Capitol Committee.

State Land Planning Commission

Because of the rapidly increasing concern on the part of the general public with all phases of environmental protection, the 1971 legislature created the State Land Planning Commission, consisting of legislators and private citizens, the latter appointed by the governor. Its purpose is to study the feasibility of using computers or some alternative means of compiling statewide land-use data. From this storehouse of information, goals and policies for land use should then be formed, taking into consideration population growth and distribution, urban expansion, open space, resource preservation, and other factors of statewide development patterns. For details of the composition of the commission, see the table at the end of chapter 3.

STATE COMMISSIONER OF INSURANCE

The office of the commissioner of insurance is the only one of the executive departments that was not created by the state constitution. The first state legislature, 1889-90, required the secretary of state to serve as ex officio insurance commissioner. Then in 1907 the present office was established and made an elective one. Therefore, the insurance commissioner became the ninth state executive official. He and his employees make up the state Insurance Department.

Of the many kinds of insurance in which people may invest, one hears most about life, fire, theft, and automobile liability and accident insurance for private individuals. The insurance companies invest the money that is paid to them, and they use the interest on their investments to pay the claims of the persons who take out insurance policies. A large sum of money is put into insurance—$1,011,870,142 in the state of Washington in 1969.[10]

If the officials of insurance companies do not use good judgment in their investments or if they are dishonest, most of the people in the state will suffer some kind of financial loss. Consequently, the function of the commissioner of insurance is to make certain that the insurance companies are doing legitimate business and able to pay the justifiable claims against them.

In order to do this, the commissioner of insurance hires many trained examiners who inspect the books of all insurance companies having their headquarters in this state. They also make an examination at various periods of companies whose headquarters are outside the state, but who are licensed to sell insurance here.

In addition to determining that the companies themselves are sound, the Insurance Department must be certain that the many insurance agents who sell insurance for the companies are competent. For this purpose, the Insurance Department requires that each insurance agent, broker, or adjuster pass a written examination on the kinds of insurance which he intends to sell. Those who pass the examination are then issued licenses by the Insurance

10. State of Washington, *Insurance Commissioner's Seventy-sixth Annual Report* (1970).

Department. If there are charges later that an agent has not observed the insurance laws of this state, he may be brought before the commissioner of insurance for a hearing. If the complaints are proved true, his license may be suspended or revoked.

An insurance company that is solvent and whose agents are honest and capable may be charging rates that are unreasonable in view of the risks involved in that particular kind of insurance. The commissioner of insurance is responsible for seeing that rates are not exorbitant, and he may hold hearings or make any necessary examinations to determine such questions.

The 1955 legislature gave to the insurance commissioner the added responsibility of checking the health and welfare funds operated by labor unions or other employee groups to see that the money is not mismanaged.

National Association of Insurance Commissioners

Many of the insurance companies licensed to sell insurance in our state have their headquarters in another state. Consequently, it is necessary for the commissioner of insurance to be familiar with the insurance laws of other states as well as those of our own. As a means of pooling such information, the heads of the insurance departments of all of our states and territories formed the National Association of Insurance Commissioners, which meets twice a year. The members discuss the insurance laws of the various states and try to determine which are the best ones. It makes for greater efficiency if the insurance laws are the same in all states, and the insurance commissioners try to secure uniform legislation throughout the United States. In our state, the insurance commissioner has an opportunity to suggest such laws to the state legislature in his report.

Even though the headquarters of an insurance company may not be in this state, the company is required to pay taxes to the state of Washington if it sells insurance here. The amount of tax is set according to our tax laws and to those of the company's home state. This is another reason for the securing of information concerning the insurance laws of other states. Keeping accurate and detailed records of these laws is one of the functions of the Division of Statistics, a section of the Insurance Department.

State Fire Marshal

The insurance commissioner has the ex officio title of state fire marshal, and in this capacity it is his duty to work for the prevention of fire hazards in any locality where there is no comprehensive local fire prevention and safety code. He or his deputies may enter any building except a private dwelling to inspect it for fire hazards, and he may order that changes be made to eliminate any such dangers. The chief of each fire department or the county sheriff in rural areas is required to report to the state fire marshal all fires of undetermined origin or ones where arson is suspected, and he may investigate these or any other fire. In 1953 the legislature also gave him authority to regulate the granting of permits for supervised public displays of fireworks.

Certain types of boarding houses or sanitariums must also have their fire prevention methods approved by the state fire marshal. For example, any individual or group applying to the Department of Social and Health Services for permission to operate a children's home must first have a certificate of approval from the state fire marshal, and the same precaution is specified for sanitariums for alcoholics and the mentally ill.

QUASI-JUDICIAL AGENCIES

One can see from this discussion of the executive departments that they have the power to force people to obey their regulations as long as these conform to state laws. In order to decide whether or not a person has broken a rule, the department holds a hearing at which the accused person may try to justify his action. This procedure is so similar to that of a court that a department which has this power is called a quasi-judicial agency—that is, it has some characteristics of a court. Individuals may also demand a hearing on a department's action or failure to act.

As our civilization becomes more complex, quasi-judicial agencies are being used more and more frequently, because experts in a particular field are better able to decide complicated technical questions than are ordinary jurors or judges. For example, a layman would have to study for months before he would know enough about the technicalities of insurance finance to make a correct decision in such a case, but the experts in the Department of Insurance already have this knowledge. Consequently, it saves the state time and money to have them decide arguments over insurance regulations. Similar examples in fields represented by most of the other executive departments could be pointed out, and the administrative departments, discussed in the following chapter, also have this power.

Ordinarily, the individuals who are accused of having broken a regulation of a governmental agency would rather have the matter settled by the department than by the regular county superior court because of the saving to them in time and money. People in this country, however, are very much opposed to letting our civil courts lose power even for the sake of efficiency. Consequently, the state laws specify that any person may appeal the decision of a quasi-judicial body to the superior courts. In addition, the legislature has declared certain violations of departmental orders to be crimes, and they have to be reported to a prosecuting attorney or the attorney general for prosecution in superior court.

The usual penalty which one of these quasi-judicial agencies may impose is to revoke a license that it has granted. The legislature does permit some of the departments to assess fines for certain specific violations of rules, and the departments may also compel a person to stop a practice that is against their rules by issuing a *cease and desist* order. This type of action, though, like any of their others, may be appealed by the defendant to the superior court, if he so wishes.

SUGGESTED READINGS

Original sources for a study of any branch of our state government are official state documents corresponding to those listed for the territorial period at the end of the preceding chapter: *Session Laws of the State of Washington; Reports of the Supreme Court of the State of Washington; Revised Code of Washington;* and *Journals of the State Senate and House of Representatives.*

Helpful current materials on the operation of a given executive department may be secured from the head of the agency. The secretary of state issues brochures on various topics of general interest, in addition to the lists of state officials, maps of congressional and legislative districts, and laws on certain subjects. The biennial or annual reports of the commissioner of public lands, Department of Natural Resources, superintendent of public instruction, insurance commissioner, state treasurer, and state auditor contain helpful information on the activities of the individual offices. When funds are available, some of the departments issue serial publications for the use of public school students and members of the general public interested in a specific subject. *The Totem,* a monthly publication of the Department of Natural Resources, is an example.

Pamphlets on minority problems are issued by the office of the state superintendent of schools, the governor's Advisory Council on Urban Affairs, the governor's Indian Advisory Committee, and the Washington State Commission on Mexican-American Affairs.

TABLE I
EXECUTIVE BRANCH

Official*	Salary as of 1972	Vacancy, How Filled	Qualifications Required	Present Official (1973)
Governor	$32,500 plus $12,000 for maintenance of gov.'s mansion	Succeeded by lt. gov., sec. of state, and so forth. After elective officials, speaker of house, pres. pro tem of senate; then someone elected by legislature.	Qualified voter	Daniel J. Evans (R)†
Lieutenant governor	$10,000	Gov. appoints successor until election.	Qualified voter	John A. Cherberg (D)
Secretary of state	$15,000	Gov. appoints successor until election.	Qualified voter	A. Ludlow Kramer (R)
State treasurer	$15,000	Gov. appoints successor until election.	Qualified voter	Robert S. O'Brien (D)
State auditor	$16,500	Gov. appoints successor until election.	Qualified voter	Robert V. Graham (D)
Attorney general	$23,000	Gov. appoints successor until election.	Qualified voter and member of the state bar.	Slade Gorton (R)
Superintendent of public instruction†	$22,500	Gov. appoints successor until election.	Qualified voter	Frank B. Brouillet (N)
Commissioner of public lands #	$20,000	Gov. appoints successor until election.	Qualified voter	Bert Cole (D)
Commissioner of insurance	$16,500	Gov. appoints successor until election.	Qualified voter	Karl Hermann (D)

* All are elected for a four-year term.
+ (R) = Republican; (D) = Democrat; (N) = Nonpartisan.
† With his staff constitutes State Department of Education.
# With his staff constitutes State Department of Natural Resources

3. State Administrative Departments

The administrative branch of our state government consists of officials, departments, or other types of groups which handle details of state business too numerous for the nine elected executive officials to administer. The administrative branch is, then, an extension of the executive branch, discussed in the preceding chapter. As far as the organization is concerned, the difference between the executive and administrative departments is that the heads of the executive offices are elected by the people, whereas the heads of the administrative departments or committees are appointed.

Since we now have over 120 administrative departments, boards, commissions, committees, and so forth, it is obvious that the voters could not know enough about candidates for that many offices to vote for them. As we noted earlier, voters often have difficulty in being thoroughly familiar with details of the nine who are elected now. Thus, the legislature provided that the governor could appoint the heads of the main departments, believing that he could better choose people who are competent and well trained for the work involved. As various additional boards and advisory committees were established, the legislature specified how they were to be manned—usually by appointees of either the governor or the head of some administrative department already in existence. For some, the governor is required to have the consent of the senate for his appointments, and there is an indication of this in Tables 2 and 3 at the end of this chapter.

The work of the administrative departments has gradually widened as social and industrial developments have created new fields where governmental regulation has been judged necessary. From time to time the legislature set up individual departments, until by 1921 they seemed to be something of a hodgepodge. In that year the legislature decided to reorganize the administrative branch by combining some boards, abolishing others, and creating new departments. The series of laws covering these agencies is known as the *administrative code*. At that time, the legislature was influenced by the fact that a number of other states, and particularly Idaho and Oregon, had attempted similar reorganizations a few years earlier. The object in such states had been to eliminate overlapping of functions in existing state agencies, to reduce the number of departments in the interest of efficiency and economy, and to achieve a clear-cut organizational system.

In Washington, the 1921 legislature combined the existing state administrative agencies into ten departments: public works, business control, efficiency, taxation and examination, health, conservation and development, labor and industries, agriculture, licenses, and fisheries and game. Practically all of the remaining state functions were assigned to the state elective officials, who were formed into nine ex officio committees: equalization, finance, highways, capitol, archives, parks, voting machine, state library, and state law library.

Since 1921 the number of primary departments has been increased by one only, although some duties have been shifted from one department to another and the names have often changed—in some cases, more than once. As of 1972, the eleven "code departments" are: agriculture, commerce and economic development, ecology, fisheries, game, general administration, highways, labor and industries, motor vehicles, revenue, social and health services. The large number of current agencies is made up mainly of boards and commissions, whose duties have become interwoven with those of the administrative and executive departments to a cumbersome degree. Therefore, in recent years, there have been recommendations for another reorganization plan, and the legislature in the 1969 and 1971 sessions attempted to combine many of the agencies dealing with air and water pollution into the Department of Ecology, and to include the proliferated health and welfare units in the Department of Social and Health Services. An earlier attempt at streamlining combined separate agencies into the Department of Natural Resources.

CONSERVATION OF NATURAL RESOURCES

The Department of Natural Resources, discussed in chapter 2, deals mainly with the problem of conservation of resources of state-owned land. The urgent needs for conservation of our resources of soil, water (including marine life), animal life, minerals, air, and all other natural phenomena that can be diminished by use, however, extend to those under the control of private individuals; and the state agencies that regulate their exploitation will be described in this chapter. The conservation and development of our human resources is also an essential phase of the problem of the general welfare of the state, and a discussion of the governmental units involved in this program will form the second part of this chapter. The third section will deal with the state fiscal agencies.

The state agencies devoted to the conservation of our natural resources are centered largely around the main occupations of the residents of the state. In addition to lumbering (whose regulation was discussed in chapter 2), these are agriculture, fishing, and mining. All of these depend on keeping a constant supply of raw materials or on developing better ways of using them. The state agencies in a given field are created to take the lead in such work and also to see that the public is protected from the sale of diseased or harmful products.

The recent widespread realization that clean air and water are essential to the continued existence of plant, animal, and human life has introduced the difficult problem of maintaining a balance between modern technology and healthful, beautiful surroundings. The subject of ecology has therefore become important to all of these state agencies.

Department of Agriculture

Two considerations—maintaining the kind of soil, water, and air in which healthy, vigorous plants and animals can be grown, and protecting buyers from goods of poor quality—are stressed in the state Department of Agriculture, one of the largest and oldest of the administrative departments, having been established in 1913. Even before that time, agricultural problems had concerned the legislature. The territorial legislature in 1870 had provided that if a horse was suspected of having glanders disease, a jury was to be called to examine the animal. If it agreed that the horse had the affliction, the owner was required to kill the animal. Moreover, anyone who knowingly brought a diseased animal into the territory was subject to a fine.

The state legislature began to create agricultural agencies almost as soon as the state was admitted in 1889. The 1891 legislature, for example, established a State Board of Horticulture to aid fruit and vegetable growers. In 1895 a dairy commissioner was authorized to inspect milk products for impurities; a State Grain Commission was established; and a State Board of Stock Commissioners was created to make rules for recording brands, shipping stock, and controlling cattle depredations in counties where such services were desired. In 1909 the State Agriculture Experiment Station was given control of the quality of seeds and feedstuffs; and the Railroad Commission was empowered to fix prices to be charged by public warehousemen and to appoint an inspector to weigh and grade grains, the responsibility previously of the State Grain Commission. In 1913 these miscellaneous functions, plus others, were gathered together under the jurisdiction of the new state Department of Agriculture.

The department has devoted itself mainly to licensing the type of food sold rather than to problems of agricultural education because the federal government provides the farmer with many educational aids. (Washington State University at Pullman is a land grant institution—that is, Congress gave it land and money on condition that, among other things, it teach agriculture. Experiments on types of soils, new crops, soil conservation, dairy methods, and so forth are constantly being made at the university, and the farmers of the state are able to take advantage of the new discoveries through the extension program, paid for in part by the United States Department of Agriculture, a federal rather than a state agency.) The state Department of Agriculture also conducts research in connection with the control of animal and plant diseases and publishes the results.

The director of the state Department of Agriculture, who is appointed by the governor with senate consent, is responsible for licensing persons to sell all types of agricultural produce—livestock, meat, dairy products, fruits, vegetables, eggs, feeds, fertilizers, livestock remedies, honey, seeds, hay, and grain. The purpose of licensing the sale of food is to have control over its quality, to see that it is clean and healthful. The procedure is that the department establishes standards for grading the various kinds of food within certain specifications set by state law. Then it has the power to refuse to issue a license to a farmer or merchant whose produce does not meet the standards required. Where a license is necessary, the legislature has made it a criminal offense to sell without one. Moreover, a license may be revoked by the department in the manner of the quasi-judicial agencies discussed in chapter 2.

Agricultural industries are very important to the state, as this statement by the director makes clear: "One of the state's top three industries, agriculture has a multi-billion-dollar impact on Washington's economy. In 1970, the farm-gate value of agricultural production was a record $898,659,000. As the products of this highly-diversified industry are stored, processed and distributed, their value is increased many fold."[1]

The way in which the department maintains its standards for these agricultural products in its function of consumer protection can be illustrated from its work with livestock and dairy products. Neither meat nor milk from diseased cattle can be sold; consequently, tests have to be made for tuberculosis and brucellosis (Bang's disease), particularly, the two ailments in cattle which seem to affect humans most easily. Formerly, department employees used stamping methods to test all herds in the state for brucellosis, and any affected cattle were quarantined. (Quarantine, in this sense, means that the owner cannot sell any products from such cattle until they are

_____
1. State of Washington, *1971 Annual Report, Natural Resources and Recreation Agencies* (1971).

pronounced well. If they cannot be cured, they are killed to prevent spread of the disease.) Testing for brucellosis on cattle ranches is extremely expensive, and in 1955 the department introduced a more satisfactory means of locating diseased cattle, which is now used throughout the country. Each animal is tagged when it is sent to market, and blood samples are taken from the cows in the slaughterhouses. If laboratory analysis reveals infection, the owner of the herd from which the animal came can be ascertained by the tag. Milk samples from all dairy herds are also collected four times a year and tested for brucellosis infection; and as a result "Washington achieved brucellosis-free and hog cholera-free status in 1967."[2] The methods used by the department to prevent hog cholera are: prohibiting the importation of hogs where that disease (or others) exists, and monthly inspection of farms where garbage is fed to hogs to see that the regulations requiring cooking of the garbage are observed.

The department, in cooperation with the United States Department of Agriculture, also conducts research to find ways of combating other diseases in cattle, horses, pigs, sheep, poultry, and so forth, and makes regulations to control the sale of any diseased animal and to stop the spread of disease as much as possible. During the 1968-70 biennium the programs of the United States Department of Agriculture were integrated with those of the state Department of Agriculture to a greater degree. Because our state was an early leader in the country in providing superior protection for consumers, the federal government accepted Washington's requirements as equal to federal standards. Consequently, under the United States Wholesome Meat Act, all meat inspectors in the state were given state civil service status and trained and licensed by the United States Department of Agriculture. The same procedure was instituted for poultry plant inspection under the Federal Wholesome Poultry Products Act, and Washington was the fourth state in the union to be certified under these federal programs. Washington is now (1972) also eligible for certification for the federal egg inspection program.

All meat sold in the state must be inspected by these state-federal inspectors except for meat sold directly to consumers by farmers from animals slaughtered on their own farms. Every person who operates a slaughterhouse or meat market in the state must be licensed to do so, and the license fees pay part of the cost of hiring a sufficient number of meat inspectors. During the 1968-70 biennium, improvements were made in ways of identifying meat from animals exempt from such inspection; to prevent its entering trade channels, it must be labeled "not inspected."[3]

2. According to the director of agriculture, in State of Washington, *Twenty-Ninth Biennial Report, Department of Agriculture, July 1, 1968 to June 30, 1970* (1970).

3. All references to specific work done by a department during a given period are taken from the annual or biennial reports of that department, unless otherwise indicated. Reports from certain departments, specified by the legislature, are published in a series

In addition to taking milk samples from dairy cows to be tested for brucellosis, the department attempts to insure that farmers follow sanitary methods in handling milk or butter even though the cows are healthy. Anyone who sells Grade A dairy products must have a license to do so. The department's employees inspect farms, creameries, and other dairy establishments to make certain that they are clean and that the equipment is adequate for the grade of milk sold. The inspectors also see that the percentage of butterfat in the milk products is as much as the law requires. The inspection of refrigerated lockers for sanitary methods of food handling and proper temperature maintenance is also included in their jurisdiction.

New programs adopted during the 1968-70 biennium in regard to dairy products were establishing standards for frozen desserts and conforming to the national abnormal milk program for mastitis control through the Interstate Milk Shippers Organization.

The 1949 legislature provided that any city, township, or county that wants a local milk inspection service unit instead of the general inspection from the Department of Agriculture may ask the director for a certificate of approval. With the consent of the secretary of the Department of Social and Health Services, the director may define the boundaries of the local unit, and, if he is satisfied with the health officer, the laboratory equipment, and other facilities provided, he may accredit the local milk inspection service. The director of agriculture may cancel any such certificate of approval after thirty days' notice if the unit proves inadequate or remiss. Cities may also make similar arrangement for meat inspection, and if they wish to maintain higher standards they may do so.

On big cattle ranches where the herds graze over a large area, the owner usually brands the calves with some particular mark which can be recognized as his own. He may register this brand with the state Department of Agriculture, and it acts then as a trademark. No one else may use this brand or claim cattle that have it.

Since 1947 public livestock markets have also been included in the livestock agencies requiring inspection, and fur-bearing animals raised on fur farms likewise come under the jurisdiction of the department.

The legislature requires that fruits and vegetables be sold under safeguards for the consumer's health. In order to prevent the spread of infectious diseases, inspectors of the state Department of Agriculture test fruits and vegetables that are shipped into or out of the state and destroy any carrying an infectious disease. Because any out-of-state shipment becomes a part of interstate commerce, under federal regulation, the state Department of Agriculture works under a cooperative agreement with the United States

---

called Washington Public Documents, issued biennially.

Corn harvest near Stanwood, Snohomish County. Grain corn is one of Washington's most valuable crops. (Photo by Washington State Department of Commerce and Economic Development)

Department of Agriculture whereby both state and federal inspectors may inspect produce whether it is intended for intra-or interstate shipment.

The state Department of Agriculture grants licenses to farmers selling fruits, vegetables, grain, seeds, and nursery stock, if their produce is healthy. If it is not, the horticulture inspectors may quarantine a farmer's produce until it can be disinfected or healthy stock substituted.

In 1969 the legislature divided the state into eleven horticulture inspection districts to which the director is required to assign one or more inspectors-at-large.[4] The director is allowed to adjust the boundaries or abolish specific districts as long as he leaves at least six. There are also deputy horticultural inspectors who are paid from state, county, and federal funds. If a county wishes to pay for an additional inspector, the county commissioners have the authority to hire one or more.

No plant may be brought into the state without inspection at a point of entry unless our department has reciprocal agreements with another state for mutual exchange of plants. In such instances, an out-of-state nurseryman must have a license from our department and use containers marked with this

4. District 1 consists of Walla Walla, Columbia, Garfield, Asotin, Whitman, Benton, and Franklin counties; district 2, Spokane, Lincoln, Stevens, Ferry, and Pend Oreille counties; district 3, Adams and Grant counties; district 4, Chelan and southern part of Douglas County; district 5, Yakima, Kittitas, Klickitat, and Skamania counties; district 6, Clark, Cowlitz, and Wahkiakum counties; district 7, Lewis, Pacific, Thurston, Mason, and Grays Harbor counties; district 8, Pierce, Kitsap, Jefferson, and Clallam counties; district 9, King County; district 10, Whatcom, Snohomish, San Juan, Skagit, and Island counties; district 11, Okanogan and the northern part of Douglas County.

information and describing the contents. The director of agriculture is also required to fix standards for grades or classifications of plants. It is then unlawful to sell fruit or vegetables marked as a particular grade or class unless it meets those requirements. In addition, in 1961 the legislature gave the director permission to adopt rules to insure that certified or registered plant stock is genetically pure and breeds true to strain. He may establish crop improvement nurseries to grow stock for sale at cost, with the surplus to be given to commercial producers of certified or registered plants. Nobody may offer for sale stock said to be registered or certified unless it has been inspected under the direction of the director and approved.

The state Department of Agriculture in collaboration with the Statistical Reporting Service of the United States Department of Agriculture issues bulletins of statistics on various types of agricultural production.[5] In 1969 Washington's wheat crops were valued at $120,065,000, which made this state the largest producer of wheat in the country for that year, with the yield reaching 44.6 bushels per acre, the highest recorded. Orchard crops came next in importance, financially, the gross value being $108,643,000 for 1970, with the final processed figure estimated to be about $325,929,000. Apples accounted for 61.1 percent of the state's fruit crop, with pears, sweet cherries, and grapes following in that order. The amount of grapes planted each year is increasing, the rise in 1970 being 2,500 additional acres. For field crops, potatoes are also being planted in greater numbers, in 1970 rising 25 percent in value.

The department supervises the manufacture of sprays or dusts for combating insect pests or plant diseases, and licenses commercial applicators of such materials. All insecticides for sale in the state must be registered with the state director of agriculture. The department has, of course, recognized the recent emphasis on finding pesticides that will not have the danger of latent harm to animal or human life. In fact, the director said that the period of 1968-70 introduced us to the ecological revolution. One result of the increased concern of people everywhere in regard to everything that affects the environment was to direct even more attention toward pesticides. The state of Washington, already operating as comprehensive a pesticide regulatory program as any state in the nation, was in a position to demonstrate that effective controls existed and to respond promptly to ban or further restrict DDT. The result was an executive order by Governor Evans creating a temporary State Pesticide Review Board and directing the board to determine essential uses. Regulations resulted banning home, shade tree, and aquatic use and requiring permits for the very limited uses approved. Registration of Lindane vaporizers was also banned and a start was made

5. For titles of reports giving statistics on specific agricultural products, see the section of Suggested Readings at the end of this chapter.

toward substituting pesticides that are less toxic to bees and other pollinating insects for the control of ear worm in sweet corn. Many other problems in regard to these and other pesticides remain to be solved, and tests and research continue.[6]

Other specific agricultural products that are licensed or inspected by the state Department of Agriculture in order to control their quality and cleanliness are feeds, fertilizers, livestock remedies, honey, hay, grain, and warehouses.

In addition to seeing that our food materials are healthy and uncontaminated when they leave the farms, the department is also responsible for inspecting various food-processing plants to make certain that good sanitation practices are observed in the preparation of food products. Specific plants required by law to be inspected are flour mills, bakeries, macaroni plants, and confectioneries to see that white flour is enriched with the stipulated vitamins. Employees of the department also examine all food-manufacturing or -packing plants and canneries to check on the degree of sanitation observed.

Testing foods for branding or adulteration also comes within the scope of the department's authority for food sold within the state. Its regulations are modeled on federal requirements for foods involved in interstate commerce. Antifreeze mixtures for use in motor vehicles are included in the items the department is to test for misbranding.[7]

Food sanitation needs to be checked up to the point where food is actually consumed in public eating houses, and this necessity causes another seeming instance of duplication of function between two state departments. The Department of Agriculture is concerned with the way food is handled in a restaurant, but, even though the food itself may be kept clean, patrons can become ill if the dining room or the kitchen utensils are dirty or if a restaurant employee has tuberculosis or is a typhoid carrier. The requirements in connection with the cleanliness of the employees is the concern of the state Department of Social and Health Services. Consequently, inspectors for both departments have the authority to check restaurants for their respective phases of sanitation. To avoid a double inspection, in 1947 the two departments agreed that inspectors from the Department of Agriculture are responsible for food sanitation up to the point where it reaches a public eating house and that employees from the Department of Social and Health

6. For the boards created by the legislature to regulate the use of pesticides in general or to recommend measures regarding them, see *Pesticide* Control Board and *Pesticide* Advisory Board in Table 3 at the end of this chapter. Entries in it are arranged alphabetically according to the italicized word in each title.

7. See the State Board of *Pharmacy* in Table 3 as the state agency responsible for inspecting drugs and cosmetics, formerly a function of the state Department of Agriculture.

Services shall inspect restaurants, taverns, and other types of public eating places as part of their general supervision of any conditions which might encourage the spread of contagious diseases.

In addition to the food itself and the premises where it is sold or eaten, the general public is also concerned with the devices to measure or weigh agricultural produce. If scales are not accurate, either people will pay for more merchandise than they get or the seller, in turn, will be cheated. Consequently, the state legislature requires the Department of Agriculture to inspect weighing and measuring devices, including gasoline and other fuel tanks. Weighmasters who weigh trucks with their loads also have to be licensed by the department. The director of agriculture has the ex officio title of state sealer of weights and measures, and he employs trained persons to test such machines. If they weigh correctly, a seal is put on them that is not to be broken. If the machine is inaccurate and cannot be repaired, it is destroyed. The inspectors also investigate complaints by individuals who believe that they have received short weight on items purchased. Sample checks are made of packaged goods in retail stores to see if the packages have the weight claimed on their labels. A city may have its own inspection service for weights and measures with the approval of the director of agriculture.

The state Department of Agriculture is responsible for checking on merchants who sell produce for farmers on a commission or cash basis. The kinds of complaints investigated generally concern failure on the part of buyers to pay farmers for the produce bought. To protect the farmers, the department requires that each trucker carry a manifest of cargo book, showing the type of license he has, how the goods are paid for, and other information that enables the farmer to know that the buyer is a bona fide commission merchant who is dependable.

Commodity Commissions. An additional function given to the department by the 1955 legislature is the establishment of commodity commissions to issue marketing orders in regard to a particular commodity. If at least 5 percent or one hundred commercial producers of a given agricultural item petition the director of agriculture to make a marketing order, he is required to hold hearings and conduct referenda on the question until he gets the reaction of the producers. If the response is sufficiently favorable for him to issue a marketing order, he is required to set up a commodity commission to consist of not fewer than five nor more than thirteen people, two-thirds of whom are affected producers. The director is an ex officio member of each commission.

The commission enforces the terms of the order, which may include advertising to maintain present markets or create new ones for any state agricultural product; carrying on research to find more efficient methods of producing, handling, or marketing the commodity; naming labeling require-

Team of draft horses at the Western Washington State Fair in Puyallup, Pierce County. (Photo by Washington State Department of Commerce and Economic Development)

ments to improve standards and grades; and taking necessary action to prevent unfair trade practices. Producers may agree to such terms themselves, in which case they become the commission to enforce them.

Agricultural commissions in existence as of 1972 are: Washington State *Apple* Advertising Commission; Washington State *Beef* Commission; Washington *Blueberry* Commission; *Bulb* Commission; Washington State *Dairy* Products Commission; Washington State *Fruit* Commission; *Fryer* (chickens) Commission; Washington *Hop* Commission; Washington *Mint* Commission; Washington Dry *Pea* and Lentil Commission; Washington State *Potato* Commission; Washington State Seed *Potato* Commission; Washington *Tree* Fruit Research Commission; State *Wheat* Commission.

The apple, bulb, and dairy commissions were created individually by the legislature before the 1955 law allowed the director of agriculture to name additional commissions as the demand arose. The 1969 legislature also established the beef and tree fruit research commissions. The director ordered the formation of the remaining ones. These agencies use funds from dues or assessments made against the producers concerned, rather than from the state treasury. For further details, see Table 3.

In 1930 the legislature allocated to 4-H fairs, junior livestock shows, and community fairs part of the money from the parimutuel funds received by the State Horse Racing Commission. The director of agriculture appoints and serves as chairman of the five-man Fairs Commission, which advises him on the distribution of this money.

Local county agricultural experts, called county agents, are appointed through the Agricultural Extension Service of Washington State University and are paid from county, university, and federal funds. County agents carry on the educational phases of agricultural aid, and their duties will be discussed in chapter 7, "County Government."

Department of Ecology

The 1969 legislative session made a definite attempt to streamline the organization of the administrative branch by combining many of the individual units into larger agencies. In the field of conservation of natural resources, the Department of Ecology was created to take the place of the Department of Water Resources (which the 1967 session had substituted for the Department of Conservation), the Water Pollution Control Commission, the Water Resources Advisory Council, the Weather Modification Board, the Air Pollution Control Board, plus the pollution duties of the Department of Health.[8]

The director of the Department of Ecology is appointed by the governor with senate consent, and the duty of his department is to undertake studies dealing with all aspects of environmental problems involving land, water, or air; to manage and develop the air and water resources of the state in an orderly, efficient, and effective manner; and to maintain a coordinated program of pollution control for these and related land resources. As part of the coordinated program, the director is required to consult with the secretary of social and health services to assure that the agencies concerned with preservation of life and health may integrate their efforts—along with those of the federal government, other states, and the Canadian provinces—toward improvement of environmental quality.

The specific functions of the earlier departments concerned with conservation of natural resources are being maintained, for the most part, by the new Department of Ecology through divisions corresponding to the previous departments. One of these, the management of water resources, has been performed by many different agencies under various titles and organizational systems. It can therefore serve as a useful example.

Division of Water Resources. In 1917 the office of state hydraulic engineer was established. In 1921 the legislature created the state Department of Conservation and Development, which carried that title until 1957, when it was called the Department of Conservation. Before that year the department had been responsible for conservation measures in regard to timber, water for irrigation and power, and minerals. In that year, however, the responsibility for timber regulation was transferred to the Department of Natural Resources under the administration of the commissioner of public lands, as we saw in chapter 2.

8. Which was also abolished and made a part of the Department of Social and Health Services. The Columbia Basin Commission was deactivated at that time.

Because of the varied climate in our state, we have some land that is too wet to be farmed without draining and some that is too dry to be cultivated without irrigation. Draining swampy land has been a simpler task than getting water to dry land. In fact, the latter process was the beginning of our current system of dams that supply water for both irrigation and generating electricity. The Department of Conservation and its successor, the Department of Water Resources, supervised the state's reclamation activities until the establishment of the Department of Ecology, which continues this function through its Division of Water Resources.

From the time of Marcus Whitman's mission near present Walla Walla, settlers in the dry central part of the state have used irrigation to raise their crops. Our state government has been involved in some way with this growth of irrigation from the beginning of statehood. The first state legislature passed a law allowing farmers, with the approval of the Board of County Commissioners, to organize into irrigation districts, which are units of local government having the power to levy taxes, elect a board of directors, buy and sell property, construct irrigation works, and do other acts necessary to a public corporation.[9]

Since most local groups have not been able to finance irrigation projects without help, the state furnishes aid through the Division of Water Resources. When the division gets a request for funds, it investigates to see if the district is sound financially and if the loan would serve to increase land use as planned. If the division approves the district's proposal, it may lend money within the appropriation made for that purpose by the legislature.

Because we need a great deal of water for irrigation, the rivers supplying the water are very important, and arguments arise constantly as to who has the first right to water from a given stream. The building of a dam or even the construction of an additional irrigation ditch near the source of a river may affect the water supply for irrigating hundreds of farms farther downstream. The legislature has passed a detailed system of water-rights laws, and countless cases which concern them have to be settled in court. In order to avoid as many such suits as possible and to distribute the available water according to existing water rights, the legislature has stipulated that the division shall supervise the use of public waters within the state.

The division works through local water masters and stream patrolmen.[10] When disputes over water rights occur, the supervisor of the division acts as

9. Similar arrangements are in effect for diking and drainage districts and also for many other types of districts.

10. In counties where so much irrigation is done that a water master cannot take care of the problems of his county, the supervisor of water resources appoints stream patrolmen, who check their streams daily in the low-water season to see that water rights are observed. They work under the direction of the water master who, in turn, is responsible to the division.

referee and recommends a ruling to the county superior court, which may either sustain or overrule it. The division also issues permits to appropriate water, to construct reservoirs, to construct electric generating plants, and to sell electric power. When the county commissioners receive a petition to form an irrigation district, they are required to notify the director of the Department of Ecology, who asks the supervisor of water resources to investigate the amount of water available for the proposed irrigation system and to make a recommendation as to the feasibility of forming a district. When the supervisor of water resources receives an application to divert water from a stream for any purpose, he is required to notify the director of fisheries and the director of game, and if they think that the diversion will lower the water level to a point where fish will be affected, they instruct him not to issue the permit.

Electric Power. The Department of Ecology also has the authority now to regulate the production of electric energy by any private or public power company within the state (except a federal agency).[11]

It considers the sale of electricity as a public utility and tries to integrate the sale of electric facilities to the best advantage. It studies the present potential hydroelectric resources of the state and the amount of power now available, and aids public and private power companies to develop the greatest possible amount of electric power. One specific field of study is the feasibility of using steam-generating plants for atomic energy, made possible through agreements with the federal Atomic Energy Commission concerning the use of energy produced at the Hanford site.[12]

In our state, cities and public utility districts may build their own generating plants for electricity. Such districts are organized in a manner similar to that for irrigation, diking, and drainage districts. They function as local governmental units which may build dams or use other means to furnish a source of power for electricity production. They may also contract for the purchase of electricity from public or private agencies for sale in the district. A board of directors to manage the production and sale of power is elected for each district.

When a public utility district wishes to build a dam or other public work as a means of producing power, it must have permission from the Department of Ecology, whose engineers study the plan to decide if it seems workable. Moreover, sometimes a public utility district and a private power company

11. Formerly, the Department of Conservation and the State Power Commission divided this function, but the 1957 legislature abolished the State Power Commission and concentrated power supervision in the Department of Conservation (now the Department of Ecology) with a Power Advisory Committee, now discontinued.

12. In 1964 the federal commission built a dual-purpose reactor at Hanford to produce electric power from the waste steam generated in making plutonium. For details of an advisory group on this subject, see *Thermal* Power Plant Evaluation Council in Table 3.

both want to build a generating plant at the same place, and the Department of Ecology then has to decide which one appears to have the better resources and plan for undertaking. If the project affects the use of water involved in a federal generating system, the federal Power Commission may also have to make a decision in the matter.

Although the diking and drainage districts take care of excess water under normal conditions, in an unusually wet season, floods often strike various sections of the state, and some constant means of flood control is necessary. Flood-control measures are provided by the division of water resources within the Department of Ecology. The work consists of administering funds appropriated by the legislature for construction of dikes and other works to prevent floods; studying the river systems of the state in order to make recommendations for a long-range program of flood control; encouraging the organization of flood-control districts; and enforcing regulations concerning water-works construction in flood-control zones.

A group of residents in an area where floods are common may establish a flood-control district according to a plan similar to that for an irrigation district. A certain amount of state money is provided to match funds raised from district taxes if the plans for their flood-control projects are approved by the division. The Division of Water Resources may also designate an area as a flood-control zone if the flood danger is great enough. In such a zone, no dam or any kind of obstruction may be built in a stream without the consent of the division.

Interstate Compact Commission. The use of water in our area has implications for our neighboring states and Canada, since the Columbia and its tributaries flow through the entire Pacific Northwest. The present treaty with Canada on the joint water rights of Canada and the United States forms the basis for the use of the water and power from the Columbia River by both countries. In regard to the surrounding states, including California, conservationists have considered for a number of years an interstate agreement to divide water resources among them.

The United States Constitution forbids two or more states to make a compact without the consent of Congress, and bills for the division of water and for the Bonneville Power Administration to sell hydroelectric power over a wider area have been before Congress for a number of years. Studies have been made of probable population increase and growth of businesses in the Pacific Northwest, and statisticians and scientists are using the results to try to predict how much water and power this area could spare in the future without depriving itself, if water from the Columbia and Snake rivers were to be diverted to California and the Southwest.

When Congress is satisfied that a fair and workable compact has been devised and approves it, our Interstate Compact Commission, authorized by our legislature (and those of other nearby states) will consider ratifying it. If the various state legislatures accept it, the commission, or a similar one, will put it into effect. For the composition of our state commission, see Table 3.

Water Pollution Control. Contamination of rivers, lakes, and parts of Puget Sound had become sufficiently threatening even before the present heightened concern over environmental quality that the legislature began in the 1960s to create agencies to combat pollution. The first one was the Pollution Control Commission, designed initially to combat water pollution only. At that time the directors of the departments of agriculture, conservation, fisheries, game, and health made up the commission. Later an Air Pollution Control Board was added, and, of course, these same directors were concerned with its regulations.

When the 1971 legislature created the Department of Ecology, it gave to the department the responsibility for controlling both water and air pollution, and abolished the Water Pollution Control Commission and the Air Pollution Control Board. A third program of the department which affects both water and air pollution is solid-waste management—the disposal of refuse such as glass, plastics, and other materials that disintegrate slowly or leave a residue when burned. Even the burning of wood products in large amounts pollutes the air.

In order to combat water pollution, the Department of Ecology requires a waste discharge permit from any industrial or commercial operator who dumps waste into the waters of the state; plans adequate sewage drainage basins; gives tax credit to industries that go beyond the minimum requirements of clean waste disposal; enforces orders regarding water contamination; and investigates and cleans up any large oil spillage in the waters of the state. [13]

Because the legislature has placed the primary responsibility for control of air pollution in the hands of local agencies, the role of the state Department of Ecology in that area is primarily to provide technical advice to the local agencies and to assist them in their programs. The legislature has also given the department authority to set the standards for certain sources of air contamination and to enforce compliance. The department has concluded that the most dangerous pollutants at the present time are kraft pulp mills, aluminum reduction plants, and motor vehicles. Consequently, the department has limited the amount of pollutants permitted from pulp and aluminum reduction plants and forbids anybody to remove any device now required by the federal government to reduce emission of noxious elements

13. The Oil and Gas Conservation Committee and the mineral and geological research function of the earlier Department of Conservation (subsequently the Department of Water Resources and now the Department of Ecology) were transferred by the 1969 legislature to the Department of Natural Resources.

into the air. In the meantime, the department is working on a program to ascertain if such devices are actually installed in cars and are working properly.

The 1971 legislature required anybody conducting a commercial operation that discharges waste other than sanitary sewage into the water or air to file an annual report with the department, describing the enterprise and defining the pollutants. The director then shall see that the operator provides reasonable and known methods of treatment for these wastes. Commercial water-well contractors must also have a license.

The director reported that by 1971 all major pulp mills on Puget Sound were following the requirements of the department in regard to the amount of sulphite waste liquor that may be discharged into the Sound.[14] Some requests for permits by other types of commercial operators have been denied. The emphasis is on trying to find a viable means of operation that will allow the commercial development and at the same time maintain high environmental quality.[15]

State Soil and Water Conservation Committee. The State *Soil* and Water Conservation Committee is responsible for aiding our farmers in establishing soil and water conservation districts to counteract soil depletion. The committee is now attached to the Department of Ecology, but it has followed the pattern described above for the other agencies allied with the Department of Ecology, having earlier been a part of the departments of conservation and water resources.

The state soil and water conservation districts are established by the landowners of the area concerned, and they are governed by a board of supervisors chosen by the members of a district. In 1972 there were 67 such districts. Their purpose is to enable farmers to know the best ways of conserving and increasing soil fertility and maintaining the right amount of moisture. Basic plans are prepared for such conservation procedures for specific areas, and all farmers are urged to follow them.

The districts differ from irrigation and other types of reclamation districts in that the soil conservation districts do not levy taxes for their upkeep. The tours, publications, radio and television broadcasts, and other means used to demonstrate to farmers the most effective procedures for soil conservation are sponsored by voluntary contributions. Then when a district can demonstrate that a proposed project qualifies for federal aid, it is funded by the federal Soil Conservation Service. The state also appropriates money to

14. *1971 Annual Report, Natural Resources and Recreation Agencies.* Unless otherwise noted, information and quotations in this section are from this report.

15. For information on controlling pollution from exhaust fumes of motor vehicles, see the section on the state Department of Motor Vehicles, one of the code departments. See also *Pollution* Control Hearings Board in Table 3.

maintain the State Soil and Water Conservation Committee.

The committee's function is to acquaint the supervisors of the soil conservation districts with their responsibilities, to recommend soil conservation programs, and to further cooperation between the various state, county, and federal agencies concerned with any aspect of soil conservation. In the past the committee has been largely concerned with giving advice to individual farmers, but now with the increased awareness of the need for total community effort to raise the quality of our environment, it is being called upon to advise local conservation groups on "more complex total resource problems and needs of communities and groups of people." The committee is therefore encouraging the local districts to support river basin surveys and all other aspects of long-range planning for environmental quality in which fertile, well-drained, or irrigated soil and pure water are two of the fundamental bases. The main areas of committee service are soil fact-finding; securing the correct amount of moisture for varying types of soil in the state; preventing soil erosion; preventing floods; and making the necessary surveys to determine what procedures in all of these areas will bring the most over-all good.[16]

Department of Commerce and Economic Development

The 1957 legislature felt that encouraging industrial development and attracting tourists to the state was sufficiently important to create an agency for that purpose. It therefore established the Department of Commerce and Economic Development, with a director who is appointed by the governor with senate consent.

The primary duty of the department is to advertise the state in order to increase the number of tourists visiting Washington and to arouse the interest of industrialists in establishing commercial plants in our state. In connection with the latter purpose, the department is authorized to conduct research to further development of existing products and to provide for the processing of new ones. Plans for public work projects acceptable during an economic recession are also to be formulated.

In the *1968-70 Biennial Report* of the department, the director says of these functions: "As we enter the 1970's, there is the immediate problem of the economic downturn in the state, especially in the Central Puget Sound region. Programming needs relative to these conditions not only involve the Department of Commerce and Economic Development, but other state agencies and the federal government as well. . . . During the next biennium,

16. Additional information on the committee's activities can be found in *Convention Proceedings, 1970 Annual Meeting of the Soil and Water Conservation Districts* and *Washington's Resources: Our Challenge,* a joint publication of the committee and the federal Soil Conservation Service.

the Department will expand its current efforts in such fields as trade and tourist promotion, assistance to public and private entities in industrial development and developing effective state legislation to assist the economy."

Specific programs for the past several years are: stimulation of world trade through Washington ports, which has shown a steady increase, the total two-way trade having exceeded $2,000,000,000 during the biennium, providing one-third of the nation's favorable balance of trade (excess of exports over imports); publication of brochures to attract tourists, who spend $365,000,000 a year in the state; informational services to firms seeking new locations and investment opportunities within the state, forty-two of whom invested $480,000,000 in new businesses in the state and provided new jobs for 5,400 people; assistance to local communities in planning programs to stimulate new businesses, including ones for racial minorities, in learning of possibilities for use of nuclear power for industrial plants, and in improving the environment in communities where economic decay has set in; and aid to public and private agencies for general planning programs.

Department of Fisheries

Conservation of our fish resources has been a problem for our governmental agencies since territorial days. As early as 1871, the territorial legislature passed a law forbidding anyone to place in any fresh-water stream a fish trap or net that would reach more than two-thirds of the way across and thus block passage of fish through the river. If a dam was built, a passageway for fish had to be left. In 1877 the legislature established closed seasons for taking salmon and created the office of fish commissioner to enforce the regulations. Money from fines imposed by the office was to go into building hatcheries. In 1881 the office was abolished, but it was reestablished by the first state legislature (1889-90) under the direction of a Fish Commission. In 1921 the commission was superseded by the Department of Fisheries and Game. In 1932 sportsmen's organizations sponsored a successful initiative proposal to provide a separate Department of game to supervise the hunting of land animals and the taking of game fish. Since that time, the Department of Fisheries has been responsible only for the care of food fish—largely salmon and shellfish.

The director of the state Department of Fisheries, who is appointed by the governor with senate consent, makes regulations in regard to permissible types of fishing gear and to times and places for taking food fish, either by individuals or by commercial firms. The department licenses commercial fishermen, and the department's employees plus any game warden, sheriff, constable, or police officer may without a warrant arrest any individual who is violating a state law or departmental regulation and may without a search

Reef netter raising net to take out catch of salmon. Reef net-
ting for salmon, an adaptation of an ancient Indian method of
fishing, is carried on only in Puget Sound. (Photo by Washington State Department of Fisheries)

warrant examine his possessions for fish caught unlawfully.

The fishing industry is sufficiently valuable to our state that great care is taken to conserve the supply of fish, not only for financial reasons but also to maintain an important source of food. In 1970, 136,325,320 pounds of fish were taken for a final commercial value of over $100,000,000. Because of decreasing runs, salmon is no longer the top-ranking fish in quantity, if bottom fish are not segregated as to type. However, salmon is still the most important single variety.[17]

Because of the nature of the salmon's life cycle, regulating the catch of fish in the state is not sufficient to preserve the industry. The fish are hatched in fresh water, migrate to the sea where they live for three years or more (depending on the species), then make their way back up a river to some point in fresh water where they spawn and die. The building of dams for irrigation and electric power has produced a serious problem for the fishing industry, since the spawning grounds above a dam are blocked. Wherever possible, fish ladders are constructed—a series of ledges built so that the salmon can jump from one to the next in order to reach the top of the dam. These have been of considerable help in getting the mature fish to their spawning grounds, but many of the young fish (fingerlings) get caught in the turbines or are killed in the spillways as they go downstream to the ocean.

The Department of Fisheries has found that they can be protected, to a considerable extent, by discharging electric impulses above a dam to attract the fingerlings and guide them into a safe passageway. It is sometimes possible to by-pass a dam, as, for example, at Mayfield Dam on the Cowlitz River, where sets of vertical aluminum louvers were placed at the entrance to the power canal to guide the fish into a pipe that carries them around the dam to the river below. However, the high dams, such as Grand Coulee, are too formidable a barrier for fish passage, and scientists will have to continue their research to find ways of solving the problem.

People used to think that a salmon returned to spawn at precisely the spot where it had hatched, and they were convinced, therefore, that the construction of dams would soon limit our supply of salmon to those whose spawning grounds are normally near the mouth of the Columbia. However, scientists now believe that the environment is what determines the spawning grounds—a particular kind of gravel and algae, the oxygen content of the water, and, perhaps, the electric field at a given spot. To test this idea, the department began more than ten years ago to clip the fins of young fish raised in hatcheries or to tag them in some way before they were released in a

17. Salmon, 31, 937,354 pounds in 1969 with a catch value of $12,373,046; bottomfish, 47,454,774 pounds, $2,993,991; halibut, 9,916,084 pounds, $3,991,758; other food fish and livers, 27,084,430 pounds, $1,400,321; oysters, 5,760,833 pounds, $2,289,354; other shellfish, 22,589,721 pounds, $4,980,570.

stream in order to identify them if they were caught several years later when they returned upstream to spawn.

Enough time has elapsed now to show that salmon will spawn in a place other than that where they were hatched. For example, at Priest Rapids Dam, a six-thousand-foot channel was dug along the left bank of the river just below the dam. Fish are trapped there as they come upriver to spawn and shunted up fish ladders into a series of ponds. The biologists were relieved to find that the first run in 1963 were willing to use these ponds as spawning beds, even though the salmon would, under normal conditions, have proceeded farther upstream. The baby fish are drawn into another pond where there is sufficient natural food to support them until they are released the following spring below the dam to start their trek to the ocean and back as mature fish.

According to the director, the return of sockeye salmon to Lake Washington, where they are now in sufficient numbers to be taken commercially, is a very encouraging development that has grown out of an experiment begun in 1936. In that year sockeye fingerlings were planted in the Cedar River, flowing into Lake Washington. From Lake Washington they continued to the Pacific Ocean, presumably, for their life span. At first only a few returned through Lake Washington on their way to spawn in the Cedar River, but then suddenly in 1958 around 20,000 mature sockeyes were counted in the river. In 1964 the return jumped to 50,000, and by 1968 it was estimated that 175,000 were on their way to Cedar River to spawn. Consequently, a commercial fishery was opened in that year and is continuing to increase. [18]

Along with attempts of this kind to provide an intermediate fishing ground where salmon can be caught near the beginning of their return trip from the sea, the department is maintaining hatcheries where experiments are conducted on rearing fish in one place for their entire lives. Some are kept in fresh water to see if they can survive without the interval in the salt water of the ocean (similar to the successful program of raising land-locked salmon in Lake Michigan); others are placed in salt water as fingerlings and are kept constantly in it. Some fish live under both conditions, and it is hoped that eventually both types will add to our supply of fish by forming a fresh-water and a salt-water variety with which the dams do not interfere. Streams are also stocked with salmon from hatcheries at various points in our rivers. In 1970 the department's hatcheries raised and released 126,498,234 young salmon. The department is also clearing rivers which have become so clogged by landslides, logjams, or other obstructions that fish can no longer use them, for if such rivers are cleared, they bear fish again. In habitable rivers the department screens irrigation ditches to keep the fish out of that kind of trap.

18. State of Washington, *Department of Fisheries, 1969 Annual Report* (1969).

In addition to these activities related to the fish population, the department is concerned with measures to increase oyster production.

Cleaning Lake Washington has been a spectacular example of what a city can do to reverse the cycle of pollution that had threatened to kill marine life in the lake and to make it unusable for swimming as well. It took ten years and an expenditure of millions of dollars to undo the damage done by the dumping of refuse into the lake, but once this was accomplished, fish flourished in its waters again, and people could also enjoy bathing in it once more.

Building hatcheries, conducting research, and stocking streams with fish require a large amount of money and a staff of well-trained experts. The federal government, through the United States Fish and Wildlife Service, contributes funds to help in increasing salmon and steelhead trout numbers in the lower Columbia to compensate for the loss of spawning grounds above the dams farther up the river. Another interstate agreement, made with approval of Congress, is the Pacific Marine Fisheries Commission, a group with representatives from Washington, Oregon, and California, which recommends conservation programs to the legislatures of these states. The work of replenishing the salmon supply is even of international scope. In 1937 Congress allowed our state to join the International Pacific Salmon Fisheries Commission, a combined Canadian-United States body, to open a section of the Fraser River blocked by a railroad slide in 1913. By clearing the river and regulating the catch, the commission has caused the sockeye run to return to the pre-1913 figures.

Department of Game

Laws for the protection of game animals were passed surprisingly early. In 1868, for example, the territorial legislature set certain months as a closed season when no elk, deer, partridge, grouse, prairie chicken, or quail could be killed for sale. At that time, the enforcement of the law was left up to individuals. If a person suspected that someone had killed an animal out of season, he was to make a complaint against him in the civil courts, and, if the suspect was convicted and fined, the informant got half the fine and the county received the other half. The first state legislature (1889-90), however, instructed the governor to appoint a state game warden who, in turn, was to appoint a deputy game warden for each county to enforce the game laws. In 1899 the state fish commissioner was made ex officio state game warden, and, as we have seen, in 1921 the Department of Fisheries and Game was created.

The Department of Game has the function for game fish (mainly trout) and land animals that the Department of Fisheries has for food fish—to license persons to kill them in certain seasons and in specified numbers, and to conduct research to maintain an adequate supply. Its deputies have the same privileges of arrest as do those of the department of fisheries. In order to make it convenient for people to get their hunting and fishing licenses, the department authorizes a large number of persons to sell them—county auditors, storekeepers, resort owners, and others.

The department maintains game farms where wild animals are protected and where research can be done to determine the most desirable conditions for them. Pheasants are raised and released each year to increase the number for the hunting season. The legislature includes fur-bearing animals, if they are not raised commercially on fur farms, among those under the protection of the Department of Game.

Recent projects of the department include extending elk fences in the Asotin, Oak Creek, and Nordberg game ranges; fencing various game ranges; making major repairs on the Lewis County and Whidby Island game farms; constructing fish-rearing facilities on the Green River, at Shelton Barnaby Slough, and in Chambers Lake; and purchasing land in various parts of Chelan County for future hatchery construction. [19]

During 1971 the department released bighorn sheep in eastern Washington, wild turkeys in western Washington, Chilean Tinamou near Castle Rock (for the first time), and cottontail rabbits in the Colville Valley (a reintroduction because the rabbits had been eliminated previously from the use of pesticides). It is trying to produce giant steelhead fish, regarded as the prime sport fish in the state's streams, by breeding the largest steelheads in the Cowlitz hatchery and releasing them, hoping that their progeny will provide an increased number of fish weighing over twenty pounds. Its research continues to the limits of its budget to try to keep pace with the increased number of hunters and fishermen, from 130,000 in 1933 to almost 1,000,000 today.

State Parks and Recreation Commission

The purpose of the State Parks and Recreation Commission, created by the legislature in 1913, is to supervise the operation of the state parks already in existence and to study the needs of the state for public recreation spots. The commission may buy land and create state parks, as it sees fit, within the budget allowed it by the legislature. The commission may appoint a parks director.

Usage of state parks has more than tripled in the past decade, from 7,000,000 park visitors in 1960, when the state's population was 2,800,000

19. State of Washington, *Department of Game, Twentieth Biennial Report, July 1, 1968 through June 30, 1970* (1970).

to 23,000,000 visitors in 1970, when the population was only 600,000 more than in 1960. This tremendous increase in numbers and in diversity of recreational needs makes it very difficult for the commission to find ways of meeting the public demand.

The upsurge of concern with environmental quality has resulted in an unusually high number of suggestions from individuals and groups that the commission acquire specific spots for recreational areas. The park planners investigated ninety potential park sites and approved seventeen, subject to legislative appropriations for their purchase. Considerations of snowmobiling and other new forms of outdoor recreation have led the commission into working with the Washington State Arts Commission and the State Highway Commission to try to integrate recreational development with highway construction and with a combination of art and parks projects.

Two new parks were developed during 1971—Steamboat Rock and Ike Kinswa—and the environmental education centers at Deception Pass, Moran, Fields Spring, and Sequim Bay State Parks were modernized. Road improvements in twenty-six parks were made, using $224,887 of special road-maintenance funds.

The commission, working with the governor's Advisory Council on *Historic* Preservation, prepared a statewide plan for the restoration and preservation of historic sites, which was submitted to the federal agencies responsible for allotting federal funds for these programs. As a result, our state was granted the fifth largest amount in the country, $108,141, when the first federal funds for that purpose were apportioned among the states in 1970. The retired state ferry, *S. S. San Mateo*, was made one of these sites, to be located on Lake Union in Seattle to serve as a maritime interpretive center. The advisory council nominated 112 sites to be placed on the National Register of Historic Places, and 17 of these were accepted, bringing to 28 the number of Washington's historic spots so honored.

The commission tries to combine use of state-park lands with needs of other agencies or individuals. For example, suitable park lands are leased for agriculture or grazing, salvaged timber sales, or other commercial operations as long as they do not interfere with the recreational purposes of the specific sites. Cooperation with other state agencies included arrangements with the State Highway Commission to provide for overnight camping and recreational facilities at highway safety rest areas and in skiing areas on highways through the Cascades; with the superintendent of public instruction to make nine state-park resident youth camps into outdoor learning laboratories for the state's public schools, three to be used for year-round environmental education; with the army corps of engineers for that group to build campsites at places where they have engineering projects, an example being Lyons Ferry State Park.

Staffing of the recreational areas is aided greatly by special employment programs for young people: a project of the State Parks and Recreation Commission itself to hire young men and women for summer work; a job-training program sponsored by the Employment Security Department; the federal college work study programs and those for soldiers discharged from the armed forces; and the state Youth Development and Conservation Corps Program, sponsored by cities, counties, and school districts, which from 1961 to 1971 has assigned more than 6,300 young people—many of them handicapped by social or emotional problems or mentally retarded—to maintenance work in state parks or other recreational areas.

There has been a 30 percent increase in park attendance over the past five years and only a 20 percent increase in campsites. Consequently, each summer weekend, people who want to camp in state parks are turned away. The commission approved entrance or day-use fees in the major parks, which is expected to go into effect in 1972. (For additional information, see *Columbia* River Gorge Commission in Table 3.)

Oceanographic Commission of Washington

In 1967 the legislature created the Oceanographic Commission of Washington, consisting partly of members of the state house of representatives and senate and partly of members of the general public appointed by the governor. (For its specific composition, see Table 3 at the end of this chapter.) Its duties are to develop a coordinated program in oceanography in order to find new uses for and encourage commercial utilization of the state's marine resources and to study problems related to the development, pollution, and public recreational use of waterfront areas.

The commission is authorized to act only as a research agency. The staff, which includes experts in the field of oceanography, can request that the Oceanographic Institute of Washington, a nonprofit research and educational corporation, implement a particular project, if the institute approves it and can finance the undertaking.

During 1971 the commission tried to promote "increased understanding of the ocean and Washington waters by decision-makers in government and the private sector, and . . . economic recovery through environmentally safe development of the natural and man-made marine resources of the state."

The commission undertakes many specific projects, for example, exploration of Cobb Seamount, a 9,000-foot extinct volcano fairly near the ocean surface 270 miles west of Grays Harbor. This work has been done in conjunction with federal agencies and also in cooperation with agencies of neighboring states who have joined in an organization called Sea Use Council to provide much of the money for the project outside of federal appropriations. The expectation is that the marine resources of the volcano can eventually be utilized on a commercial basis. Another project has been a contract for wave spectra analysis to provide additional information about the strains on ships caused by ocean waves. The results will be used by naval architects to design better ships. A third activity has been a systems analysis of the question of oil transportation and handling in Washington waters. The commission also continues to sponsor research on food production or possibilities for other uses of ocean resources.

Interagency Committee for Outdoor Recreation

In 1964 the voters through an initiative measure passed the Marine Recreation Land Act, one part of which was the establishment of the Interagency Committee for Outdoor Recreation. Its purpose is to plan a long-range system of outdoor recreation and then to approve proposals for specific projects presented to it by state or local government agencies. The committee has authority to acquire and develop outdoor recreational sites.

In order that the other state agencies concerned with recreation will have a means of coordinating their efforts, the heads of the departments of game, natural resources, parks and recreation, fisheries, highways, commerce and economic development, and ecology are members of the committee, three of which (game, natural resources, and parks and recreation) present projects to the committee for funding. (For the complete composition of the committee, see Table 3 at the end of this chapter.)

The committee appropriates funds that come from bond issues approved by the voters, federal funds, unclaimed marine fuel tax money, local agency contributions, and state appropriations. As of 30 June 1971, three state agencies, 55 cities, 20 counties, four port districts, one school district, and one university had received grant-in-aid assistance through the committee, and over 110,000 acres of land had been acquired.

PUBLIC WELFARE

We have now discussed the state agencies which try to develop natural resources for the use of our people. But the people themselves have to be able to take advantage of these resources if the goal of their maximum use is to be reached. If industries are to grow, individuals have to be healthy enough to work in them, and, if the recreational facilities are to be enjoyed, people have to have a certain amount of money for their use. To what extent a government can guarantee sufficient food, clothing, shelter, medical care, and recreational facilities for everyone is a difficult question that we all have to consider.

Insurance systems of the kind provided by federal social security seem to have met with more favor, generally, for providing medical care and old-age assistance than direct financial grants, although proposals for establishing a minimum income for everybody are also under present consideration. In the types of insurance plans already in use, the individual and (or) his employer contribute a certain amount of money to the insurance fund, and some government agency provides the remainder. Current systems were started too late, however, to provide old-age assistance for many people who are now retired, and only certain occupations are covered. Health insurance, which is largely on a voluntary basis, except for the elderly under Medicare, has also developed fairly recently. Even these arrangements do not cover young people who are physically or mentally handicapped to the point that they cannot earn enough money to contribute to an insurance program. Handicapped children or ones whose parents cannot or will not provide for them come in such a group. Consequently, our state legislature appropriates money for various welfare projects to try to promote the well-being of underprivileged groups, including racial minorities.

State Department of Social and Health Services

As was the case with agencies dealing with natural resources, those concerned with public welfare had grown to the point where there were a large number of units whose functions overlapped. This proliferation made the system cumbersome, and people in need of help often found it difficult to get in touch with the many agencies involved with the various aspects of public assistance. The duplication of effort was also considered inefficient and unnecessarily costly. Consequently, the 1969 legislature, after having studied recommendations by various public and private agencies for streamlining the organization of the welfare system, established the Department of Social and Health Services to supersede the Department of Public Assistance, the Department of Health, the Department of Institutions, the Veterans' Rehabilitation Council on Occupational Education. All of these agencies were abolished except the Coordinating Council on Occupational Education.

Inasmuch as overhauling an organization composed of this large number of important agencies takes considerable time, the work of the former departments is continuing at present in much the same manner, with the labels of divisions within the department.

Division of Public Assistance. When the Department of Public Assistance handled financial aid to persons who were unable to work or to secure jobs that would support them, it was the largest of the individual public welfare agencies. As a part of the present Department of Social and Health Services, it still maintains that position. Originally called the state Department of Social Security,[20] it was established during the depression of the 1930s, when widespread unemployment reached such a height that local and even state governmental agencies could not cope with the problem of providing a minimum of food and shelter for those out of work.

· Before that time, the board of county commissioners in each county was responsible for taking care of those in the county who could not support themselves. The legislature allowed the commissioners to establish county poor farms and hospitals, or to give direct financial assistance to indigent persons. When severe unemployment occurred in the 1930s, however, many counties did not have enough funds to prevent groups of people being threatened by actual starvation. To meet this situation, the federal government created the Social Security Administration, which allotted relief funds to a corresponding state agency to be created by state legislatures—in Washington, the state Department of Social Security.

In 1969 the Department of Public Assistance became the Division of Public Assistance within the Department of Social and Health Services. The other divisions are: health, institutions, veterans' affairs, and vocational rehabilitation. The head of the Department of Social and Health Services is called the secretary of social and health services instead of director. He is appointed by the governor with senate consent and is named as the chairman and executive officer of the State Board of Health and registrar of vital statistics.

Financially dependent persons receiving financial support from the state Division of Public Assistance in 1969 were divided as follows: children, 47%, persons over sixty-five years of age, 15%; blind, 3%, and those otherwise unemployable, 13%. "Over 85 per cent of recipients were not in the labor market at all because they were too old, too young, or too disabled." In addition to these not in the labor market are mothers of children under five years of age who do not have a father in the home. "These represent about 6 per cent of all recipients. Of the remaining recipients, the majority are seriously handicapped in seeking work by lack of education and training." Thirty-two thousand additional people could not meet the cost of their medical needs.[21]

The old-age-assistance program of the Division of Public Assistance provides financial and other assistance to indigents over 65 years of age. The purpose of this support for the elderly is to "help them remain at home with

20. Later the name was changed to Department of Public Welfare, and then to Department of Public Assistance.

21. State of Washington *Human Resource Agencies, 1970 Annual Report* (1970). Unless otherwise noted, information and quotations in this section are from this report.

family and friends or to find and use suitable, alternative living arrangements. Some persons are helped to find nursing homes, boarding homes and needed specialized care. Funds for unusual requirements are provided where necessary, including housekeeping and attendant care, meals delivered to homes, and restaurant meals. Many persons are helped to develop resources such as social security, veteran's benefits, and railroad retirement."

The division also licenses institutions providing services and facilities for child care, group homes, maternity homes, day-care centers, child-placing agencies, family foster homes, nursing homes, and family day-care homes to be certain that they meet adequate standards for safety and health protection.

The division provides financial assistance to severely disabled persons over eighteen, with the primary goal of making them physically and emotionally able to take care of themselves and, wherever possible, to hold a job. For blind persons or those in danger of becoming blind, the work of the division in addition to financial aid, falls into the two categories of training the blind person for a job and of preventing blindness in cases where surgery, special lenses, or some other form of treatment is recommended as a deterrent.

The program for assistance for dependent children pertains largely to families where the father is incapacitated or unemployed or has deserted his family, or families in which the parents are divorced or separated. Often the mothers do not have the education or training to get a job that pays enough for them to hire satisfactory baby sitters or to pay for day-care centers. Of all children in this program 36 per cent are younger than six years, and 22 per cent of the mothers are physically, mentally, or emotionally incapacitated. Only 6 per cent of the mothers are employed. The average period of assistance for such families is thirteen months. Only 16 per cent receive assistance for five years or more.

In addition to the children who need help because of the absence of a wage-earner in the family, there are those who are neglected or abused by their parents or are in danger of becoming delinquent from neglect. For this category, the division tries to help the parents change their attitudes or to remedy a situation that is causing the abuse, and the department believes that "An intensive program of such services would tend to overcome the growing rate of referrals to courts and subsequent removal of children from their homes." If it appears that this training cannot be done, however, the division places the children in foster homes or allows them to be adopted, if possible. Adoptive services are used, also, for orphans.

The division gives direct financial aid to eligible, needy persons who do not meet requirements for the federally matched assistance programs, and provides medical care for persons on public assistance. The food stamp program is a recent supplemental means of improving the diet of low-income people. The division issues food stamps to persons certified by local public assistance offices, believing, on the basis of experience and research, "that the diets of low-income families are improved, farmers sell more food, grocery stores get more business and the entire economy gets a boost from the added food purchases of stamp customers."

Inasmuch as the ultimate goal of financial assistance is to make the recipient self-supporting, the division joins the state Employment Security Department in administering the work incentive program, under which the mothers or other persons receiving aid for dependent children also receive counseling and job training, where feasible, to enable them to get and hold a job that will pay enough for them to support their children. Day-care facilities may be provided for the children during such training periods. If the father or other person legally responsible for the support of the children has disappeared or refuses when he is employed to give financial aid to his family, the division has an enforcement unit which attempts to locate the absent parent and collect support money from him.

Children in families where aid is needed may have more difficulty in avoiding situations leading to juvenile delinquency than ones in stable homes where both parents are able-bodied and interested in their welfare. The division maintains several programs aimed at preventing such results. An example is the summer youth opportunity, which provides summer employment for 800 youths between the ages of sixteen and twenty from families receiving financial assistance. Another example is the new careers program in which the division hires approximately eighty persons to work in public service programs and at the same time allows them to attend school two days a week.

Division of Veterans' Affairs. United States war veterans make up about 15 per cent of the state's population—over 477,000 men and women, including around 300 who served in the Spanish-American War. They are eligible for benefits from state as well as federal sources, but many of them are not aware of these possibilities for aid, and if they cannot find work, they eventually are declared eligible for some kind of general public assistance. The Division of Veterans' Affairs in the Department of Social and Health Services attempts to assist the state's veterans, their dependents, and beneficiaries to meet requirements for federal and state benefits. During 1970 this division, with the aid of private veterans' organizations, processed 31,642 individual claims for veterans' benefits equaling $45,927,348. They provided 626,157 additional services, including counseling, answering inquiries, completing forms, interviewing, reviewing cases, and attending hearings.

Division of Vocational Rehabilitation. This division attempts to aid handicapped individuals to become self-supporting. The assistance may consist of medical and psychological evaluation of the person's difficulties, or surgical, psychiatric, or hospital care with additional therapy where such treatment is needed. If a physical deformity or other disabling ailment can be alleviated to the point that the handicapped person can be employed, the division is authorized to furnish training in a school or college or in a sheltered workshop or in the individual's home.

The division works with many other public and private agencies in locating and rehabilitating handicapped persons, and 80 percent of the division's budget comes from federal funds. During 1970 almost 25,000 people, most of them young, were helped, and nearly 2,600 were rehabilitated. It is estimated that the increase in the number of disabled persons will shortly be such that the present staff and facilities could serve only about one out of six handicapped people in the state. Consequently, the division has established the following priorities for areas of concentrated aid: public assistance recipients, the model city (a project in Seattle's Central Area where the worst poverty exists), migrant workers, and people in correctional institutions. In an attempt to reach more people the department is hiring aides to help take some of the work load from people who have professional training in treating handicapped persons. The main categories of disability, in addition to those mentioend above, are: deafness, amputations, mental illness, alcoholism, mental retardation, heart disease, speech impairments, drug addiction, epilepsy, and kidney ailments requiring artificial kidney services.

Division of Health. The Division of Health within the Department of Social and Health Services corresponds to the former state Department of Health, which is responsible for measures to promote public health in general. In most of the divisions discussed above, aid for individuals with medical problems represents part of the services given, but there are also problems of public welfare affecting everyone, regardless of his financial status or type of work, and public health is one of the most important of these.

The most obvious community health problem is that of contagious or infectious diseases. In the past, if a person had smallpox, diphtheria, polio, or any other communicable disease, he had to be kept as isolated as possible in order not to spread the disease. Now inoculation has made these diseases almost nonexistent. However, there must be some systematic check to make certain that everybody is vaccinated for the diseases considered most dangerous, and the Division of Health supervises this program through the public schools. Scientists continue to discover means of preventing additional contagious diseases, and the division arranges vaccination programs, such as the statewide "Measles Must Go" campaign in 1969, when 127,000 children under the age of twelve years were vaccinated. During the measles epidemic of 1964, 6,000 cases of measles were reported, but in April of 1970, after the vaccination program, only 150 cases were tabulated. The assistant secretary for the division predicts that rubella, the disease that produces defects in children before birth, will also soon be eradicated through inoculation. In another area, the division tries to get people to have their pets vaccinated for rabies in clinics established by the division.

As part of its program in public health education, the division sends out public health nurses who are experts in caring for people with specific diseases—such as tuberculosis, cancer, cerebral palsy, and so forth—and these experts train the local public health nurses and others in new or improved methods of care. The federal government, through the United States Public Health Service, also provides nurses to demonstrate new techniques for particular diseases. Improvement of mental health is another phase of the division's responsibility, and it advises local communities on mental health programs.

In addition, in the campaign against tuberculosis, the division sets up clinics throughout the state where people may have X-rays taken to show whether or not they are tubercular. In 1968 the number of tuberculosis patients needing hospitalization had decreased to the point that Mountain View General Hospital in Tacoma was closed. The Division of Health is responsible for seeing that food handlers are free from tuberculosis and are not typhoid carriers, and by agreement with the Department of Agriculture the Health Division's employees inspect all phases of sanitation in an eating house, whether they apply to the food itself or to the handlers. If a county or city maintains its own sanitation inspectors, the employees of the Division of Health offer advice and assistance to the local sanitarians.

With the current emphasis on education to prevent disease, the division in its maternal and child health program encourages young expectant mothers to attend prenatal clinics and to bring their children to clinics for examination and health guidance before they are ill. The crippled children's service organizes health clinics for diagnosis of such disabilities and assists the parents in arranging for funding of treatment for congenital defects. Around 5,000 children receive this type of care in the state each year.

Additional phases of the work of the division includes a statewide program for the study, treatment, and rehabilitation of alcoholics; the elimination of hazards in water supplies, sewage disposal systems, and swimming pools, including a statewide plan for the collection, storage, and disposal of garbage; and the organization of family-planning clinics to teach parents to limit the size of their families to what they want and can afford.

The legislature adds specific regulatory functions to the health agencies from time to time. For example, in 1959 it required the division (then the state Department of Health) to license persons who sterilize used rags for sale as "wiping rags." The 1961 legislature added responsibility for mosquito control. The division is also the state radiation control agency. It appoints a state radiological control officer to evaluate radiation health hazards. His office is required to keep a file of all licenses issued by the United States Atomic Energy Commission and a file of registrants possessing ionizing materials. The legislature also created an Advisory Council on *Nuclear* Energy and Radiation to recommend programs to develop and regulate the sources of atomic radiation and to review regulations of all agencies to see that they are consistent. Although nuclear power plants are ordinarily regarded as the most dangerous sources of radioactivity affecting animal and human health, a larger amount comes from the medical or industrial use of radioisotopes and X-rays. The division therefore frequently surveys such facilities in connection with approving them for use. Likewise the legislature created the Western Interstate *Nuclear* Board to represent this state in working on an interstate agreement on uniform regulations, which, with the approval of Congress, can be put into effect.[22]

In addition to the duties described above that pertain in some way to public health, the division maintains the Bureau of Vital Statistics, one of the few administrative units required by the state constitution. The bureau was created to keep an official record of all births and deaths within the state. The procedure is that doctors report a birth or death to local registrars who, in turn, forward the information to the state registrar of vital statistics. Birth certificates are necessary to people who wish to get passports or who must prove their identity for social security cards, inheritances, and many other purposes. Death certificates are essential, too, so that the cause of death may always be certified and any foul play detected. The county auditors also use local registrars' reports of deaths as a check on the list of registered voters. The 1959 legislature added a registry of handicapped children to the records to be maintained by the bureau.

The Division of Health operates McKay Memorial Research Hospital at Soap Lake as a contagious disease hospital and as a research laboratory for the study of Buerger's disease, cerebral palsy, arthritis, skin diseases, and medicinal qualities of the water of Soap Lake. Indigent patients and veterans

22. Additional advisory bodies regarding public health are: *Thermal* Power Plant Site Evaluation Council, which develops guidelines for location of thermal power plants; Advisory Council on *Atomic* Energy; Washington State *Hospital* Advisory Council, whose function is to advise the State Board of Health regarding minimum standards and regulations for the construction and operation of all types of hospitals; and the *Furniture* and Bedding Advisory Council, to recommend regulations for the sale of furniture and bedding to insure that such articles are offered for sale only where they are clean and sanitary. For the composition of these boards, see Table 3.

are cared for free of charge, but others pay for the hospital services.

State Board of Health. Although the Division of Health in the Department of Social and Health Services enforces regulations for public health, it does not set sanitary qualifications. These are decided upon by the State Board of Health, a separate group required by the state constitution. The State Board of Health consists of the assistant secretary of the Department of Social and Health Services in charge of the Division of Health plus four persons experienced in health and sanitation matters who are appointed by the governor.

The board sets up an outline of the regulations for the control and treatment of drug addicts, such rules to be binding on county and city health officers and any others involved in the apprehension and custory of drug addicts. The board is also required by the 1959 legislature to license anyone who produces or sells narcotic drugs.

The Board of Health makes rules for the procedures to be followed in rendering wiping rags and certain other commodities—such as mattresses and bedding—sanitary, and the Division of Health enforces the regulations concerning their sale through its licensing power. The State Board of Health also specifies procedures for determining that food handlers are not disease carriers and decides the quarantine rules for certain diseases. Once the board has adopted rules in such matters, the Division of Health sees that they are obeyed within the state.

Division of Institutions. The management of our state institutions has been entrusted to a number of agencies since 1897 when the State Board of Audit and Control was created. It operated under various titles until 1921 when the Department of Efficiency was set up not only to manage the state institutions, but to supervise banks throughout the state. In 1935 the Department of Finance, Budget and Business was given supervision of institutions, banks, the state budget, and purchasing of state supplies. In 1947 the function of budget-making was transferred to the director of the budget in the governor's office; then the name of the department was changed to Department of Public Institutions, and it was given the care of state archives. In 1955 its name was changed to Department of Institutions, and its duties in connection with banks, purchasing, and archives were transferred to the new Department of General Administration. In 1969 the Department of Institutions was abolished, and its functions were given to the Division of Institutions within the Department of Social and Health Services.

Except for our colleges and universities, all of the state hospitals, prisons, remedial schools, and other institutions already mentioned are under the management of the Division of Institutions. Until fairly recent years, such state institutions were usually regarded as simply a place of custody—an institution where convicts, insane, mentally retarded, and the indigent sick could be confined so that they would not bother others in the community. There they were forgotten by most people, and, in addition to having no opportunity to better their own condition, the inmates had hardly any chance of learning to be a benefit rather than a liability to society. Today in our state, at least, emphasis is being placed on rehabilitation of those who have lost their place in a law-abiding community or are physically or mentally unable to take care of themselves. An additional goal is to prevent the crime and the disability, and exciting gains are being made in that direction. Such programs are costly, but when they are successful they are much cheaper than the cost of maintaining an individual in an institution indefinitely. Besides the financial consideration, there is the tremendous achievement of having individuals living an independent, productive existence instead of having their lives largely wasted.

The Office of Adult Corrections in the division administers the Washington State Penitentiary in Walla Walla; the Washington State Reformatory in Monroe; the Washington Corrections Center at Shelton; and four forest honor camps operated in cooperation with the department of natural resources at Yacolt (Larch Mountain Honor Camp), at Washougal, at Loomis (Okanogan Honor Camp), and at Clallam Bay.[23] In these facilities both the work and training release program and a program for vocations of a more academic nature were increased and strengthened during 1970. Walla Walla Community College offers an associate of arts degree program for the penitentiary inmates who may be able to benefit from such training and be prepared to hold a responsible job when they are released. An intensive educational program is also in effect at the Washington Corrections Center for young first offenders, and the parole success for them has reached a figure of more than 80 per cent.

Psychiatric treatment has also been made available at the state penitentiary and is increasingly effective. Another type of rehabilitation program is one for training handicapped persons in the correctional institutions to be self-supporting when they are released. This project involves contracts between the Division of Institutions and the Office of Vocational Rehabilitation of the Division of Public Assistance. The honor camps have benefited the participants and the general public, as well, through the work done in state forests in clearing trails and performing other tasks to improve the usefulness of the recreational areas.

The Office of Juvenile Rehabilitation operates the correctional institutions to which courts send minors who have broken a law. They are: the Cascadia Reception and Diagnostic Center at Tacoma; the Maple Lane School (state

---

23. The office will also administer a corrections center for women that will be opened soon.

school for girls) at Centralia; the Green Hill School (state training school for boys) at Chehalis; the Fort Worden Treatment Center (for boys and girls) at Port Townsend; the Echo Glen School (for younger boys and girls); and five youth forestry camps for boys (Cedar Creek and Naselle near Littlerock, Mission Creek near Bremerton, Spruce Canyon near Colville, and Indian Ridge). In addition, the office maintains five group homes for paroled juveniles who do not have a proper home environment to which they can return. A subsidy to counties, authorized to provide funds for care of juvenile offenders outside institutions, is proving to be successful in many instances in preventing later commitment to a correctional institution.

The office works closely with community law enforcement agencies and with civic groups to provide counseling centers throughout the state for service to maladjusted and delinquent children and their parents to try to solve the problems before they reach the state of institutional commitment.

With this type of help, a young person who has committed his first crime can often be prevented from repeating an unlawful act. Under such circumstances, the court will put him on probation instead of imposing the usual sentence and assign probation counselors to work with him. If counties of Class III and smaller cannot afford to pay for the work of as many counselors as are needed, money from a state fund for that purpose is apportioned to the counties by the office of juvenile rehabilitation according to a formula specified by the legislature.[24] This program has reduced the percentage of juvenile parole failure from more than 40 percent to less than 25 percent and has given our state national recognition as a leader in the effective rehabilitation of juvenile offenders. Since 1967 the Office of Probation and Parole within the Division of Institutions has been responsible for supervising all persons on parole, regardless of age, and in 1970 the office instituted a statewide program for the use of volunteers from the general public to act as parole aides. This added involvement with parolees by individual citizens has increased the understanding by the public of a convict's problems and is very helpful in their rehabilitation.

The Office of Mental Health in the division administers the three state mental hospitals: Western State Hospital at Fort Steilacoom; Eastern State Hospital at Medical Lake; and Northern State Hospital at Sedro Woolley. In 1967 the legislature passed the Community Mental Health Services Act by which the state gives support to counties which will establish mental health services, to include education, in-patient and out-patient care, and rehabilitation. The office also plans an intensive program on drug-abuse.

The Office of Veterans' Homes within the division operates two homes for indigent honorably discharged veterans: the State Soldiers' Home and Colony

24. See chapter 7 for information on the various classes of counties. Cities are also classed according to population; for those figures, see chapter 8.

at Orting and the Washington Veterans' Home at Retsil. Veterans of the First World War make up 65 percent of the inmates; consequently, they are reaching the age where increased nursing and medical care facilities are necessary, and these are being provided. In a project at Orting a number of the veterans have become volunteer foster grandparents to retarded children in the nearby Rainier School.

The Office of Handicapped Children within the division provides care for children who are mentally retarded, blind, or deaf through Lakeland Village at Medical Lake, Rainier School at Buckley, Yakima Valley School at Selah, Interlake School and Fircrest School at Seattle (mentally retarded only), and School for the Blind and School for the Deaf, both in Vancouver. In addition, the office gives consultation services and financial support to thirty-four centers where retarded children can receive help at the community level.

The goal for all of these schools is to give the handicapped children the maximum training possible. Research in new approaches to the problem indicates that many who were previously thought to be completely dependent on institutional care can learn to take care of themselves and even handle jobs in laundries, restaurants, and other commercial enterprises. Because there is a long waiting list for the state training schools, the office is allowed to use private day centers or group training homes in order to get help for these children as early as possible. The Office of Handicapped Children and the Division of Vocational Rehabilitation cooperate closely so that those from the schools or homes for the retarded or deaf may be given additional training for specific jobs whenever they are capable of holding them.[25]

Employment Security Department

Although many of the former departments concerned with public welfare were made divisions of the present Department of Social and Health Services, some of them were retained as separate departments. This is true of the Employment Security Department, whose aim is to find jobs for those who are out of work and to supervise the state system of unemployment insurance.

It has been demonstrated that a healthy person finds greater satisfaction in being employed than in being idle, because he feels independent in earning his living and useful to society in performing a needed task. Obviously it is better

25. For additional regulatory or advisory boards, see Washington State Council in *Aging*; State Comprehensive *Health* Planning Advisory Council; Mental *Health* and Mental Retardation Advisory Council; State *Hospital* Advisory Council; Institutional *Industries* Commission; *Interfaith* Advisory Committee; State Welfare *Medical* Care Committee; and *Youth* Development and Conservation Committee.

for society to have as many people as possible employed in order that public welfare funds may be used to a greater extent to support or rehabilitate handicapped individuals than to care for employable persons. The Department of Employment Security, therefore, maintains a type of employment agency where employers may submit requests for workers and where the unemployed may apply for work. It also studies labor conditions in order to be able to advise an individual on the type of job and area in which he will be most likely to find work. The department counsels people in search of employment, and especially veterans, in order to determine the kind of work they could do best. In 1970 the Employment Security Department in the state of Washington placed approximately 164,000 people in jobs, 117,000 in agriculture and 47,000 in nonagricultural employment. During this period, the department held over 31,000 counseling interviews and gave approximately 21,000 aptitude and proficiency tests.

Like the other phases of public assistance undertaken through the use of federal and state, rather than county, funds, the plan for insuring a person against the loss of his job was adopted during the depression of the 1930s. Legislators reasoned that a tax paid by employers according to the total amount of wages paid would be the most feasible method of creating a principal from which benefits could be paid to persons when they lost their jobs through no fault of their own. Congress established the program on a national scale for participating states. The state Department of Employment Security collects the taxes from employers and sends a portion to the federal government for administration of the employment security agencies in the various states. The remainder goes into the trust funds within the state from which unemployment benefits are paid. Congress appropriates additional funds for specific related programs—such as Job Corps, work incentive programs, and so forth—administered on the state level by the department.

The area of interest of the department includes "education, training, health, social services, administration of laws and regulations governing conditions at work sites (such as antidiscrimination agencies and those which administer labor practices legislation), safety standards, workmen's compensation, and regulations governing the employment of women and minors." This is true because ordinarily an unemployed person is handicapped by lack of education, health, racial discrimination, or other factors relating to his social situation. Consequently, the department needs a staff for "family and personal counseling beyond the scope of vocational counseling, medical and health services, child care, transportation and legal aid." The department refers its clients to the other welfare agencies responsible for such aids, but in most instances their services are already in demand beyond their maximum capacity.

Appeal Tribunal for Employment Security Department. Many questions arise as to the length of time for which a person is eligible for unemployment compensation, and there are various disputes that affect employers or employees. For this reason, the legislature requires the commissioner of employment security to set up an impartial appeal committee, called a tribunal, to hear disputes. A salaried examiner presides over the tribunal and he makes the final decision in the questions brought to the department.

Department of Labor and Industries

Unemployment compensation is a comparatively recent step in the program of improving living conditions for workers in the state, but the problem of the general welfare of industrial workers was in the minds of the writers of our state constitution. Article II, Section 35 states that "The Legislature shall pass necessary laws for the protection of persons working in mines, factories, and other employments dangerous to life or deleterious to health, and fix pains and penalties for the enforcement of the same." At first, there were inspectors for each type of mine or factory covered; then in 1897 the legislature created a Bureau of Labor to make regulations for the protection of our labor forces; and in 1921 the bureau was superseded by the Department of Labor and Industries under the control of a director who is appointed by the governor with senate consent.

One phase of the work of the department concerns the enforcement of certain state laws. If the legislature passes minimum-wage or maximum-hour legislation for a particular industry, the employers cannot pay less than the minimum wage prescribed or require an employee to work more than the specified number of hours without overtime pay. Most of these regulations also have to meet the requirements of the United States Department of Labor, if federal contracts are involved or if the goods produced are destined for interstate commerce. There are also standards of health and safety to be met.

In addition to enforcing such laws, the department acts as a mediation board to settle disputes between employers and employees; these problems usually involve the interpretation of labor laws and regulations or complaints as to wages or working conditions. According to the director, "The very name of the department suggests its two primary involvements with outside agencies. On the labor side, the department works closely with the Washington State Labor Council and its affiliated organizations. On the industry side, a solid working relationship has been established with the Association of Washington Business."

Another main function of the department is to supervise the state industrial insurance program, created to provide funds to pay for medical care if a workman is injured at work or becomes ill. Pensions, payments for time

Workers at Kaiser Gypsum in Seattle. (Photo by Washington State Department of Commerce and Economic Development)

lost at work, and other disability compensations are also provided. The medical aid fund is financed half by employers and half by employees. Payments for time lost because of accidents are made entirely from funds provided by the employers. About half the state's total labor force is now covered by state industrial insurance.

Apprenticeship Division. The Apprenticeship Division of the department administers the apprenticeship program, which is charged with placing young persons in work-training jobs in various occupations. The legislature instituted such a project in 1941, when it created the Washington State Apprenticeship Council to set policies for a statewide program. In 1970 there were more than 5,300 apprentices registered in the state plan, learning a skill with some employer and receiving journeyman's wages while becoming proficient in their trade. Recently the need for maintaining minority representation in the group of apprentices has been emphasized.

See Table 3 at the end of this chapter for the composition of the following related agencies: *Electrical* Advisory Board; Board of *Boiler* Rules; Institutional *Industries* Committee; Board of *Industrial* Insurance Appeals;

Factory Built *Housing* Advisory Board.

Washington State Human Rights Commission

The 1971 legislature changed the name of the Washington State Board Against Discrimination in Employment to Washington State *Human* Rights Commission. It consists of five members who are appointed by the governor. The board's function is to investigate complaints concerning discrimination in employment because of race or religion, and the board is empowered to create advisory groups to encourage community effort in racial tolerance, and to publish results of its investigations or other materials which will work toward that end.

The educational aspect of the commission's work is the one currently stressed. A weekly TV program, called "It Begins with You", "fulfills a need for information on discriminatory practices and the resulting frustrations and unmet hopes of minority individuals." Two special programs featured Yakima-area Mexican-American leaders discussing specific problems faced by the Chicanos in eastern Washington.

An example of the commission's efforts on behalf of equal housing opportunities for black residents is its hearings in Tacoma. It found in one case that the availability of property was misrepresented to a black couple and in another that a black couple was openly denied housing because of their race. Each couple was awarded $350, satisfactory arrangements were made for housing the couples, and cease-and-desist orders were issued to the property owners to prevent their continuing with discriminatory practices.

The commission summarizes its position in the following statement: "Although our state is experiencing an economic recession, we cannot afford to diminish our effort to improve the plight of our minority citizens. This work is controversial and complex, but it also presents an unusual opportunity to make good on the promises of our American institutions. There is no more important work on the domestic scene at the present time."

Office of Economic Opportunity

Another agency concerned with improving the economic condition of disadvantaged persons is the Office of Economic Opportunity. It is funded primarily from federal appropriations under the Economic Opportunity Act, with additional state funds. The director of the state office is appointed by the governor under a law passed by the 1965 legislature.

The primary functions of the office include "general and specialized technical assistance to 30 Community Action Agencies which serve local communities, Indian communities and migrant families. OEO serves as an advocate for the poor in assisting state, federal and local agencies in developing programs and better delivery of services."

In 1970 there were twenty-nine community action groups participating in the program. These groups are organized as nonprofit private corporations governed by community-elected boards of directors. Consequently, their activities vary, depending on the specific needs of each area. They include economic development, Neighborhood Youth Corps, Project Headstart, day care, legal services, services for the elderly, family planning, youth drop-out prevention, basic education, vocational training and placement, counseling, Operation Mainstream, tutoring, health and food assistance, neighborhood centers, and community organization.

Two important programs in the community action projects are the New Careers and the Volunteer Services. For a period of four years (two two-year cycles), disadvantaged persons received experience and training while assigned to jobs in state agencies—such as Social and Health Services, Personnel Department, Employment Security Department, the Office of Economic Opportunity—and in colleges. In 1970, 73 out of the original 100 completed the program and are working in jobs or are eligible for jobs formerly requiring a college degree.

In 1969 Washington was the first state to name a volunteer services coordinator for the entire state, and since then a large number of persons have been trained and assigned to both public and private agencies, where they add to the scope of the aid given to disadvantaged persons. This program has emphasized schools and institutions for the retarded, and parole and probation agencies.

In a number of instances the Office of Economic Opportunity has pointed up a local need that has then been filled through state-local development funds. Some of these projects are: City-bound, an educational program for urban disadvantaged youth in Tacoma and Pierce County; Pioneer Trading Post, a training and employment project for rural elderly people in Okanogan County; Martin Luther King Half-way House, the first "half-way" house in the nation for graduates and returnees from Job Corps; Drop-out Prevention, work assistance and experience for disadvantaged youth in forestry in northeastern Washington; and North by Northwest, nationally recognized "on the sea" training and employment in maritime skills. Also, in the Lummi Management Aid, management training and technical assistance are provided for the Lummi tribe (this project is now serving as the model for twelve other programs in the nation). Grays Harbor County has a Youth Mini-Industry, which is a youth center and mini-industry training and education for drop-outs. Other efforts toward providing employment in urban areas are the Comprehensive Employment Development in Seattle's Skid Road, which is a comprehensive approach to employment and social services developed by residents of "the Road," and the Central Employment Service, emphasizing counseling and job placement with attention to employer-employee relations concerned with minority problems.

Board of Prison Terms and Paroles

We learned in chapter 2 that the governor has the aid of the Board of *Prison* Terms and Paroles in deciding whether or not a prisoner in the reformatory or penitentiary should serve his full sentence. The court may set a maximum sentence, but if it does not do so within six months after a person is admitted to a state penal institution, then the board sets a maximum term not lower than that set by law for such an offense. The board also sets a minimum sentence, within certain limits. For example, sentence for a first felony committed when armed with a deadly weapon may not be less than five years. The authority of the Division of Institutions within the Department of Social and Health Services, therefore, does not extend to the length of time a prisoner is to be there.

In order to decide on a minimum sentence for each convict, the Board of Prison Terms and Parole studies the prisoner's life history, the type of crime, his attitudes toward society, and his probable actions if released. If a convict can become a useful citizen, it is to everyone's advantage to release him. If he is likely to repeat his crime, however, society is better off if he serves the maximum sentence.

If the Board of Prison Terms and Paroles believes that an inmate of these penal institutions can leave without harm to society after a short imprisonment, it releases him, usually on parole. Under this system, he reports to a parole officer at regular intervals. The parole officer helps him to get work and advises him in the many problems faced by an ex-convict. It was stated in connection with the governor's power that he may pardon any convicted criminal or revoke his parole, regardless of the action of the Board of Prison Terms and Paroles.

Between 1 July 1968 and 30 June 1970 the board conducted 8,410 "in-person" hearings and 14,722 "administrative actions." "In-person hearings include Admission (minimum term), Parole Revocation Sentence Determination (new minimum term), Progress, Disciplinary, Parole, and 'On Site' Parole Revocation hearings. Administrative actions are largely divided between the administrative institution hearings and parole reviews." During 1969-70, there were 1,264 persons paroled, and 691 parolees were accused of having violated the terms of their parole.

The board says of its plan for the future: The ultimate goal of the Board and the criminal justice system is to increase the safety of the community by reducing incidence of crime. Rehabilitation of offenders provides one of the most promising means to this end. It is to this effort—the rehabilitation of the offender and reduction in crime—that the Board commits itself. Within this ultimate goal, the Board has established specific goals as follows: fix optimum minimum terms; parole when ready; promote and assist reintegration into the community; conduct parole revocation hearings with focus on fairness, due process and public safety; increase expertise in the decisional process; increase skill in hearing process; provide coordination within the criminal justice system; review Board practices, procedures and policies.

Planning and Community Affairs Agency

The Planning and Community Affairs Agency is responsible for planning the best development of counties and cities. The legislature has assigned the agency to the governor's office as the coordinator for state programs relating to communities and federal programs dealing with local government units in the state.

During 1970 the planning agency's activities included: reviewing and administering $3,524,310 in federal grants for twenty cities, twenty-one counties and regional planning bodies, and six Indian tribes; holding a six-week institute for Mexican-Americans in eastern Washington to learn "about participation in the community decision-making process"; sponsoring action programs to stimulate business for black people in Pasco, Tacoma, Seattle, Spokane, and Vancouver; organizing the Puget Sound Coalition, a workshop involving college teachers, students, and the general public in an effort to solve the problems of "poverty, housing, government, land use, transportation, and environmental exploitation"; statewide citizen seminars on community development and environmental quality.

The agency emphasizes the need to make comprehensive planning part of the regular decision-making process of county, city, and regional governmental units. It tries to see that local planning is in general agreement with the state's long-range goals. The projects include land-use planning, health, nuclear power plant locations, Columbia River Gorge preservation planning, and scenic rivers and islands developments, as well as the whole field of law and justice in relation to economic status. It supersedes the state Census Board, which was abolished. A state census is made every ten years in between the federal census. See also the State *Planning* Advisory Council in Table 3.

State Personnel Board

It has been pointed out that when an elective official has the authority to appoint administrative assistants, he naturally wants them to follow his own policies, which often have a relationship to his political ideas. However, the

American people have a fear of such appointments, because if they are made to pay political debts, the recipients may not be qualified for the job or a corrupt political machine may develop. For this reason, the system that is ordinarily referred to as "Civil Service" was instituted at the various governmental levels to try to prevent excessive appointments on a political basis.

In our state a 1960 initiative placed under state civil service nearly all state employees except elective officials and top administrative heads. The 1961 legislature, however, amended the initiative to exempt from civil service requirements the following additional groups: all employees of the legislature and the courts; the academic personnel of institutions of higher learning; officers of the Washington State Patrol; confidential secretaries of directors and assistant directors plus their administrative assistants in all agencies for which the governor appoints the head; students; part-time employees; the public printer and his employees; and members of advertising boards—for example, the Washington State Apple Advertising Commission. The 1971 legislature added to these exemptions liquor vendors appointed by the Washington State Liquor Control Board and executive assistants for personnel administration and labor relations in all state agencies.

Until 1969 the Department of Highways had its own personnel board, but in that year the legislature abolished the Highways Personnel Board and transferred its duties to the State Personnel Board. The 1969 legislature created the State Higher Education Personnel Board to supervise selection of personnel in nonacademic positions in colleges and universities, and named the State Board for Community *College* Education to perform that function for community college nonacademic personnel.

The State Personnel Board was created to supervise the selection of efficient government personnel for the state agencies under the merit system. It works out job classification schedules and prepares standards for training and experience for each classification. It also makes up registers of persons eligible for employment by the state departments concerned and tries to see that appointments are made solely on a merit basis by sending to prospective employers lists of eligible applicants from which the employer chooses the one who seems best qualified. The board recommends to the governor a list of three persons rating highest on an examination on personnel management, and from that list the governor selects a director of personnel to head the Department of Personnel, which administers the merit system under the board's direction. For the composition of the board, see Table 3 at the end of this chapter. See also *Employee* Suggestion Awards Board.

Employees' Retirement Boards

As we have seen, retirement systems of various kinds are in effect for people in private industry, and similar arrangements are under way for many government employees. As a result, the Washington Public *Employees'* Retirement System Board was created to administer the fund for state and county employees and to invest the money in such a manner as to increase the amount of interest from it whenever possible.[26] (A separate board called the State Employees' Insurance Board handles the funds for insurance other than retirement benefits.) Until 1971 law enforcement officers and fire fighters had a separate board for managing their retirement funds, but in that year they were included in the employees under the administration of the Washington Public Employees' Retirement System Board.

Certain groups of public employees still have separate boards for managing their retirement funds: teachers, under the board of trustees of the State Teachers' Retirement Fund, unless they choose to transfer to the Public Employees' Retirement System, and the staff of the various institutions of higher education under the administration of their regents. In addition, the Public Pension Commission has the assignment of studying the entire pension system for all public employees in the state and recommending to the legislature changes which it believes would be beneficial. For the composition of these various boards see Table 3.

Boards of Regents or Trustees for Institutions of Higher Education

Each of our state universities and state colleges has a separate group of regents or trustees which acts as a board of managers for their particular school. For the number of regents for each institution, see the heading board of *regents* or the heading boards of trustees of state *colleges* in Table 3. Community colleges (formerly called junior colleges) have a board of trustees for each school, and there is a coordinating group called State Board of Community *College* Education.[27]

State Library Commission

We have other types of state institutions that serve an educational purpose—libraries and historical societies. The legislature created a State

26. The Washington Public *Employees'* Retirement System Board has now replaced the boards for the Statewide City Employees' Retirement System, the State Patrol Retirement System, and the Volunteer Firemen's Retirement System.

27. For local school administration, see chapter 7. For details concerning education advisory groups, see the headings *School* Emergency Construction Commission; Coordinating Council for Occupational *Education*; State Advisory Council on Vocational *Education*; Council on Higher *Education*; Commission on Higher *Education*; Western Interstate Commission of Higher *Education*; *Education* Commission of the States; State Higher *Education* Personnel Board; and Washington State *Educational* Television Commission in Table 3.

Library Commission to set the policies for a state library and to act as an advisory group on a statewide library program. The commission consists of the superintendent of public instruction and four commissioners who are appointed by the governor. The commission appoints the state librarian, who is in charge of the state library in Olympia.

The state library acts both as an official library for the use of state officials and as an aid to libraries throughout the state. As part of its function as a legislative reference library, it is required to keep copies of legislative bills and other official documents for the use of the legislators. As part of its general library service, it lends books directly to schools or groups in a community having no local library, and it helps in organizing county or regional libraries or in improving the services of those in existence. With the approval of the State Library Commission, the state library allocates funds appropriated by the legislature for public library service to tax-supported libraries throughout the state.

State Board for the Certification of Librarians

Any public library that serves a community of four thousand or more or any library under the control of the state (except law libraries) may not employ full-time professional librarians unless they either have library training or can pass an examination in library techniques. The legislature created the State Board for the Certification of Librarians to grant certificates to librarians who can meet these requirements.

State Law Library

A state law library was established to serve as a reference library on matters of law and court procedure. It is intended primarily for the use of the supreme, appellate, and superior court judges, the attorney general, and all lawyers throughout the state, although any official may use it. The Law Library, situated in Olympia, receives copies of all the *Session Laws,* journals, state supreme court reports, and other official documents, and it has charge of selling copies of the court reports (*Washington Reports*). It is directed by the state law librarian, who is appointed by the state supreme court. The State Law Library Committee, which used to appoint the law librarian, was abolished by the 1959 legislature.

Statute Law Committee

In order for people to use legal material of the kind described above, summaries must be prepared of our laws and state supreme court decisions, so that a person can tell what laws are in force at the present time and what the judicial interpretations of them are. Such a compilation is called a code, and it must be extremely accurate and well organized if it is to serve as an official statement of our laws. Giving a number to a law on a certain subject so that any later law passed will appear under that number is one of the difficult parts of preparing a code, and the legislature established a Statute Law Committee to prepare and maintain a *Revised Code of Washington* according to such a system. For its membership see Table 3.

Commission on Uniform State Laws

When laws differ from one state to another on subjects having interstate application, much difficulty and confusion results. The legislature created the Commission on Uniform State Laws to study subjects on which uniform laws throughout the country would be desirable and to recommend passage of such laws.

The *1969-70 Biennial Report* of the commission contains a list of laws already passed by the Washington State legislature in accordance with recommendations of the commission and a list of recommendations not yet in force in this state. Examples of ones in existence now are: divorce recognition from other states; code of military justice (for the state militia); and reciprocal enforcement of family support. Examples of ones currently proposed are: adoption; consumer credit code; deceptive trade practices act; and interstate compromise of death taxes act. The commissions from various states meet together to draw up the proposed uniform laws. For the composition of the commission in this state, see Table 3.

State Historical Societies

There are three state historical societies in Washington: the Washington State *Historical* Society in Tacoma, the Eastern Washington State *Historical* Society in Spokane, and the State Capitol *Historical* Society in Olympia. The purpose of the Washington and the Eastern Washington State Historical Societies is to collect and preserve books, maps, charts, papers, and materials that illustrate the history of our state, with the Washington State Historical Society emphasizing statewide history and the Eastern Washington State Historical Society devoting itself largely to the history of the Inland Empire.

The State Capitol Historical Association has the same function as the other two historical societies, except that it specializes in materials pertaining to the history of our state capitol. It maintains the State Capitol Museum. A curator or director is appointed by each of the historical society boards. For the composition of the boards of trustees for the historical societies, see entries in

Freeway through north Seattle. Mount Baker is visible in the upper right-hand corner. (Photo by Forest and Whitmire, Yakima)

Table 3 for each society, entered alphabetically under the word *Historical.*

Washington State Printing Plant

It is obvious that a great deal of printing is necessary in the publications of the *Session Laws, Washington Reports,* reports of executive and administrative departments, and the many other official documents referred to above. The state printing plant was created by the legislature to handle the printing, and it is operated by the state *printer,* who is appointed by the governor. For the composition and function of the State *Printing* and Duplication Committee, see that heading in Table 3.

State Highway Commission

An important phase of the state's public welfare program is the construction and maintenance of good roads. In fact, easy travel by highway, air, railroad, and water has become such a necessity that we have governmental agencies to deal with problems of all these. Aid for roads comes from both federal and state funds. Federal money is given for building of transcontinental highways, with which we are all familiar. U. S. Highway 30, which follows approximately the route of the old Oregon Trail, is of particular interest to the Pacific Northwest. In addition, the state acts as agent for the federal government in the use of federal funds appropriated to aid certain road projects, such as county roads, city streets, and primary and secondary state highways.

Like public welfare, roads throughout the state were first largely local projects under the direction of the county commissioners of each county. If the roads were good in one county and bad in another, it mattered only to the county residents, for the most part. As the use of automobiles increased the scope of travel, however, nearly everyone was traveling outside his county and demanding good roads for the whole state. In 1905 when automobile travel had just begun, the legislature created a State Highway Board and then replaced it in 1921 by the Department of Public Works. In 1923 the supervision of highways was removed from that department and given to the state highway engineer. In 1929 the department was established under a director of highways, appointed by the governor. The task of providing a satisfactory system of state roads had become so difficult by 1951, however, that the legislature decided to divide the responsibility for our state road policies among a group. It then established the State *Highway* Commission, consisting of five members appointed by the governor. The commission, in turn, appoints the director of highways. The county commissioners are still in charge of county roads.

When the State Highway Commission thinks that a state road should be built over a given route, it sends a recommendation to the legislature. If the legislature agrees, it designates the road as a primary or secondary state highway and authorizes the commission to let contracts for its construction. The director, working with the commission, supervises construction and attends to maintenance of all state highways. The commission also fixes maximum speeds for automobiles on state highways, within limits set by law. Local authorities have the power to alter these within their jursidiction, to a certain extent.

Our roads are paid for largely by the fees for automobile licenses and the gasoline tax collection. A certain percentage of the money received from gasoline taxes is allocated to the counties and cities for county roads and city streets. The director of highways supervises the expenditures made by the counties and cities from this fund.

With the growing concern over the pollution that results from the exhaust fumes from the thousands of cars on our highways—particularly freeways and city streets—agitation has increased in recent years to curtail the building of freeways and substitute some type of mass transit, subways, or faster train or bus service in cities, to reduce the number of cars traveling in metropolitan areas. In the meantime, when the Department of Highways finds that a state highway project will affect the quality of the environment, the highways director is to prepare an environmental report for the director of ecology, who writes a review statement for the Department of Highways, which then calls a public hearing. The report by the director of ecology must be made available to the public through news media. [28]

Washington Historic Sites and Markers Commission

It was mentioned that the State Parks and Recreation Commission locates and marks spots of historic interest in the state. Many such places are on state highways, and the legislature wishes to have them marked in a uniform fashion. It therefore created the Washington *Historic* Sites and Markers Commission to decide where such markers shall be placed and to supervise their construction. No marker may be put up along a state highway without the approval of the commission. The highway commission itself prescribes regulations for erecting and maintaining private advertising signs or directional signs in a scenic area or near an interstate highway. No sign may be erected in these places without a permit from the commission.

Washington State Patrol

It is also becoming more and more necessary that traffic regulations be observed in order to lessen the number of deaths and injuries from highway accidents. The agency responsible for enforcing traffic regulations outside of incorporated towns in our state is the Washington State *Patrol,* and the chief of the State Patrol employs sufficient patrol officers to cover all of our rural roads and highways. There are five patrol districts in the state, each of which is in the charge of a district captain who is assisted by a sergeant with his detachment of patrolmen. They can issue tickets for speeding or for any other violation.

The patrol not only enforces traffic laws, but it tries to prevent traffic accidents. Research is conducted to find out what are the main causes of accidents, and efforts are made to educate people in avoiding such risks. Before 1965 the State Patrol was also in charge of issuing drivers' licenses, but

28. Various advisory groups at both the state and the local levels are concerned with all aspects of the highway transportation system. At the present time these are mainly composed of county or city officials plus staff members of the Department of Highways, and will be discussed in chapters 7 and 8.

at that time the legislature transferred the responsibility to the Department of Motor Vehicles.[29]

Washington State Aeronautics Commission

Other types of transportation need regulations, also, to protect the public welfare. Aviation, for example, has now reached the point where state as well as federal supervision is necessary. In this state, the Washington State Aeronautics Commission has the power to establish flying regulations in the interest of safety. It requires aircraft owners to register each plane, and it licenses airports so that the owners can be required to meet safety standards. The commission also encourages the establishment of airports and air facilities, and coordinates the activities of the federal government, cities, and individuals in the development of aeronautics.

Board of Puget Sound Pilotage Commissioners

Since we have ocean-going vessels coming into our harbors and boats operating on various sections of Puget Sound, it is necessary to have well-trained pilots who know the channels in the river or inlet in order to prevent accidents. The legislature created the Board of Puget Sound *Pilotage* Commissioners to license pilots for boats operating in the waters of this state. The board consists of the director of labor and industries plus four members appointed by the governor.

Washington Toll Bridge Authority

Sometimes expensive bridges are paid for by charging a certain amount for each person or automobile crossing them. Such a charge is called *toll*, and in this state the Washington Toll Bridge Authority decides matters of tolls. It has the right to establish and construct a toll bridge on any of our public highways or to operate a ferry if it is considered necessary. The authority consists of the governor, director of highways as a nonvoting member, two members of the State Highway Commission, and two members appointed by the governor.

The 1961 legislature required the director of highways to appoint, with the approval of the State Highway Commission, an assistant director of toll facilities to supervise the operation of toll bridges and ferries.

29. For the composition and function of advisory groups in connection with problems of the State Patrol, see the following headings in Table 3: Washington Traffic *Safety* Commission; State Commission on *Equipment*; State *Communications* Advisory Committee; Washington *Law* Enforcement Officers' Training Commission.

Toll facility aid districts may be established to pay for the retirement of bonds issued by the toll bridge authority. If the authority recommends the creation of such a district, the county commissioners of the affected counties hold hearings and an election to determine if the people want the district. If they do, the district is put into operation.

Washington Utilities and Transportation Commission

As we have seen, even at the time when the state constitution was written, there was fear that governmental agencies would be unduly influenced by corporations. At that time, railroads were the only type of corporation seemingly powerful enough in the new state to appear threatening. Consequently, in Article XII of the state constitution, which attempts to prevent any corporation from becoming a monopoly or burdening the people with excessive rates, railroads are mentioned specifically. Section 13 states, "All railroad, canal, and other transportation companies are declared to be common carriers, and subject to legislative control." In Section 18 the legislature is directed to pass laws to establish reasonable maximum freight and passenger rates. The constitution also gave the legislature authority to create a railroad commission.

From 1889 to 1905 the legislature tried to regulate railroad rates and service within the state by passing specific laws to accomplish this purpose. By 1905, however, it became evident to the legislators that some more efficient system of supervision was necessary, and the legislature created the Railroad Commission, which was given authority to regulate the rates, services, and facilities of railroad and express companies. In 1911 the legislature changed the name of the agency to the Public Service Commission of Washington and gradually began adding different types of public service corporations to the list of those to be regulated by the commission. To emphasize its wide coverage, the legislature in 1921 gave it the name of Department of Public Works of Washington, which included the supervision of the construction and maintenance of highways. However, the task of road construction was great enough even then that a separate Department of Highways was established at the next session of the legislature, 1923. In 1935 the name of the Public Works Department was changed to the Department of Public Service of Washington, and in 1945, toward the end of World War II when all existing means of transportation and utility companies were being pushed to the utmost, the legislature tried separating the two functions into a Department of Transportation and a Department of Public Utilities. Their problems were sufficiently related, however, that in 1949 the legislature combined the two departments into the Washington Public Service Commission and in 1961 changed its name to the Washington Utilities and

Orcas Island ferry. (Photo by Washington State Department of Commerce and Economic Development)

Transportation Commission.

The present commission consists of three members appointed by the governor with senate consent for staggered six-year terms. The governor names one of the commissioners as chairman. Not more than two of the three may be from the same political party.

The following types of companies come under its jurisdiction for regulating rates and services within the state, subject to federal regulations by the Interstate Commerce Commission for companies that serve more than this state: railroads; motor freight carriers, with garbage and refuse collection companies (other than city garbage-collection systems) considered as a separate category; intercity and intracity bus companies; wharfingers and warehouse companies having watercraft landing to receive or discharge freight; storage warehouses; steamboat passenger and ferry companies; port districts (for some of their charges); gas companies; electrical companies; telephone companies; telegraph companies; water companies.[30] Utilities owned by cities, counties, service districts or cooperatives serving only their stockholders are, for the most part, autonomous and are not under the regulation of the commission.[31]

State Department of Motor Vehicles

Until 1965 the Department of Licenses handled the registration of motor vehicles as well as the certification of persons engaging in professions or

30. According to State of Washington, *Eleventh Report, Washington Utilities and Transportation Commission* (1970).
31. For the composition and function of the State Anti-*Monopoly* Board, see Table 3.

skilled work requiring licensing for the protection of the public and for state revenue. However, the great increase in the number of automobiles in the state made licensing them seem important enough for the legislature to create a separate Department of Motor Vehicles, which has now absorbed the other functions of the former Department of Licenses, which was abolished.

Motor Vehicle Functions. The state Department of Motor Vehicles licenses cars and automobile drivers. Drivers were formerly licensed by the State Patrol. The department issues ownership certificates and license plates; administers the laws for drivers' licenses, drivers' financial responsibility in accident cases, and driver improvement; and takes charge of the collection of liquid fuel taxes.

The department is administered by a director of motor vehicles, who is appointed by the governor with senate consent. He may appoint county auditors as his agents for the issuance of motor vehicle licenses.[32]

Professional Licensing Function. We have seen that most of our state departments or boards have the power to license people who sell goods or services as a means of controlling the quality of the product. Many of these, like the Department of Agriculture, examine the qualifications and performance of persons selling agricultural goods or services and issue licenses to those they approve. However, there are many professional people and skilled workers whose services or products are not covered by any existing agency in their own field. The legislature therefore allows the Department of Motor Vehicles to license such persons. Either the legislature creates an examining board in a particular profession or skill which gives examinations and then instructs the department to issue the proper license, or the legislature allows the department itself to create such examining boards when there is a call for a specific license. For the latter type, the department asks the governor to appoint three persons to pass on the qualifications of the applicants.

Examples of types of practitioners for which the legislature has established examining boards and their respective certifying groups are listed below:

LICENSED PRACTITIONERS AND THEIR CERTIFYING GROUPS

Practitioner	*Certifying Group*
Certified or licensed public accountants	Board of *Accountancy* for certified or licensed public accountants
Architects	State Board for Registration of *Architects*
Barbers	*Barber* Examining Board
Beauty parlor operators	*Beauty* Culture Examining Committee

32. For related agencies, see *Driving* Instructor's Examination Committee; *Reciprocity* Commission; and Mobile Home and Recreational *Vehicle* Advisory Board in Table 3.

Practitioner	*Certifying Group*
Participants in boxing or wrestling matches	State *Athletic* Commission
Chiropractors	State Board of *Chiropractic* Examiners
Collection agencies	Washington State *Collection* Agency Board
Dentists	Washington State Board of *Dental* Examiners
Employment agencies	*Employment* Agency Advisory Board
Engineers	State Board for Registration of Professional *Engineers* and Land Surveyors
Funeral directors and embalmers	*Funeral* Directors and Embalmers Examining Committee
Landscape architects	State Board of Registration for *Landscape* Architects
Librarians	State Board for the Certification of *Librarians*
Physicians	Washington State Board of *Medical* Examiners
	Examining Committee in Basic *Sciences*
Nurses	Washington State Board of *Nursing*
	Washington State Board of Practical *Nurse* Examiners
Nursing homes	State Board of Examiners for *Nursing* Home Administrators
Optometrists	State *Optometry* Board
Osteopaths	Committee of *Osteopathic* Examiners
Pharmacists	Board of *Pharmacy*
Physical therapists	State Examining Committee of Physical *Therapists*
Practicing psychologists	Examining Board of *Psychology*
Real estate dealers and agents	*Real Estate* Examining Commission
Sanitarians	Washington State Board of Registered *Sanitarians*
Veterinarians	Washington State *Veterinary* Board of Governors
Water well construction operators	*Water* Well Examining Board

For building contractors, electricians, alien and short firearms dealers, and certain types of corporations, such as mining firms, the Department of Motor Vehicles appoints examining committees as needed.

Each of the above boards may revoke as well as issue licenses, but the 1955 legislature established' a separate body to investigate complaints of unprofessional conduct on the part of physicians and surgeons—the Washington State *Medical* Disciplinary Board. If the board finds the person guilty, it may order the Department of Motor Vehicles to revoke or suspend the doctor's license. As in other similar cases, he may appeal the board's decision to the superior court. A hearings board was also created to hear complaints against beauty parlor operators—the *Beauty* Culture Hearing Board.

In recent years, the trend toward the use of a centralized licensing agency has been extended even to older licensing units. For example, the Department of Labor and Industries decides whether or not an electrician meets the requirements for his work, and, if he does, it requests the Department of Motor Vehicles to issue his permit. The Department of Fisheries is required to follow that procedure in licensing commercial fishermen, and there are numerous other such instances. If a complaint is filed against any license holder, the director of licenses asks the governor to appoint an examining committee for the profession involved. The 1967 legislature added specific hearing boards for barbers, beauty parlor operators, and chiropractors.

Additional Regulatory Bodies

In this state, corporations may be formed to provide cemeteries, and the legislature in 1953 created a State *Cemetery* Board to inspect the financial proceedings of such firms.

In addition to regulating various types of corporations, the state government also takes responsibility for supervising the sale of some specific commodities that may harm individuals. Liquor is one of these, and the Washington State *Liquor* Control Board was created by the legislature to operate the state liquor stores and to license restaurants or clubs to sell liquor.

Regulation of certain types of commercial amusements is also necessary to protect the public welfare. Some of these, such as boxing and wrestling matches, were mentioned in connection with the Department of Motor Vehicles, which licenses them. Another separate agency with a similar purpose is the Washington *Horse* Racing Commission, which makes rules to govern horse races and licenses the operators, owners, trainers, and jockeys connected with horse races. By this means, the commission can penalize any race-track operator who does not follow the state laws in regard to gambling, treatment of racing animals, and so forth.

Organized Militia

Regulation of any activity through licensing or the establishment of rules for operation is considered part of the police power of a government because it is a control used for the benefit of the public. All of our state administrative agencies discussed so far would fit into this group in some way. In the United States, our feeling of responsibility for obeying laws has been such that no physical force is necessary, ordinarily, to compel the great majority of people to observe laws or to pay a fine for rules that they may have broken. Those who do defy laws can usually be handled by the police officers who act in connection with our city and county governments, which will be discussed in chapters 7 and 8.

If the local police cannot keep order, the governor, as commander-in-chief of the state militia, may call that group into action. Article X, Section 1 of the state constitution stipulates that all able-bodied male citizens of this state between the ages of eighteen and forty-five are liable for this type of military duty. The 1963 legislature included female members of the national guard as part of the state militia and defined state citizens as ones who are United States citizens or who have declared their intention of becoming ones.

The training of the organized militia[33] is under the control of the adjutant general, who is appointed by the governor to serve at his pleasure. The only restriction on the governor's control of the national guard is that it may be called into federal service, in which case the president becomes commander-in-chief.

Department of Civil Defense

Ordinarily the legislature reserves the label "department" for one of the main agencies included in the administrative code. The name Department of Civil Defense was given, however, to a unit created in 1951 outside of the administrative code group. Its purpose is to coordinate the activities of all civil defense organizations within the state and to cooperate with those of other states and of the federal government. The head of the department is appointed by the governor with senate consent. A Washington State Civil *Defense* Council acts as an advisory group to the department.

Washington State Arts Commission

In 1961 the legislature created the Washington State *Arts* Commission to plan for cultural development in the state and recommend to the legislature

33. Called the national guard.

and state officials pertinent programs. For its composition, see Table 3 at the end of this chapter.

FISCAL AGENCIES

In the preceding chapter, we discussed some of the state elective officials whose work relates to the management of or accounting for the state's receipts and expenditures. Those most directly concerned with the state's finances are the governor, in the preparation of the budget, the state treasurer, in the disbursement of funds, and the state auditor, in the auditing of the books of state and local officials. However, the commissioner of public lands, in his surveys of the value of state lands for the consideration of the Board of Natural Resources, has an important connection with the management of the state's finances. In fact, all of the executive and administrative officials receive fees of some kind and are required to submit annual or biennial reports to the governor and the legislature of their receipts and disbursements. In the administrative branch, in addition, there are agencies whose function is to deal, either exclusively or to a major degree, with fiscal matters. They are the Department of General Administration; the Department of Revenue; and the State *Finance* Committee.

Department of General Administration

In 1955 when the legislature divided the work of the Department of Institutions, it created a new Department of General Administration to handle the supervision of banks, the purchasing of state equipment and supplies, and the care of state records (archives)— duties previously performed by the Department of Institutions.

The director of the Department of General Administration is appointed by the governor with senate consent. The director selects a supervisor of banking, who appoints bank examiners to inspect banks and trust companies to make certain that they are sound and operating within the law. Another supervisor performs the same function for savings and loan associations. New banks and trust or loan companies must be chartered or licensed by these supervisors before they begin operations.

In the interests of economy, the legislature established the Division of Purchasing within the department to act as a central purchasing agency for all state departments and institutions. The supervisor of the division asks for sealed bids for the purchase of supplies and equipment in order to buy in large quantities and have as much competition as possible for the purchases. If all departments pool their orders for a particular item, it can be purchased in quantity and therefore secured at a lower price. The 1961 legislature required that any state or local governmental unit shall buy products made by blind persons in a nonprofit agency whenever they are available in equal price and standards to commercial goods.

The Division of Engineering and Architecture within the Department of General Administration plans and supervises the erection and maintenance of all buildings in Olympia used by state agencies. The division also performs this service for other state institutions that do not have their own architectural divisions—for example, the various penal and remedial institutions, the district offices of various state agencies, and the state colleges.

Another function of the Department of General Administration is to preserve the official records of any state office. The director appoints a state archivist to maintain these records as state archives. He also has the responsibility for deciding which records of counties, cities, or other local governmental units may be destroyed and which must be preserved.

Records Committee

The volume of books, papers, and archives of all kinds maintained by state officials increases to such an extent that space cannot be provided to keep all of them; therefore, the legislature created the Records Committee to decide what old records have no further value from an administrative standpoint. The committee then advises the state archivist that these documents may be destroyed. This committee supersedes a former group known as the Committee on the Destruction of Obsolete Records. The state archivist selects records having historical value, and these are never destroyed unless, in some instances, microfilm copies may be substituted.

State Department of Revenue

The legislature created the state Department of Revenue in 1967 to replace the former State Tax Commission. The present department is under the control of a director appointed by the governor with senate consent; the State Tax Commission consisted of three members appointed by the governor with senate consent. The Tax Commission enforced laws and regulations regarding the collection of all state taxes, and this included supervising the appraisal of property for the collection of local real and personal property taxes in each county. The difficulties of achieving uniform assessment of real property, particularly, from one county to another were the main impetus that led the legislature to substitute a Department of Revenue under the direction of a single person for the more cumbersome administration of a group of three people.

Almost everybody is familiar with the local procedure for assessing taxes on real and personal property. The county assessor lists the acreage and buildings owned by each person, plus livestock and other chattels in the personal property category. Then he assigns a value to them. This is called appraising the property. The county Board of Equalization hears complaints from owners and makes necessary corrections. We are then required, by law, to pay taxes on 50 percent of the assessed valuation of our holdings, which before 1967 was supposed to be set at the market value they would have had as of approximately 1941.

The State Tax Commission, acting as the State Board of Equalization, was required to try to see that a house valued, for example, by an assessor in one county at $10,000 would be appraised at approximately the same figure by the assessors in all of the other counties. However, this was not the case. Consequently, in 1955 the legislature ordered the State Tax Commission to require each county assessor to revalue the property within his county by 1 June 1958. A study in 1963 revealed that there was still a wide variation. At that time appraisals appeared to be lowest in San Juan County—14.69 percent of the actual value of the property—and highest in Grant County—25 percent.

According to the director, when the department was created in 1967 these inequities were still in effect. He states: "Large areas of many counties had not been revalued for more than ten years, up to thirty years in extreme cases. (In some counties today the assessor doesn't know when most of the values were placed on the rolls.)

"Not a single county was observing the constitutionally established yardstick for establishing assessed values at 50 percent of true and fair value. Different assessors used different ratios, and some used varying ratios within a single county." [34]

Consequently, in 1969 the legislature appropriated $2,850,000 to begin a program of financial aid to counties to make a revaluation of property. Each county's method for carrying out the valuation project had first to be approved by the Department of Revenue. The 1970 special session of the legislature made another appropriation to continue the project for those counties that would accept it under the conditions stipulated by the department, and by the third quarter of 1970, thirty-five of our thirty-nine counties had received state funds to make approved revaluations of property. Twenty counties had part of their revised appraisals on the 1970 assessment roll, and as a result of that proportionate change, property values in the state were increased $1,732,000 and assessed values rose $865,900,000.

When the state constitution was written, real and personal property taxes were the basis of our tax system because practically everybody who had

34. State of Washington, *Department of Revenue, Second Biennial Report, 1970* (1970).

money owned as much property as he could. However, as cities increased in size and space for building decreased sharply, rental units in apartments or other types of buildings became much more common. In addition, the mobility of our population, stimulated by new means of fast transportation and accentuated by the movement of people during World War II, has resulted in a proportionate decline in the number of property owners. Consequently, many property owners feel that property taxes are now wrong in principle because they apply only to a particular segment of the population. In order to try to keep property taxes low, the legislature proposed a constitutional amendment, which was approved by the voters, limiting the tax levy on real property to forty mills on each dollar of assessed valuation. Levies in excess of that amount must be approved by the voters of a taxing district in special elections.

In the past, when property taxes failed to produce sufficient revenue for rising costs of local and state governments, the legislature turned to a sales tax, which in 1971 was 4.25 percent, with counties and cities having the authority to add a local sales tax. In 1970, 25 counties and 199 cities and towns had added the local tax. The consumer pays sales tax on most goods purchased. Many economists consider a sales tax an undesirable kind of tax from the standpoint of a person's ability to pay, since it affects persons of low income equally with those of high income. From the standpoint of collection, however, governmental agencies prefer a sales tax because the collections are made by business firms rather than by governmental employees, and the public often seems to be less aware of a sales tax, which ordinarily is paid a few cents at a time, than of a tax paid all at once in a larger amount.

These factors (ability to pay and economy in collection) are reversed if a state income tax is used. A graduated state income tax has been declared unconstitutional by our state supreme court on the basis of the constitutional requirement that taxes be "uniform" on a particular kind of property. In 1935 the legislature proposed a constitutional amendment to permit a state income tax, but the voters refused to pass the amendment. At the present time, during every session of the legislature the question of proposing another similar amendment or of passing a flat income tax law, which would, presumably, be constitutional, is debated and the leaders of both major political parties have expressed themselves in favor of some type of state income tax, but by 1972 none was in effect.

In addition to the sales taxes, there are certain state taxes on businesses and members of various occupations, a tax on admissions to movie theaters and other places of amusement, a tax on cigarette sales, one on inheritances or large gifts, and various other types of transactions. However, intangibles—stocks and bonds mainly—are not taxed by the state, and proposals have been made to include them in taxable personal property. The total net amount of taxes collected by the department for 1970 was $648,212,758, and the ratio for property taxes collected by counties, school districts, and certain other local taxing districts for 1970 was: schools, 57.90 percent; counties, 11.46 percent; cities and towns, 13.09 percent; state, 6.27 percent; roads, 5.22 percent; port districts, 2.70 percent; fire districts, 1.72 percent; other, 1.64 percent.

There have to be procedures for deciding what share of taxes paid by businesses that operate in more than one county goes to each county concerned and how much of the property taxes collected by counties goes to the state. When the State Tax Commission was in existence, it acted as a board of equalization to decide these matters. Now the director of the Department of Revenue with members of his staff act as the state board of equalization. For example, certain kinds of businesses—railroad, telegraph, telephone, motor transport, airplane, electric light and power, gas, water, pipeline, heating, and steamboat companies—operate in more than one county, almost without exception. Each county where such a service exists wants a fair share of the taxes the company pays to the state. The amount would depend, to a certain extent, on the volume of business done in a particular county as well as on the actual value of the company's property in the county. Its holdings in a county containing a large city would obviously have a higher value than similar property in a rural county.

The State Board of Equalization also determines how much of the property taxes collected by each county shall go to the state. The board first adds up the total property value of each county as submitted by the assessor. The state tax rate is then applied to half this amount, and the result is the amount of taxes due the state from all of the counties.

Here we meet again the problem of the proportion each county should pay. If the state tax were divided equally among the thirty-nine counties, some with a small population or low valuation would be paying a greater rate of tax than would the big or wealthy counties. Consequently, the State Board of Equalization works out a ratio of tax payments based on the total property value of each county. Each one then pays to the state that amount from the taxes it collects, and the remainder goes for county, city, and certain district expenses.

The State Board of Equalization also has the power to raise or lower the valuation of any class of property in any county as reported by the county assessor if it appears that discrepancies exist.

Board of Tax Appeals

The legislature created a state Board of *Tax* Appeals to hear complaints from individuals or corporations about decisions made by the Department of Revenue. The board consists of three persons appointed by the governor with senate approval.

State Finance Committee

The State *Finance* Committee, created in 1895 under the title of the State Board of Finance, decides how to invest state funds so that they are safe and remunerative within the limits set by law. The committee also approves banks where state funds are to be deposited, called state depositaries. The committee consists of the governor, the lieutenant governor, and the state treasurer.

Administrative Board

Obviously, the governor can more easily determine the policies of the officials who administer these departments, committees, and commissions than those of the executive departments, since the governor appoints most of the administrative department heads and may dismiss many of them if he wishes. The law authorizing the appointment of each state official specifies whether his term of office is at the governor's pleasure or whether he may be removed only for cause, and if so, under what conditions. In Tables 2 and 3 at the end of this chapter, these details are given.

Because the governor tries to appoint people whose views on the work to be done (which may not necessarily be their political views) coincide with his own as much as possible, he naturally relies on their advice to a considerable extent. Therefore, the legislature has provided that the heads of agencies designated as "code departments" shall constitute an official advisory board to the governor. It comes the nearest to a governor's "cabinet" of any group we have. In 1972 these officials are: the directors of ecology, agriculture, fisheries, game, highways, motor vehicles, general administration, commerce and economic development, labor and industries, revenue, and the secretary of social and health services.

Although the agency for administering unemployment insurance is called the *Employment* Security Department, its head is named commissioner instead of director, and the legislature did not include the agency in its list of code departments. The Department of Civil *Defense* is likewise not a code department.

The *Administrative* Board is instructed to make recommendations for unifying the work of the administrative departments. We have noted that the Legislative Council proposed measures for achieving a more streamlined organization for the executive and administrative departments, and we shall consider further recommendations for improving the efficiency of the legislative and judicial branches in chapters 4 and 5.

SUGGESTED READINGS

For a discussion of original sources for study of state agencies, see the first paragraph of the Suggested Readings for chapter 2.

Administrative departments issue helpful reports and bulletins on the current work of their agencies and the status of the occupation or activity with which they are concerned. Recently, most of the agencies connected with conservation of natural resources have issued their reports in a combined booklet entitled *Annual Report, Natural Resources and Recreation Agencies.* This may be secured from the Department of Ecology or any of the other related agencies. Departments concerned with public welfare are following a similar procedure. Their publication is called *Annual Report, Human Resources Agencies* and may be secured from the Department of Social and Health Services or any other agency associated in the report. Olympia is the headquarters for all of the administrative departments. For the agencies that do not include their annual or biennial reports in these consolidated publications, one needs to write to the individual department or board in Olympia to receive its bulletins.

In addition to the regular departmental reports, bulletins on specific subjects are issued by many state agencies. The Department of Agriculture, for example, publishes an annual series called *Washington Agricultural Statistics,* which deal with individual crops, indicating the amount produced, its value, and the main problems encountered in the production and marketing. Similar pamphlets give information on livestock production and other phases of agricultural industries.

TABLE II

STATE ADMINISTRATIVE DEPARTMENTS

Department	Director (How Chosen)	With Senate Consent?	Term of Office	Monthly Salary*	Name of Director
Agriculture	Apptd. by gov.	Yes	At pleasure of gov.	$1,250.00	Donald W. Moos
Commerce and Economic Development	Apptd. by gov.	Yes	At pleasure of gov.	$1,666.66	Daniel B. Ward
Ecology	Apptd. by gov.	Yes	At pleasure of gov.	$2,500.00	John A. Biggs
Fisheries	Apptd. by gov.	Yes	At pleasure of gov.	$1,250.00	Thor C. Tollefson
Game	Apptd. by Game Commission	No	At pleasure of commission	$1,500.00	Carl N. Crouse
General Administration	Apptd. by gov.	Yes	At pleasure of gov.	$1,250.00	William E. Schneider
Highways	Apptd. by Highway Commission	No	Indefinite; may be dismissed by commission after formal charges and hearing	$1,666.66	George H. Andrews
Labor and Industries	Apptd. by gov.	Yes	At pleasure of gov.	$1,250.00	William C. Jacobs
Motor Vehicles	Apptd. by gov.	Yes	At pleasure of gov.	$1,875.00	Jack G. Nelson
Revenue	Apptd. by gov.	Yes	At pleasure of gov.	$1,875.00	George Kinnear
Social and Health Services	Secretary apptd. by gov.	Yes	At pleasure of gov.	$3,041.66	Sidney E. Smith

* The legislature now allows the Committee on Salaries to set the maximum compensation for administrative officials, and the figures for the more recently created departments (Ecology, Motor Vehicles, Revenue, and Social and Health Services) are based on its recommendations to the governor. The figures for the older departments are taken from vol. 2 of the 1967 governor's budget, the last issue of that section printed for public distribution.

TABLE III

STATE BOARDS, COMMISSIONS, AND COMMITTEES

Group	Composition	How Chosen	Qualifications	Term of Office	Compensation	Function
Board of *Accountancy**	5 members	Apptd. by gov.	US citizens; Wash. residents; 3, CPA; 1, LPA; 1, PA. CPA's must have 10 years' experience; others, 5.	CPA's, 3 years; others, 2; not more than 2 consecutive terms for all	$25 per day pay plus regular expense allowance †	To examine accountants for competency and approve licenses for ones who qualify as LPA, CPA
Administrative Board	Gov. plus directors of code departments. See Table 2					
Washington State *Aeronautics* Commission	7 members	Apptd. by gov. with senate consent	No more than simple majority from same political party; 1 from each cong. dist.	5 years; gov. may remove for cause	$40 per day pay plus regular expense allowance	To make regulations for flying in state; register pilots

*Titles of agencies are arranged alphabetically according to italicized word in heading.

†Some boards receive pay for each day spent on duty plus travel allowance, which is ordinarily ten cents a mile. However, the amount of pay set by the legislature varies with the degree of training necessary for the work and also with the pay scale in operation at the time the law was passed. Therefore, in 1970 the legislature (first extra session of the 1969 legislature) passed a general law in an attempt to make the amounts more uniform. The regular expense allowance may thus be $25 per day for lodging and travel within the state ($35 outside the state) for persons not receiving additional per diem rates or it may be travel only—ten cents per mile. In this table, if the legislature specified a particular amount of pay for an agency member for days spent on official business, it is listed. However, the director of program planning and fiscal management has some discretionary powers in interpreting the distinctions between the terms used for "per diem" remuneration and "expenses" by the legislature.

TABLE 3—Continued (2)

Group	Composition	How Chosen	Qualifications	Term of Office	Compensation	Function
Washington State Council on *Aging*	Not to exceed 80	Apptd. by gov. except for 4 chosen from legis. (2 senators apptd. by pres. of senate; 2 reps. apptd. by speaker of house	1 from each legislative dist. plus additional number, not to exceed 20 (now attached to Dept. of Soc. and Health Serv.)	Gov.'s appointees, 4 years; legislators, 2 years	$25 per day pay plus regular expense allowance	To advise dir. of soc. and health services, gov., and other state officials on programs for aged
Washington State *Apple* Advertising Commission	13 apple men plus dir. of ag. as nonvoting member	Elected by apple men of the state from 3 geographical districts	US citizens; state residents; 4 apple dealers; 9 apple producers (at least 25 years old); all with 5 years' apple experience	3 years	Not more than $20 per day pay plus regular expense allowance	To advertise Washington apples and to enforce marketing orders if apple men authorize them
Apprentice-ship Council	6 members plus employee of the Div. of Vocational Educ. of the State Dept. of Educ. and of Dept. of Employment Sec. as nonvoting members	6 apptd. by dir. of labor and ind.	3 from employer and 3 from employee organizations	3 years	Regular expense allowance for 6 non-state employees	To set standards for agreements between employers and apprentices learning a trade; approve appointment by dir. of lab. and ind. of supervisor of apprenticeship

TABLE 3—Continued (3)

Group	Composition	How Chosen	Qualifications	Term of Office	Compensation	Function
State Board for Registration of *Architects*	5 members	Apptd. by gov.	State residents for at least 8 years; 8 years' experience as architects.	5 years; gov. may remove for cause	$25 pay per day plus regular expense allowance	To examine applicants for licenses as architects and approve those qualified
Washington State *Arts* Commission	21 members	Apptd. by gov.	1 from senate; 1 from house; others to represent various categories of the arts and different geographical sections as much as possible	3 years	Regular expense allowance	To plan for cultural development and recommend program to legis.
State *Athletic* Commission	3 members	Apptd. by gov.	None specified	4 years. Gov. may remove at will	Regular expense allowance	To approve applications from boxers and wrestlers for matches
Advisory Council on *Atomic* Energy	5 members	Apptd. by gov.	None specified	At pleasure of gov.	$15 pay per day plus regular expense allowance	To advise gov. on programs for peaceful uses of atomic energy within the state

TABLE 3—Continued (4)

Group	Composition	How Chosen	Qualifications	Term of Office	Compensation	Function
Barber Examining Board	5 members	Apptd. by gov.	Must hold valid barber license in state; state resident for at least 3 years immediately preceding appt.; practicing barber, 5 years immediately preceding appt.; not connected with renting or selling barber appliances and supplies or any barber school or college for one year immediately preceding appt.	5 years. Gov. may remove for cause	Regular expense allowance	To examine applicants for barber licenses and approve those qualified; to adopt reasonable rules for sanitation of barber shops or schools with approval of dir. of motor vehicles
Barber Hearing Board	3 members	Apptd. by gov.	None specified	5 years	Regular expense allowance	To hear appeals from decisions of Barber Examining Bd.
Beauty Culture Examining Committee	5 members	Apptd. by gov.	US citizens; state residents 3 years; at least 25 years old; operators with at least 5 years' experience; instructors not connected with any beauty school or dealer; no two members graduates of same beauty school	5 years. Gov. may remove for cause	$20 pay per day plus regular expense allowance	To examine applicants for beauty parlor operator's license and approve those qualified

TABLE 3—Continued (5)

Group	Composition	How Chosen	Qualifications	Term of Office	Compensation	Function
Beauty Culture Hearing Board	3 members	Apptd. by gov.	Same as for Beauty Culture Examining Committee	5 years. Gov. may remove for cause	$20 pay per day plus regular expense allowance	To hear appeals from decisions of Beauty Culture Examining Comm.
Washington State *Beef* Commission	8 members plus one nonvoting ex officio member from Dept. of Ag.	8 apptd. by gov. from recommendations of related organizations; 1 apptd. by dir. of ag.	3 beef producers; 1 dairy (beef) producer; 3 feeders; 1 livestock salesyard operator; 1 meat packer; US citizens and residents of state; over 25 years old; engaged in occupation for 5 years; producer members cannot be directly involved in other phases of the business	3 years	Regular expense allowance	To establish beef revolving fund to pay expenses of program to increase consumption of beef; develop more efficient methods for producing and processing; eliminate transportation rate inequalities on feed; properly identify beef and beef products (10 cents a head assessment on all cattle sold in Wash.)
Washington *Blueberry* Commission	5 members plus dir. of ag. as nonvoting member	Elected by blueberry growers	Blueberry producers	3 years	Regular expense allowance	To advertise Wash. blueberries and enforce marketing orders if blueberry producers authorize them

TABLE 3–Continued (6)

Group	Composition	How Chosen	Qualifications	Term of Office	Compensation	Function
State Board of *Boiler* Rules	5 members	Apptd. by gov.	1 from owners; 1 from manufacturers; 1 from boiler insurance companies; 1 mechanical engineer; 1 from boilermakers	4 years. Gov. may remove for inefficiency or neglect of duty	$20 pay per day plus regular expense allowance	To make rules for construction, installation, and use of boilers and unfired pressure vessels in the state
Washington Toll *Bridge* Authority	Gov., aud., chr. of Util. and Trans. Comm., chr. of Highway Comm., dir. of gen. admin.	Ex officio				To set amount of fee for toll bridges in existence and to establish ones authorized by legis.
State *Building* Financing Authority	Gov., treas., lt. gov.	Ex officio				To arrange for financing the construction of buildings authorized by legis.
Bulb Commission	7 members plus dir. of ag.	5 elected by narcissus, tulip, and iris bulb growers in state; 2 chosen by elected group	7 members must be bulb producers	3 years	$20 pay per day plus regular expense allowance	To advertise Washington bulbs and to enforce marketing orders if bulb producers authorize them

TABLE 3–Continued (7)

Group	Composition	How Chosen	Qualifications	Term of Office	Compensation	Function
Canal Commission	5 members plus dir. of ecol.	Apptd. by gov. with senate consent	Not more than 3 from same political party; geographical distribution to be considered	6 years. Gov. may remove for incompetence or neglect of duty	$25 pay per day plus reg. expense allowance	To investigate feasibility of developing system of canals in state and construct those authorized
State *Canvassing* Board	Sec. of state, aud., treas.	Ex officio				To tabulate votes for state office candidates.
State *Capitol* Committee	Gov., lt. gov., comm. of pub. lands	Ex officio				To make contracts for construction of buildings on state capitol grounds as authorized by legis.
State *Cemetery* Board	5 members	Apptd. by gov.	Minimum of 5 years' experience (immediately preceding appt.) in active administrative management of a cemetery corp. or member of its bd. of directors. At time of appt. shall be pres., gen. man., or vice pres. of cemetery corp.	4 years. Member disqualified if he quits executive post	Regular expense allowance	To inspect the financial procedures of cemetery corps.

TABLE 3—Continued (8)

Group	Composition	How Chosen	Qualifications	Term of Office	Compensation	Function
State *Census* Board	3 members	1 apptd. by gov.; 1 by pres. of UW; 1 by pres. of WSU	1 from faculty of UW; 1 from faculty of WSU	At pleasure of appointing official	$25 pay per day plus regular expense allowance	To make a census of cities, towns, and rural areas of state between federal censuses
Chiropractic Disciplinary Board	6 members	Apptd. by Wash. Chiropractors' Assoc. plus Chiropractic Society of Wash. (3 each), plus dir. of motor vehicles	None specified	Indefinite term. Gov. may remove member for neglect of duty after written charge and opportunity for hearing	$25 pay per day plus regular expense allowance	To hear complaints of unprofessional conduct on part of chiropractors and to suspend or revoke licenses when necessary through dir. of motor vehicles
State Board of *Chiropractic* Examiners	3 members	Apptd. by gov. from list of names submitted by Wash. Chiropractors' Assoc. and/or Chiropractic Society of Wash.	US citizens; state residents; licensed chiropractors within state	3 years	$25 pay per day plus regular expense allowance	To examine applicants for licenses as chiropractors and approve those qualified

TABLE 3–Continued (9)

Group	Composition	How Chosen	Qualifications	Term of Office	Compensation	Function
Washington State *Collection Agency* Board	4 members plus dir. of motor vehicles	4 apptd. by gov.	2 licensed collection agency members, owners or executives of an agency for 5 years preceding appointment who do not have an interest in the same agency; 2 from general public	4 years. Gov. may remove his appointees for misconduct after giving written charges and opportunity for hearing	$25 pay per day plus regular expense allowance	To suspend or revoke license for operating a collection agency if evidence warrants after hearing
Community *College* Boards of Trustees	5 on each (22 boards)	Apptd. by gov.	Gov. is to give consideration to geographical situation and interests of labor, industry, ag., and professions. Members shall not be on governing bd. of any public or private educ. institution	5 years	Regular expense allowance	To manage each community college within framework set by State Bd. of Comm. College Educ.

TABLE 3—Continued (10)

Group	Composition	How Chosen	Qualifications	Term of Office	Compensation	Function
State Board of Community *College* Education	7 members	Apptd. by gov. with senate con-	1 from each cong. dist.; US citizens and state residents; while serving, cannot be on State Bd. of Educ. or K-12 bd., or have direct pecuniary interest in educ. in the state, including membership on governing bd. of public or private schools and colleges	4 years	Regular expense allowance	To set standards of community colleges to insure degree of uniformity in offerings
Boards of Trustees for State *Colleges*	5 members for each (4 colleges)	Apptd. by gov. with senate consent	None specified	6 years	Regular expense allowance	To set regulations for operation of individual state colleges
Columbia River Gorge Commission	3 members	Apptd. by gov.	Residents of Skamania, Klickitat, and Clark counties, respectively	6 years; removable at pleasure of gov.	Regular expense allowance	To prepare comprehensive plan for preserving recreational, scenic, and historic areas of the Columbia River Gorge

TABLE 3–Continued (11)

Group	Composition	How Chosen	Qualifications	Term of Office	Compensation	Function
Advisory Council on *Commerce* and Economic Development	Not more than 15	Apptd. by gov.	State residents	Not more than 2 years	Regular expense allowance	To recommend to Dept. of Comm. and Econ. Devel. ways of increasing state's industrial development
State *Communications* Advisory Committee	5 members plus sec. of soc. and health serv.	5 apptd. by gov.	1 county sheriff; 1 chief of police; 1 county commissioner; 1 city chief exec. officer; member of Wash. State Patrol (all incumbents)	2 years	Regular expense allowance	To advise dir. of program planning and fiscal management on installing a teletypewriter communications network of state law enforcement agencies
Washington State *Dairy* Products Commission	5 members plus dir. of ag. as nonvoting member	5 apptd. by gov.	5 must be practical dairy producers; U.S. citizens; state residents; at least 25 years old	3 years	$10 pay per day plus regular expense allowance	To advertise Wash. dairy products and to enforce marketing orders if dairymen authorize them

TABLE 3–Continued (12)

Group	Composition	How Chosen	Qualifications	Term of Office	Compensation	Function
Data Processing Advisory Commission	Lt. gov., comm. of pub. lands, supt. of pub. inst., atty. gen., treas., aud., dir. of prog. planning and fiscal management, plus 12 members	7 apptd. by gov.; 5 from legis.	3, directors or agency supervisors in state govt.; 1 representing counties; 1 representing higher educ. and comm. colleges; 1 representing judicial branch; chr. of legis. council; chr. budget comm.; 1 state representative apptd. by speaker; 1 senator apptd. by pres. of senate.	No term specified	Regular expense allowance	To advise gov. and dir. of prog. planning and fiscal management on developing data processing systems to serve statewide needs of state and local govt.; to make contracts to furnish machines
Department of Civil *Defense*	Dir. plus employees	Dir. apptd. by gov. with sen. consent	Not to hold any other state office	At pleasure of gov.	Dir., whatever gov's. advisory comm. recommends	To coordinate the activities of all civil defense organizations within the state
Washington State Civil *Defense* Council	Not fewer than 7 nor more than 15 members, plus gov. as chr.	Apptd. by gov.	None specified	At pleasure of gov.	Regular expense allowance	To advise the Dept. of Civil Defense on its projects

TABLE 3—Continued (13)

Group	Composition	How Chosen	Qualifications	Term of Office	Compensation	Function
Washington State Board of *Dental* Examiners	3 members	Apptd. by gov.	Practicing dentists chosen from list made by Wash. unit of Amer. Dental Assoc.; US citizens; state residents; licensed for 5 years in state; not connected with dental school	3 years	$15 pay per day plus regular expense allowance	To examine applicants for dental licenses and approve those qualified
Driving Instructor's Examination Committee	3 members	Apptd. by gov.	1 from Dept. of Educ.; 1 from Dept. of Motor Vehicles; 1 from a commercial driving school	1 year	Not to exceed $25 pay per day plus regular expense allowance	To examine applicants for licenses as driving instructors and to approve those qualified
Commission on Higher *Education*	9 members	Apptd. by gov. with senate consent	The citizen members of the Council on Higher Education comprise the commission	6 years	Regular expense allowance	To administer state program or federal program in state for financial aid to students

TABLE 3–Continued (14)

Group	Composition	How Chosen	Qualifications	Term of Office	Compensation	Function
Coordinating Council for Occupational *Education*	9 voting members plus supt. of pub. inst. and dir. of state system of comm. colleges, nonvoting members	3 apptd. by gov.; 3 by State Bd. of Educ.; 3 by State Bd. of Comm. Colleges	One of gov's. appointees to represent labor, 1 management; ones chosen by bds. to come from respective memberships	At pleasure of appointing agency	Regular expense allowance	Sole state agency to receive federal funds for vocational educ. Under supervision of state supt., council is to administer the state plan for vocational educ. in public schools and comm. colleges within federal regulations.
Council on Higher *Education*	25 members	9 voting members apptd. by gov. with senate consent; 2 state reps., apptd. by speaker, 2 state senators, apptd. by pres. of senate; 2 members of gov's. staff, apptd. by gov.; pres. of UW, WSU, and 4 state colleges; exec. dir. of State Bd. of Comm. College Educ.; pres. of 2 private univ. or 4-yr. colleges and 1 comm. college, apptd. by gov.	Legislators must be equally divided between the 2 major political parties	9, 6 years; legislators, 2 years; gov's. staff at his pleasure; gov's. college pres. appointees, 2 years	Regular expense allowance	To facilitate planning and coordination of higher educational systems; define educational needs of state; recommend measures for adult educ. and public service programs and general goals and problems of such institutions

TABLE 3–Continued (15)

Group	Composition	How Chosen	Qualifications	Term of Office	Compensation	Function
Education Commission of the States	Gov., 1 state sen., 1 state rep. plus 4 members	4 apptd. by gov.; 1 by pres. of senate; 1 by speaker of house	None specified	4 years, at pleasure of gov.	$25 pay per day plus regular expense allowance	Interstate compact for maintaining cooperation among educators. To be in effect when 10 states ratify compact
State Advisory Council on Vocational *Education*	Not fewer than 13 members	Apptd. by gov.	To be familiar with vocational needs and problems of management and labor in the state; representative of institutions of higher learning, of local educ. agencies, of area manpower planning, of needs of physically or mentally handicapped, and of general public	3 years	Regular expense allowance	To advise Coordinating Council for Occupational Educ. on problems of federally funded vocational educ. and submit evaluation reports to national officials
State Board of *Education*	14 members plus state supt. of pub. inst.	Elected by boards of school dist. dirs. 2 from each cong. dist.	Must not be connected with any educational institution or office	6 years	Regular expense allowance	To set educational standards for the state's public school system

151

TABLE 3–Continued (16)

Group	Composition	How Chosen	Qualifications	Term of Office	Compensation	Function
State Higher *Education* Personnel Board	3 members	Apptd. by gov. with senate consent	Have interest and belief in merit principle; not hold other employment with state; not have been officer of a political party for a year; not be a candidate for partisan public office during his term	6 years	$50 per day plus regular expense allowance	To promulgate rules for employee participation in development of personnel policies; rules for dismissal or suspension or demotion of an employee, with means of appeal, promotions, sick leaves and other aspects of employment
Western Interstate Commission for Higher *Education*	3 members	Apptd. by gov. with senate consent	Must be educators in field of higher education	4 years	Regular expense allowance	To meet with similar reps. from other western states, including Alaska and Hawaii, to allocate number and type of professional schools to each state for maximum efficiency
Wash. State *Educational* Television Commission	16 members	Apptd. by gov. from list made by supt. of pub. inst.	Persons from TV industry, public and private colleges, office of supt. of pub. inst., and general public	4 years	Regular expense allowance	To promote effective educational TV; recommend to legis. needed legislation

TABLE 3—Continued (17)

Group	Composition	How Chosen	Qualifications	Term of Office	Compensation	Function
Electrical Advisory Board	6 members plus state chief electrical inspector	Apptd. by gov. with advice of dir. of labor and indus.	1 from public or private co. generating or distributing electric power; 1 from electrical installation business; 1 from manufacturers or distributors of electrical devices; 1 from general public; 1 electrician; 1 professional engineer, licensed in Wash.	4 years	Regular expense allowance	To advise on problems of electrical installation and safety
Employee Suggestion Awards Board	3 plus dir. of personnel	3 apptd. by gov.	State officers or state employees	At pleasure of gov.	None specified	To encourage meritorious suggestions by state employees for promoting efficiency and economy; prizes for best from service fund of personnel service

153

TABLE 3–Continued (18)

Group	Composition	How Chosen	Qualifications	Term of Office	Compensation	Function
State *Employees'* Insurance Board	Gov., dir. of gen. admin., dir of personnel, 1 representing an assoc. of state employees, 1 representing a state employees' union, 1 state senator, 1 state representative	2 apptd. by gov.; 1 by pres. of senate; 1 by speaker of house		None specified	"Necessary and actual expenses"	To study and draw up 3 types of state employees' health-care benefit plans
Washington Public *Employees'* Retirement System	Ins. comm., atty. gen., treas., aud., plus 3 govt. employees	Non-ex officio members elected by members of the retirement system in their classification of employment	3 employees must have been members of retirement system for five years; 1 from Class A (state employees); 1 from Class B (county); 1 from all others; (1 apptd. by Wash. State Assoc. of Counties; 1 by Assoc. of Wash. Cities)	2 years for non-ex officio members	Regular expense allowance	To administer the retirement fund for state employees and invest it to their best interests

TABLE 3–Continued (19)

Group	Composition	How Chosen	Qualifications	Term of Office	Compensation	Function
Employment Agency Advisory Board	7 members plus atty. gen	7 apptd. by gov.	5 from owners or managers of employment agencies; 1 representative of employers; 1, representing majority of workmen	4 years	Regular expense allowance	To advise dir. of motor vehicles on rules and regulations for practices and rates of employment agencies
Employment Security Department	Commissioner plus employees	Comm. apptd. by gov.	None specified	At pleasure of gov.	$1,000 per month	To operate state employment offices and administer unemployment insurance
State Board for Registration of Professional *Engineers* and Land Surveyors	5 members	Apptd. by gov.	U.S. citizens; state residents for at least 5 years immediately preceding appointment; registered professional engineers, engaged in engineering for at least 12 years and in responsible engineering or teaching for at least 5 years	5 years. Gov. may remove for misconduct, incompetence, or neglect of duty	$25 pay per day plus regular expense allowance	To examine applicants for licenses as professional engineers and surveyors

155

TABLE 3–Continued (20)

Group	Composition	How Chosen	Qualifications	Term of Office	Compensation	Function
State Board of *Equalization*	Members of Dept. of Revenue	Ex officio				To equalize tax assessments between counties
State Commission on *Equipment*	Dir. of motor vehicles, chief of Wash. State Patrol, person designated by State Highway Comm.	Ex officio				To make and enforce rules regarding proper safety equipment on commercial vehicles
Escrow Commission of the State of Washington	4 members plus dir. of motor vehicles	4 apptd. by gov. from list prepared by governing authority of Escrow Assoc. of Wash. and from list made by Wash. State Bar Assoc.; 2 from people handling escrow transactions	persons concerned with escrow matters	4 years	Regular expense allowance	To conduct exams for escrow officers. Dir. issues licenses to those who qualify. Commission may hold educational conferences for benefit of the industry

TABLE 3–Continued (21)

Group	Composition	How Chosen	Qualifications	Term of Office	Compensation	Function
Expo 74 Commission	15 members	5 apptd. by gov.; 3 by pres. of senate; 3 by speaker of house; 1 by Spokane bd. of county comm.; 1 by Spokane City Council	3 state senators; 3 state reps.; 1 county comm.; 1 member of Spokane city council	To 1975	None specified	May become directors of Expo 74, a nonprofit corporation to stage an exposition in Spokane in 1974 or shortly thereafter
Factory Built Housing Advisory Board	11 members	Apptd. by gov.	Reps. of industries and professions in factory-built housing; building-code enforcement agencies; architectural and engineering assoc.; general public	None specified	$25 pay per day plus regular expense allowance	To review the rules made by Dept. of Labor and Indus. to govern standards for factory-built housing and recommend changes if desirable
Fairs Commission	7 members plus dir. of ag.	7 apptd. by dir. of ag.	3 from east of Cascades; 3 from west; 1 member at large	3 years	$20 pay per day plus regular expense allowance	To advise dir. on youth, county, or larger fairs; allocate money to them

TABLE 3–Continued (22)

Group	Composition	How Chosen	Qualifications	Term of Office	Compensation	Function
State *Finance* Committee	Gov., treas., aud.	Ex officio				To choose depositories and investments for state funds
Washington State *Fruit* Commission	16 members plus dir. of ag.	Elected by fruit growers, dealers, and processors of state	10 assorted tree fruit producers (at least 25 years old, 5 years' experience); 2 processors; 4 dealers. U.S. citizens and state residents. Each representative of a group must not be engaged in other phases of work	3 years	$20 pay per day plus regular expense allowance	To advertise state's fruits and administer marketing orders when authorized by fruit growers
Washington Tree *Fruit* Research Commission	9 members plus dir. of ag.	3 apptd. by Wash. State Fruit Comm.; 5 by the Apple Advertising Comm.; 1 by dir. of ag.	Appointee of dir. of ag. to be in winter pear industry. All to be U.S. citizens; state residents over 25 years old; and have been fruit producers for 5 years.	3 years	Regular expense allowance	To carry on research or contract for it to benefit fruit industry or shipping of fruit

TABLE 3–Continued (23)

Group	Composition	How Chosen	Qualifications	Term of Office	Compensation	Function
Fryer Commission	8 members	6 elected by poultry raisers in state; 2 apptd. by elected group	Poultry producers	3 years	$20 pay per day plus regular expense allowance	To advertise state's chickens and administer marketing orders when approved by poultrymen
Funeral Directors and Embalmers Examining Committee	2 members plus sec. of State Bd. of Health	2 apptd. by gov.	Must hold embalmers' licenses	2 years	$10 pay per day plus regular expense allowance	To examine applicants for embalmers' licenses and approve those qualified
Furniture and Bedding Advisory Council	7 members plus sec. of soc. and health sci.	7 apptd. by gov.	1 from upholstered furniture industry; 1 from bedding industry; 1 from retail furniture industry; 1 from sterilizing and fumigating industry; 3 with no commercial affiliation with such industries	7 years. Gov. may remove for misconduct	Regular expense allowance	To recommend regulations for maintaining sanitation for secondhand furniture and bedding to be sold

TABLE 3–Continued (24)

Group	Composition	How Chosen	Qualifications	Term of Office	Compensation	Function
State *Game* Commission	6 members plus dir. of game	6 apptd. by gov.	Qualified voters, 3 from east of Cascades, 3 west. Must have knowledge of subject; not hold any other public office; no two from same county	6 years. Gov. may remove for cause; hearing required; no review by any court	$25 pay per day plus regular expense allowance	To set regulations for taking animals and fish for sport and to maintain adequate supply of game for hunting and fishing
Harbor Line Commission	Bd. of Natural Resources	Ex officio				To determine line dividing state's tide and shore lands from those under private ownership
Mental *Health* and Mental Retardation Advisory Council	At least 7 members plus sec. of soc. health serv. and supt. of public inst.	7 (or more) apptd. by gov.	Reps. of nongovernment organizations or groups concerned with functioning of community mental health or retardation facilities	3 years. Gov. may remove at will	Regular expense allowance	To advise gov. on programs for mental health of the general public and means of aiding mentally retarded
State Board of *Health*	5 members plus sec. of soc. and health serv.	5 apptd. by gov.	4 must be persons experienced in matters of health and sanitation; one to represent the consumers of health care	6 years. Gov. may remove only by process through Thurston Co. superior crt.	$25 pay per day plus regular expense allowance	To set regulations for maintaining public health

TABLE 3—Continued (25)

Group	Composition	How Chosen	Qualifications	Term of Office	Compensation	Function
State Comprehensive *Health* Planning Advisory Council	Not more than 39 public members plus representatives of appropriate depts. of state govt.	Gov. is to name the state agency to choose the personnel; gov. names chr.	At least 1 doctor; 1 dentist; 1 hospital admin.; 1 nursing home admin.; 1 osteopath; 1 optometrist; 1 chiropodist; 1 registered nurse; 1 chiropractor; majority of public members to be consumers	Public members, 3 years	Public members, $25 pay per day plus regular expense allowance; ex officio members, regular expense allowance	To advise the state planning agency named by gov. on planning and developing a comprehensive health program
State *Highway* Commission	5 members	Apptd. by gov. with senate consent	State residents; no two from same cong. dist.; not more than 3 on same side of Cascades or in same political party; no state officer or employee eligible	6 years	$40 pay per day plus regular expense allowance	To direct the construction and maintenance of state roads as authorized by legis.
Advisory Council on *Historic* Preservation	6 members plus dirs. of state parks and rec,; gen. admin.; Wash. State Hist. Soc.; East. Wash. State Hist. Soc.; State Capitol	6 apptd. by gov.	Officers of local govt to have due consideration and interested and experienced persons	At pleasure of gov.	Regular expense allowance	To recommend to gov. and Parks and Rec. Comm. measures to coordinate activities of state and local agencies and private institutions regarding historic preservation; encourage education in this field

TABLE 3–Continued (26)

Group	Composition	How Chosen	Qualifications	Term of Office	Compensation	Function
Washington *Historic* Sites and Markers Commission	Dirs. of Highways, dir. of E. Wash. State Hist. Soc.; Wash. State Hist. Soc.; ecol.; State Regent of DAR; State Pres. of Daughters of Pioneers	Ex officio				To select sites warranting commemoration as historic spots and to determine type of marker to be used
Board of Curators of Washington State *Historical* Society	Gov., sec. of state, and treas., plus 24 curators	24 elected by society membership	None specified	3 years	Regular expense allowance	To set policies and regulations for operation of Wash. State Hist. Soc.
Board of Trustees of Eastern Washington State *Historical* Society	Gov., sec. of state, and treas., plus 16 curators	16 elected by society membership	None specified	3 years	Regular expense allowance	To set policies and regulations for operation of East. Wash. State Hist. Soc.

TABLE 3–Continued (27)

Group	Composition	How Chosen	Qualifications	Term of Office	Compensation	Function
Board of Trustees of State Capitol *Historical* Assoc.	Gov., sec. of state, supt. of pub. inst., plus indefinite number of trustees (now 45)	Elected by association membership	None specified	3 years	Regular expense allowance	To set policies and regulations for operation of State Capitol Hist. Assoc.
Washington *Hop* Commission	5 members plus dir. of ag. as non-voting member	Elected by hop growers	Producers of hops	3 years	Regular expense allowance	To advertise Washington hops and enforce marketing orders if hop producers authorize them
Washington *Horse* Racing Commission	3 members	Apptd. by gov. with senate consent	Qualified voters. 1 to be horse breeder of at least 1 year's standing	At pleasure of gov.	$40 pay per day plus regular expense allowance	To take rules governing horse races and to license persons connected with them
Washington State *Hospital* Advisory Council	6 members	Apptd. by gov. from lists made by professional associations	3 to be supts. or admins. of hospitals; 1 medical man; 1 osteopath; 1 registered nurse. All to have 5 years' current experience	3 years	Regular expense allowance	To advise State Bd. of Health on minimum standards and regulations for construction and operation of hospitals

TABLE 3–Continued (28)

Group	Composition	How Chosen	Qualifications	Term of Office	Compensation	Function
Washington State *Human* Rights Commission	5 members	Apptd. by gov.	None specified	5 years. Gov. may remove for cause after opportunity for hearing	$20 pay per day plus regular expense allowance	To hear complaints about discrimination against individuals because of color or race or sex and issue necessary orders in such cases
Institutional *Industries* Commission	6 apptd. by gov.	6 members plus sec. of soc. and health serv.	2 representatives of organized labor; 2 of industry; 1 of agriculture; 1 of general public	4 years. Gov. may remove for cause	Soc. of soc. and health serv. regular expense allowance; others, $25 pay per day plus regular expense allowance	To determine industries which may be maintained by inmates of state institutions and to determine compensation for inmates working in commercial enterprises
State Board of *Industrial* Insurance Appeals	3 members (2 additional ones may be apptd. if docket is crowded)	Apptd. by gov.	1 active member of Wash. Bar Assoc.; 1 representing workmen in extra-hazardous employment; 1 representing employers of such workmen. All to be approved by organized labor and/or employer groups (1 of 2 additional members to represent labor; 1, industry)	6 years Gov. may file charges to remove. 3 superior ct. judges to make final decision	Chr., $15,000 per year; others $1,208.33 per month plus regular expense allowance	To hear appeals by workers from decisions of dir. of labor and indus. regarding industrial insurance compensation for injuries or illness

TABLE 3—Continued (29)

Group	Composition	How Chosen	Qualifications	Term of Office	Compensation	Function
Interfaith Advisory Committee	Not more than 12 nor fewer than 9	Apptd. by gov.	None specified	At pleasure of gov.	Regular expense allowance	To advise sec. of soc. and health serv. on qualifications for and duties of chaplains for state institutions and on development of religious programs in them
Interstate Compact Commission	5 members	1 apptd. by gov.; 2 state reps. apptd. by speaker; 2 senators apptd. by pres. of senate	None given	1, at pleasure of gov.	$15 pay per day plus regular expense allowance	To negotiate for interstate compact for use of water from Columbia River
State *Land* Planning Commission	19 members	11 apptd. by gov.; 4 state senators apptd. by pres. of senate; 4 reps. apptd. by speaker	Senators and reps. to be equally divided between main political parties	11, at pleasure of gov.	Regular expense allowance	To consider development of a statewide land-use data bank or alternative automated information system to assist in prediction of population growth and distribution and in preservation of resources

TABLE 3—Continued (30)

Group	Composition	How Chosen	Qualifications	Term of Office	Compensation	Function
State Board of Registration for *Landscape Architects*	5 members	Apptd. by gov.	Residents of state; 3 landscape architects; 2 in closely related professions and/or trades. 5 years' experience immediately preceding appt.	5 years. No more than 2 consecutive terms. Gov. may remove for cause	$25 pay per day plus regular expense allowance	To prepare and give exams to applicants for licenses as landscape architects. Dir. of motor vehicles issues licenses to those approved by the bd.
Statute *Law* Committee	7 members plus state law librarian, chr. of Senate Judiciary Comm., chr. of House Judiciary Comm., 1 from legis.	1 apptd. by gov.; 1 by speaker of house with consent of pres. of senate; 1 by chr. of Senate Judiciary Comm.; 1 by House Judic. Comm.; 3 by Wash. Bar Assoc.	Lawyers. Second members of house and senate judiciary committees to be different political party from respective chr. who appoint them	Bar Assoc. appointees 6 years; gov.'s. appointee, 4 years; judiciary comm. appointees, 2 years	Regular expense allowance	To maintain the Revised Code of Washington so that all laws in effect on a given subject may be located according to a classification system
Washington *Law Enforcement* Officers Training Commission	8 members plus atty. gen., chief of Wash. State Patrol, special agent in charge of the Seattle office of FBI	Appt. by gov.	2 incumbent sheriffs; 2 chiefs of police; 1 county comm.; 1 officer of city in field of law enforcement; 2 from institutions of higher learning, with one from a comm. college	At pleasure of gov.	Regular expense allowance	To plan facilities for training of law enforcement officers on a statewide basis

TABLE 3—Continued (31)

Group	Composition	How Chosen	Qualifications	Term of Office	Compensation	Function
Commission on Uniform State *Laws*	3 members	Apptd. by gov.	"Suitable persons"	None stated	Regular expense allowance	To work with commissioners from other states to propose uniform laws to respective legis. on subjects of mutual concern
State Board for the Certification of *Librarians*	State librarian; head, Dept. of Librarianship, U.W.; 1 additional member	1 member apptd. by gov. from list nominated by exec. comm. of Wash. Library Assoc.	None specified for additional member	3 years	Regular expense allow-	To set standards for professional librarians in the state
State *Library* Commission	4 members plus supt. of pub. inst.	4 apptd. by gov.	1 library trustee; 1 certified librarian (both to be active in profession); no qualifications specified for two remaining comms.	4 years	Regular expense allowance	To set policies and regulations for the state library
Washington State *Liquor* Control Board	3 members	Apptd. by gov. with sen. consent	Not more than 2 to be of same political party	9 years	Chr. $1,250 per month; others $1,208.33	To regulate operation of state liquor stores

TABLE 3—Continued (32)

Group	Composition	How Chosen	Qualifications	Term of Office	Compensation	Function
State Welfare *Medical* Care Committee	12 members	Apptd. by gov.	6 from providers of medical service; 1 legislator; 1 county comm.; 4 from general public	At pleasure of gov.	Regular expense allowance	To advise sec. of soc. and health serv. on minimum standards of medical care for persons receiving public assistance
Washington State Board of *Medical* Examiners	5 members	Apptd. by gov.	Licensed physicians and surgeons	5 years Gov. may remove for cause	$25 pay per day plus regular expense allowance	To approve medical schools in state and grant licenses to qualified doctors practicing in state; also set qualifications for physicians' assistants
Wash. State *Medical* Disciplinary Board	7 members	Elected by physicians and surgeons in the state	1 from each cong. dist.	2 years	$25 pay per day plus regular expense	To hear complaints of unprofessional conduct on part of physicians and surgeons

TABLE 3–Continued (33)

Group	Composition	How Chosen	Qualifications	Term of Office	Compensation	Function
Washington State Commission on *Mexican*-American Affairs	11 members	Apptd. by gov. with senate consent	2 from agricultural workers; 2 from general Spanish-speaking population in state; 1 from education; 1 from professional services; 1 from trade union officials; 4 from Mexican-American communities in the state	4 years	$25 pay per day plus regular expense allowance	To advise state agencies on programs to provide assistance needed by Mexican-Americans. State agencies are to assign a staff member to aid comm.
Organized *Militia*	Adjutant-gen., officers, and men	Adjutant-gen. apptd. by gov.	Officer not below rank of field officer; 10 years officer of the militia out of previous 15 years	May not be removed without cause	$1,125 per month	To command state militia (national guard)
Washington *Mint* Commission	5 members plus dir. of ag. as nonvoting member	Elected by mint growers	Mint producers	3 years	Regular expense allowance	To advertise Wash. mint and enforce marketing orders if mint producers authorize them
State Anti-*Monopoly* Board	Treas., aud., and 1 superior ct. judge	Ex officio	Judge is one hearing monopoly charge			To supervise fees charged for use of copyrighted musical compositions within the state

TABLE 3–Continued (34)

Group	Composition	How Chosen	Qualifications	Term of Office	Compensation	Function
Municipal Research Council	12 members	2 apptd. by pres. of senate; 2 by speaker of house; 1 by gov.; 7 by bd. of dir. of Assoc. of Wash. Cities	At least 1 to be an official of a city of 20,000 or more pop.; 1, 1,500 to 20,000; 1, under 1,500	2 years	Regular expense allowance	To make contracts with public or private agency to do municipal research and service
Advisory Council on *Nuclear* Energy and Radiation	7 members plus sec. of soc. and health serv.; dirs. of labor and indus., ag., and comm. and econ. devel.	7 apptd. by gov.	Reps. from industry, labor, healing arts, research, and educ.	At pleasure of gov.	Regular expense allow-ance	To recommend programs to develop and regulate sources of atomic ra-diation
Western Interstate *Nuclear* Board	1 member	Apptd. by gov.	None specified	At pleasure of gov.	Regular expense allowance	To recommend laws to legis. to encourage coopera-tion among the party states to de-velop and utilize nuclear energy for industry, medicine, etc. (Interstate compact. When 5 states ratify it, it becomes effective.)

TABLE 3—Continued (35)

Group	Composition	How Chosen	Qualifications	Term of Office	Compensation	Function
Washington State Board of Practical *Nurse* Examiners	5 members	Apptd. by gov.	3 registered professional nurses; 1 actively engaged in teaching practical nursing; 1 with experience in such teaching (both with 5 years' experience in nursing); 1 engaged in supervising practical nursing program; 4 licensed practical nurses at least 23 years old who have had practical nurse course and 3 years' experience	5 years. Gov. may remove for cause	$25 pay per day plus regular expense allowance	To examine applicants for licenses as practical nurses and approve those qualified; to formulate an approved practical nursing course
Washington State Board of *Nursing*	Not fewer than 5	Apptd. by gov.	US citizens; state residents; registered nurses with at least 5 years' administrative experience or teaching nursing, or college degree in nursing education	5 years. Gov. may remove for cause	$25 pay per day plus regular expense allowance	To examine applicants for licenses as registered nurses and approve those qualified

TABLE 3–Continued (36)

Group	Composition	How Chosen	Qualifications	Term of Office	Compensation	Function
State Board of Examiners for *Nursing* Home Administrators	9 members	Apptd. by gov.	6, privately or self-employed with at least 4 years' experience in admin. of licensed nursing homes immediately preceding appointment; 3, reps. from medical professions or health care admin. or educ.; US citizens; state residents	3 years	Regular expense allowance	To examine applicants for licenses as nursing home administrators and approve those qualified
Oceanographic Commission of Washington	12 members plus chr. of State Marine Resources and Devel. Committee, non-voting, ex officio	5 apptd. by gov.; 3 state senators apptd. by pres. of senate; 3 reps. apptd. by speaker	Gov's. appointees: 1 rep. of higher educ.; 1 private industry; 1, labor; senator and reps., no more than 2 of same political party in each group	5 years	Regular expense allowance	To encourage and develop a coordinated program in oceanography; promote private industrial enterprise on a national scale to Puget Sound as base for oceanographic work

TABLE 3–Continued (37)

Group	Composition	How Chosen	Qualifications	Term of Office	Compensation	Function
Oil and Gas Conservation Committee	Gov., comm. of public lands, dir. of ecol., treas., lt. gov.	Ex officio				To license persons to drill for oil and gas and regulate waste products. It may set production quotas, if necessary
State *Optometry* Board	5 members	Apptd. by gov.	US citizens; state residents; licensed optometrists who have practiced in state for at least 4 preceding years; no connection with school teaching optometry or optical supply company	3 years	$25 pay per day plus regular expense allowance	To examine applicants for optometrist's license and approve those qualified
Committee of *Osteopathic* Examiners	3 members	Apptd. by gov.	US citizens; licensed osteopaths	3 years	$25 pay per day plus regular expense allowance	To examine applicants for licenses as osteopaths and approve those qualified
Washington State *Patrol*	Chief plus staff	Chief apptd. by gov.	None specified	At pleasure of gov.	Chief, $916.66 per month	To enforce state traffic laws and regulations

TABLE 3–Continued (38)

Group	Composition	How Chosen	Qualifications	Term of Office	Compensation	Function
Washington Dry *Pea* and Lentil Commission	5 members plus dir. of ag. as nonvoting member	Elected by dry pea and lentil growers	Dry pea and lentil producers	3 years	Regular expense allowance	To advertise Wash. dry peas and lentils and enforce marketing orders if growers authorize them
State Public *Pension* Commission	15 members (5 state reps., 5 state senators, 5 nonlegislators	5 nonlegislators apptd. by gov.; 5 reps., by speaker of house; 5 senators, by pres. of senate	Nonlegislators: 1 experienced in actuarial principles; 1, trustee or official of a retirement system; 3, general experience in fields relating to retirement system	2 years	Regular expense allowance	To study present pension system for public employees in state and recommend laws for improvement to gov. and legis.
State *Personnel* Board	3 members	Apptd. by gov. with senate consent	Must believe in merit principle and not hold or seek public office in the state	6 years	$50 pay per day plus regular expense allowance	To supervise selection of state personnel covered by state civil service system

174

TABLE 3–Continued (39)

Group	Composition	How Chosen	Qualifications	Term of Office	Compensation	Function
Pesticide Advisory Board	10 members plus environmental health specialist from Div. of Health in Dept. of Soc. and Health Serv.; supervisor of Grain and Chemical Div. of Dept. of Ag.; dirs. of game, fisheries, natural resources, and ecol.	10 apptd. by gov.	3 licensed pesticide applicators in state (1 ground, 1 aerial, 1 structural pest control); 1 entomologist; 1 toxologist, 1 plant pathologist (all in public service); 1 from ag. chemical industry; 1 from food processing; 2 producers of ag. products which are or might be affected by pesticides	4 years. Gov. may remove for cause	Regular expense allowance	To advise on degree of ban on harmful pesticides
Pesticide Control Board	Dean of Coll. of Ag, WSU; sec. of soc. and health serv.; dir. of ecol.; dir. of ag.	Ex officio			None specified	To determine categories of pesticides for use. "Persistent" ones are limited to essential uses. Bd. makes regulations; Dept. of Ag. implements them.

175

TABLE 3—Continued (40)

Group	Composition	How Chosen	Qualifications	Term of Office	Compensation	Function
Board of *Pharmacy*	3 members	Apptd. by gov. with senate consent	Registered pharmacists for five years; US citizens; residents of state	4 years	$25 pay per day plus regular expense allowance	To examine applicants for pharmacy licenses and approve those qualified to inspect drugs and cosmetics for misbranding and to determine what preparations have a potential for abuse and register dealers in them
Board of Puget Sound *Pilotage* Commissioners	4 members plus dir. of labor and indus.	4 members apptd. by gov.	4 must be US citizens; state residents; over 21 years old. 2, owners or operators of vessels; 2, licensed pilots; 4, experience for 3 years prior to appt.	4 years	$25 pay per day plus regular expense-allowance	To examine applicants for pilot's license and approve those qualified
Planning and Community Affairs Agency	Dir. plus employees	Dir. apptd. by gov. with senate consent	None given	At pleasure of gov.	Salary set by by gov. on recommendation of Comm. on Salaries	Agency to identify long-range planning goals for state, coordinate plans of other state agencies, and participate in interstate planning programs

TABLE 3—Continued (41)

Group	Composition	How Chosen	Qualifications	Term of Office	Compensation	Function
State *Planning* Advisory Council	Not more than 15	Apptd. by gov.	Residents of state; at least one member from each cong. dist.	At gov's. pleasure	$25 pay per day plus regular expense allowance	To advise gov. and dir. of planning and community affairs agency on community affairs and planning
Pollution Control Hearings Board of the State of Washington	3 members	Apptd. by gov. with senate consent	Must have experience or training in environmental matters. At least 1 to be practicing attorney with state license; no more than 2 of same political party	6 years. Gov. may remove for inefficiency or other cause after written charges to members and to chief justice of state supreme ct. who names 3 superior ct. judges to adjudicate after public hearing	Gov. decides if bd. is to be fulltime or parttime. If latter, $75 per day pay plus regular expense allowance	To hear appeals from decisions of Dept. of Ecol.
Washington State *Potato* Commission	13 members plus dir. of ag.	9 elected by potato producers; 4 chosen by elected group	13 members must be potato producers	3 years	Pay per day not to exceed $20 plus regular expense allowance	To advertise Wash. potatoes and establish marketing orders if growers authorize them

TABLE 3–Continued (42)

Group	Composition	How Chosen	Qualifications	Term of Office	Compensation	Function
Washington State Seed *Potato* Commission	7 members plus dir. of ag.	5 elected by seed potato producers; 2 chosen by elected group	7 members must be seed potato producers	3 years	Pay per day not to exceed $20 plus regular expense allowance	To advertise Wash. seed potatoes and establish marketing orders if growers authorize them
State *Printer*		Apptd. by gov.	None Specified	At pleasure of gov.	$958.33 per month	To print official publications as authorized by legis.
State *Printing.* and Duplicating Committee	State printer, dir. of program planning and fiscal admin., dir. of gen. admin.	Ex officio				To pass on requests of state agencies to acquire printing equipment other than typewriters and mimeograph machines (legislative and judicial branches excepted)
Board of *Prison* Terms and Paroles	5 members	Apptd. by gov. with senate	Must not hold other public office or occupation; must not be officer or employee of any political party	5 years. Removable only by Thurston Co. superior ct. for cause	Chr., $1,041.66 per month, members, $1,000.00	To set minimum prison terms for convicts in terms of type, crime, and probable actions if convict is returned to society

TABLE 3–Continued (43)

Group	Composition	How Chosen	Qualifications	Term of Office	Compensation	Function
Professional Hearing Committees	2 members plus dir. of motor vehicles for each committee	2, apptd. by gov.	Qualified practitioners in pertinent profession	At pleasure of gov.	$25 pay per day plus regular expense allowance	If a complaint against a license holder is filed with dir. of motor vehicles in field for which no hearing committee is prescribed by law, dir. of motor vehicles asks gov. to appoint one
Examining Board of *Psychology*	5 members	Apptd. by gov.	US citizens; over 21 years old; in active practice of psychology for at least 3 years preceding appt.; licensed psychologists	3 years	None specified in law	To examine applicants for licenses as psychologists and approve those qualified
State *Purchasing* Advisory Committee	Dir. of gen. admin. plus 1 rep. from each of depts. of highways, soc. and health serv., natural resources, UW, WSU, Office of Program Planning and Fiscal Management	Gov. appts. reps. from the 6 state agencies upon recommendations of the head of each		At pleasure of gov.	None specified	To approve standards and specifications for materials and supplies used by state agencies and advise dir. on most efficient and economical purchasing program

179

TABLE 3—Continued (44)

Group	Composition	How Chosen	Qualifications	Term of Office	Compensation	Function
Real Estate Examining Commission	3 members	Apptd. by gov. at request of dir. of motor vehicles	US citizens who have been real estate brokers for past 5 years	At pleasure of gov.	Maximum of $25 pay per day plus regular expense allowance	To examine applicants for real estate agent's license and approve those qualified
Reciprocity Commission	Dir. of Motor vehicles, dir. of Dept. of Revenue, chr. of highway comm., chief of State Patrol	Ex officio				To make agreements with commissions of other states on rate of taxation on commercial vehicles on highways of states concerned
Records Committee	2 members plus state archivist	1 apptd. by aud., 1 by atty. gen.	None specified	At pleasure of appointing agency	None specified	To decide which state and local records may be destroyed
Interagency Committee for Outdoor *Recreation*	5 members plus comm. of pub. lands, dirs. of parks and rec., game, fisheries, highways, comm. and econ. devel., ecol.	5 apptd. by gov.	Have demonstrated interest in outdoor recreation in state	3 years	Regular expense allowance	To make long-range coordinated program for best recreational use of state's natural resources

TABLE 3–Continued (45)

Group	Composition	How Chosen	Qualifications	Term of Office	Compensation	Function
State Parks and *Recreation* Commission	7 members	Apptd. by gov. with senate consent	Qualified voters. 3 may be elected state officials; 4 must not hold any state or local public office and must understand park needs	6 years	Nonstate officials, $15 pay per day plus regular expense allowance	To administer state parks and other state recreational features
Board of *Regents* University of Washington	7 members	Apptd. by gov. with senate consent	None specified	6 years	Regular expense allowance	To set regulations for operation of UW
Board of *Regents* Washington State University	7 members	Apptd. by gov. with senate consent	None specified	6 years	Regular expense allowance	To set regulations for operation of WSU
Board of Natural *Resources*	Gov., supt. of pub. inst., comm. of pub. lands, dean of forestry, UW, dir. of Institute of Ag. Sciences, WSU	Ex officio				To approve value set on state lands and arrange for their sale or lease in best interests of the state

TABLE 3—Continued (46)

Group	Composition	How Chosen	Qualifications	Term of Office	Compensation	Function
Board of Trustees of State Teachers' *Retirement Fund*	Supt. of pub. inst., ins. comm., and 5 members	5 members chosen by State Bd. of Educ.	3 out of 5 must be classroom teachers	3 years	Regular expense allowance	To administer Teachers' Retirement Fund
Washington Traffic *Safety* Commission	Gov., supt. of pub. inst., dir. of motor vehicles, dir. of highways, chief of State Patrol, sec. of soc. and health serv., rep. of Assoc. of Wash. Cities, rep. of judiciary	Non-exofficio members apptd. by gov.		At pleasure of gov.	Regular expense allowance	To advise gov. and legis. on needs for legislation for traffic safety; Dept. of Highways implements regulations
Governor's Advisory Committee on *Salaries*	Pres. of U. of Puget Sound; pres of WSU; chr. of State Personnel Bd.; pres. of Assoc. of Wash. Business; pres. of Pac. NW Personnel Managers' Assoc. pres. of Wash. State Bar Assoc.; pres. of Wash. State Labor Council	Ex officio			Regular expense allowance	To advise gov. on amount of salary for state officials necessary to compete with private industry in securing qualified individuals; gov. cannot pay more than maximum recommended. To recommend salaries for elective officials to Legis. Council, including county officials

TABLE 3–Continued (47)

Group	Composition	How Chosen	Qualifications	Term of Office	Compensation	Function
Washington State Board of Registered *Sanitarians*	3 members	Apptd. by gov. from list submitted by Wash. State Assoc. of Sanitarians	US citizens and qualified sanitarians	3 years	Regular expense allowance	To examine applicants for license as registered sanitarians and approve those qualified
School Emergency Construction Commission	3 members plus supt. of pub. inst. and 1 member of State Bd. of Educ.	Gov. appts. 3; State Bd. of Educ., 1	None specified	At pleasure of appointing agency	Regular expense allowance	To allocate available money to school districts for school building construction
Examining Committee in Basic *Sciences*	5 members	Apptd. by gov.	Faculty of UW and WSU	At pleasure of gov.	$25 per day pay plus regular expense allowance	To examine physicians in their knowledge of basic sciences
State *Soil* and Water Conservation Committee	5 members plus dir. of ecol. and dean of College of Ag. of WSU	2 apptd. by gov.; 3 elected by district supervisors of soil and water conservation districts	Of gov's. appointees, 1 must be landowner or operator of farm; 3 elected members must be landowners or operators of a farm, 1 from eastern Wash., and 1 from western Wash.	4 years for appointees; 3 years for elected members	Regular expense allowance	To aid soil and water conservation districts in their program planning and coordinate work of local, state, and federal agencies in soil conservation

183

TABLE 3—Continued (48)

Group	Composition	How Chosen	Qualifications	Term of Office	Compensation	Function
Board of *Tax Appeals*	3 members	Apptd. by gov. with senate consent	Must have special knowledge of taxation	6 years. Gov. may remove by listing reasons with sec. of state	Chr., $1,250 per month; others, $1,208.33	To hear appeals from decisions of Dept. of Revenue
State Examining Committee of *Physical Therapists*	Not fewer than 3 members	Apptd. by gov. from list made by Amer. Physical Therapy Assoc. (Wash. unit)	Registered physical therapists in active practice of at least 5 years' experience; state residents	3 years. Not more than 2 consecutive terms	Not to exceed $25 pay per day plus regular expense allowance	To examine applicants for physical therapist's license and approve those qualified
Thermal Power Plant Site Evaluation Council	1 member at large; 1 member from county plus dirs. of ecol., fisheries, game, parks and rec., interagency committee for outdoor rec., comm. and econ. devel., util. and trans., program planning and fiscal management, natural resources, planning and comm. affairs, civil defense, ag.	Gov. appts. member at large (chr.) with senate consent; county legis. body appts. county rep.	None specified	At pleasure of appointing agency	Regular expense allowance	To develop and apply ecological guidelines in relation to location of thermal power sites and make recommendations to gov.

TABLE 3–Continued (49)

Group	Composition	How Chosen	Qualifications	Term of Office	Compensation	Function
Washington *Tree* Fruit Research Commission	5 members plus dir of ag. as nonvoting member	Apptd. by gov. with senate consent	Experience in horticultural research	3 years	Regular expense allowance	To conduct research on ways of combating diseases of fruit trees
Washington *Utilities* and Transportation Commission	3 members		Not more than 2 from same political party	6 years. May be removed only after hearing by 3 superior ct. judges apptd. by chief justice of supreme court at request of gov.	Chr., $1,250 per month; others, $1,000	To regulate the activities of transportation and public utilities companies
Mobile Home and Recreational *Vehicle* Advisory Board	7 members plus sup. of mobile home section of Dept. of Labor and Indus.	Apptd. by gov. with consent of dir. of labor and indus.	1, employee or official of mobile home mfg. company; 1, of a travel-trailer mfg. company; 1, of a company making parts for plumbing equipment; 1, of a distributor or manufacturer of heating equipment; 1, of a company making electrical equipment; 1, of a mobile home park; 1, to represent general public owning mobile homes	4 years	$25 pay per day plus regular expense allowance	To advise dir. of labor and indus. on rules for safety and installation of plumbing, heating, and electrical equipment for conformity with those of Amer. Standards Assoc.

TABLE 3–Continued (50)

Group	Composition	How Chosen	Qualifications	Term of Office	Compensation	Function
Governor's Advisory Committee on *Vendor* Rates	9 members plus sec. of Dept. of Soc. and Health Serv.	9 apptd. by gov.	Selection on basis of interest in problems relating to the Dept. of Soc. and Health Serv.; at least 2 must be CPA's	At pleasure of gov.	Regular expense allowance	To study methods and procedures for fixing rates for vendors of goods to the Dept. of Soc. and Health Serv.
Wash. State *Veterinary* Board of Govs.	5 members	Apptd. by gov. from list by Wash. State Vet. Med. Assoc.	State residents in active practice; veterinary license; not more than 1 from same cong. dist.	5 years	$25 pay per day plus regular expense	To examine applicants for veterinarian's license and approve those qualified
State *Voting* Machine Committee	Sec. of state; supt. of pub. inst.; ins. comm.	Ex officio				To supervise checking of voting machines to assure accuracy in voting
Water Well Examining Board	3 members	1, apptd. by gov.; 1, by dir. of ecol.; 1, by sec. of soc. and health serv.	Ecol. and soc. and health serv. appointees, members of staff; gov's. appointee, not employed by state and actively engaged in well-drilling activities at time of appt.	Gov.'s appointee, 2 years	Regular expense allowance	To prepare and administer exams for licensing water-well construction

TABLE 3—Continued (51)

Group	Composition	How Chosen	Qualifications	Term of Office	Compensation	Function
State *Wheat* Commission	7 members plus dir. of ag.	5 elected by wheat producers of state; 2 chosen by elected group	All wheat producers; US citizens, residents of state, over 25 years old	3 years	$20 pay per day plus regular expense allowance	To advertise Wash. wheat and establish marketing orders if growers authorize them
Youth Development and Conservation Committee	Member of State Parks and Rec. Comm., State Bd. of Educ. depts. of fisheries, comm. and econ. devel., game, employment security, ecol. comm. of pub. lands, plus 1 other member	1 apptd. by gov.	None specified	1, at pleasure of gov.	Regular expense allowance	To advise the Div. of Youth Dev. and Conservation within the Parks and Rec. Commission for setting up youth camps for boys and girls

4. State Legislative Branch

When the delegates to the state constitutional convention met in 1889, they decided to establish a bicameral (two-house) state legislature, as we have seen. The voters in the state were to elect the members of both houses, and the convention delegates had to decide how the number of members of the house of representatives and the senate were to be divided (apportioned) among the various sections of the state. They decided to use population as the basis for apportionment for both the house and the senate, and they used county lines as the boundaries for the representative and senatorial districts. One or more counties still form the districts except where the population of a county is large enough that more than one district is required within a county.

Because of the association of legislative districts with counties, many people believe that a senator in our state legislature represents the county from which he is elected in the same way that a United States senator in Congress represents the state from which he comes. The situations are not parallel, however. Every state has two United States senators, no matter what its size, but the United States Supreme Court has ruled that both houses of all state legislatures must be apportioned according to population. In our state legislature, the population of a legislative district determines the number of both its state senators and its state representatives, although in a different ratio—two representatives to one senator.

The federal district court in Seattle requires that the boundaries of legislative districts follow county, city, or census tract boundary lines. Except for large cities in the state, county lines are ordinarily used as the boundaries because they are convenient. Moreover, the use of county lines (or those of cities or census tracts—some standard and predetermined line) prevents manipulation of district boundaries to give a political party an advantage. In states where the legislative districts were drawn independently of counties or other existing local units (before the requirement by the United States Supreme Court that the principle of "one man-one vote" be followed to a greater degree), a political "boss" sometimes dictated their composition. The party in control drew the lines so that "pockets" of the opposition's strength would be distributed among the districts in such a way that they would be ineffective. This kind of apportionment is called *gerrymandering*. The term comes from the name of an influential political leader in Massachusetts, Elbridge Gerry, who was governor in the early 1880s. He drew the lines for the Massachusetts legislative districts so as to give his party control of practically all of them. A person who was looking at a map pointed to one of the most contorted districts and remarked that it looked more like a salamander. A friend replied that it looked more like a "Gerrymander" to him. People were amused by the pun, and the term became a general one.

Since representation in both houses of our state legislature is based on population, the state constitutional convention delegates had to decide if the representatives and senators should be equal in number and if an upper limit should be placed on the size of the legislature. They concluded that it should be restricted so that population increases would not make the group too large to discuss problems easily. The matter of the expense of maintaining a big legislative body worried the delegates, too. They set the number of representatives at seventy and gave the legislature power to increase the number to the maximum of ninety-nine, the size maintained until the federal district court in its redistricting procedures for the 1972 election established forty-nine legislative districts, each having two representatives. This makes the present number of house members now ninety-eight. The redistricting question, leading to the federal action, will be presented later in this chapter.

The number of state senators was made to hinge on the number of representatives. The state senate is to consist of not more than one-half or less than one-third the number of representatives. In 1889 the number of senators was set at thirty-five, half the number of representatives at that time, but the legislature did not maintain the two-to-one ratio for many years, since we had only forty-six state senators until the 1959 legislature increased the number to the maximum of forty-nine.

The delegates also had to consider what the minimum number of senators and representatives should be. If the population were to decrease or a depression or other cause were to make the legislature want to cut its own size drastically, a point where the reduction should end had to be chosen. Otherwise, the group might become so small that it would not be representative of all areas in the state or segments of the population. The convention delegates decided on sixty-three as the minimum number of representatives, and one-third of that would be twenty-one, the smallest possible number of state senators.

Inasmuch as the number of state senators and representatives from a given area depends on its population, presumably the number should be reapportioned often to keep up with shifts of population from one region to another. The state constitution reflects this need by requiring the legislature to redistrict the state every five years. The legislators are instructed by the constitution to assign to each legislative district the number of state senators and representatives to which it is entitled by its population after each federal census at the beginning of a decade. Then they are to make a similar reapportionment in the middle of each decade on the basis of a state census. The legislature, however, has not made the reapportionment every five years as required by the state constitution, and a similar situation in other states finally led to the decision by the United States Supreme Court that federal courts may regulate the matter of reapportionment in a state.

It is easy to see that redistricting is a difficult problem and one that a state legislature dislikes to tackle. Because our total number of representatives now remains the same, the legislature cannot increase the number for those districts whose population has increased without decreasing the number for those whose population has increased to a lesser degree. No district, naturally, wants to give up a state representative or senator because the loss cuts down the influence of that area in the legislature. On the other hand, cities which have grown rapidly object strenuously to having the same number of legislators as they had when they were much smaller.

In addition to the objections of a district to losing representation, there are political problems in reapportionment. Adding and subtracting legislators to fit population changes may give a Democratic or Republican section of the state additional legislators. Consequently, it is very difficult to get the legislature to agree on a reapportionment bill.

Students are sometimes puzzled as to why the legislature is not forced to follow a constitutional requirement. "After all," they say, "if the state constitution requires a thing to be done, it has to be done." This is true if some state or local official or board is made the agent to do the thing specified. The officer is then said to have a *ministerial* duty—one in which he has no choice. We have seen that the state supreme court may issue a writ of mandamus ordering a state official to perform an act required by law, and the superior courts may issue such writs to local officials. The legislature, however, is not a ministerial agency. It is a sovereign group and, as such, cannot be forced to pass a law if it does not wish to do so.

Consequently, from 1930, when the voters in this state made a reapportionment by an initiative, until 1956, no change had been made. In 1956 another redistricting initiative passed, which the 1957 legislature amended by a two-thirds vote. The amendments returned the composition of the legislative districts almost to their status preceding the passage of the initiative. In 1960 a senator from one district represented only 20,023 people, while a senator from another district represented 145,180. The range for state representatives was from 12,399 to 48,393.

We saw in an earlier chapter that, until the 1962 decision of the United States Supreme Court in regard to apportionment of state legislators, the matter of redistricting was considered to be a purely political one—a question to be decided by a state legislature or Congress, which the courts would not rule on. Therefore, if a state legislature allowed a small, rural county with very few people to have as many state representatives and senators as a large urban county did, there was nothing anybody could do about it except try to elect legislators who were pledged to make a change. (In our state, too, the people could redistrict, as they did by an initiative, but the legislature still had the power to nullify much of its effect by amending the initiative, a prerogative given it by a constitutional amendment ratified by the voters in the 1952 election.)

Then in 1962 the United States Supreme Court heard a case (Baker *v.* Carr) in which residents of cities in Tennessee claimed that their right to "equal protection of the laws" as guaranteed by the Fourteenth Amendment to the United States Constitution was denied because their state legislators represented a great many more people than did the legislators from rural areas. The federal district court in the area heard the case first and ruled against the plaintiffs because it said the federal court had no jurisdiction in such a case. The voters then appealed the case to the United States Supreme Court, which reversed that decision. It held that the Fourteenth Amendment does cover the right of a United States citizen to have equality of representation in state legislatures and that a federal court may enforce it if a state court will not. The United States Supreme Court, however, did not try to specify how apportionment should be done or how great a difference there could be in the number of citizens represented by a state legislator from one district to another. It simply said that there must be a reasonable equality between districts.

After that, various groups in our state worked to get the question of our legislative apportionment settled before the 1964 election. One move was that in the summer of 1962, a justice of the peace in Midway, Washington (James Thigpen), attempted to get a federal district court to prohibit any elections in the state until our legislature made a reapportionment that would meet the requirements specified by the United States Supreme Court. The court refused to do so because another initiative (Number 211) had been filed by the League of Women Voters in the 1962 election, and, if it passed, it would presumably have been a satisfactory solution of providing more equal representation between the urgan and the rural areas. However, that initiative did not pass in the November 1962 election. In December 1962, the federal district court ruled that the apportionment in effect then was "invidiously discriminatory."

After a series of appeals to federal courts for an extension of time in which the state legislature might make a reapportionment, the federal district court ruled that when the legislature met in 1965 it could consider no bills (other than ones to keep the legislature operating) until it passed a redistricting bill.

Reapportionment was such a thorny problem that bitter debate continued in the legislature week after week. The Democrats had a large majority in both houses, but party lines were not followed solidly because of the question of decreasing representation in the rural areas. A number of legislators knew that when two or three such legislative districts were combined, their own seats in the house or senate would be eliminated. Consequently, some Democrats voted with enough Republicans against the Democratically-sponsored reapportionment bills to defeat them in one house or the other until 26 January 1965, when one finally passed. Governor Daniel Evans, a Republican, vetoed it because, he said, it would "thwart the will of the majority and guarantee perpetual control of the Legislative process by one party."

The senate then passed a resolution asking the federal district court to nullify the governor's veto because it argued that the legislature had followed the court order requiring the passage of a reapportionment bill and that it should therefore stand as law. The house refused to pass the resolution, however, and the legislature continued to work on another bill that would be acceptable to both Democrats and Republicans and thus avoid another executive veto. The most troublesome areas for agreement were King and Spokane counties. The Republicans admitted that in the areas where crucial changes were to be made, more solid Democratic legislative districts would emerge than solid Republican ones. However, the Republicans insisted that boundary lines for the doubtful sections (called "swing" districts because they might go in either direction) be drawn so as to leave them undecided. Then either party would have a chance to win a majority of the votes. Some of the Democratic leaders proposed that their majority party pass a bill over Republican protests and by-pass the governor's veto by stipulating that the bill be presented directly to the voters for a referendum vote. The Republicans countered this suggestion with the statement that such an unusual legislative procedure would be challenged as unconstitutional and that the courts would then have to rule on whether or not a bill may go to the people without giving the governor a chance to veto it. Finally on 26 February a bill sufficiently agreeable to both parties was passed by both houses of the legislature and signed by the governor.

However, neither the 1971 regular session of the legislature nor the 1972 special session was able to agree on the next redistricting bill five years later,

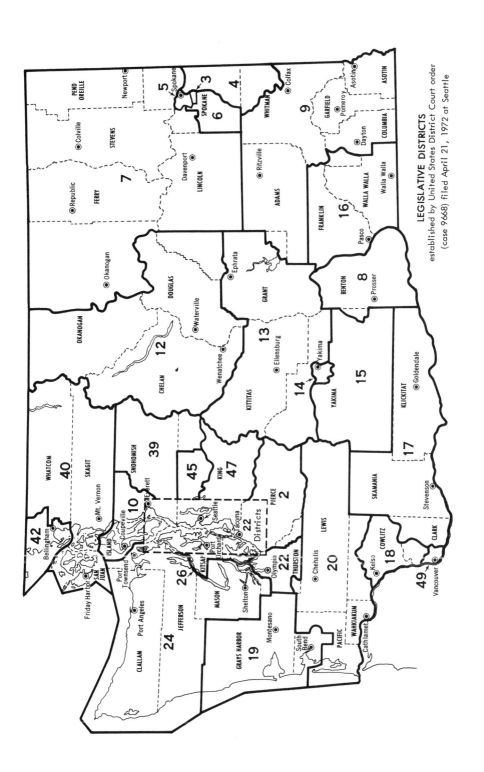

LEGISLATIVE DISTRICTS
established by United States District Court order
(case 9668) filed April 21, 1972 at Seattle

and on 26 February 1972 the federal district court in Seattle appointed a special master to redraw Washington's legislative and congressional districts with virtually equal population by 27 March 1972. The court order included guidelines specifying that each legislative district should have one-forty-ninth of the state's population—approximately 68,450 persons per district. Each district has one senator and two representatives. All except one county already had two members in the state house of representatives—Whatcom County had three house members in the previous reapportionment. The new arrangement affected the size of all but one of the 1971 districts. The 1970 federal census was the basis for population determination, and if the master could not divide the state into districts having equal population, the deviation must not be more than 1 percent. He was told not to divide any district by a river, lake, or other natural geographic barrier and not to straddle the crest of the Cascades north of the south boundary of Lewis County in forming a legislative district. He was also to avoid all contacts with congressmen, legislators, or candidates for public office or anyone who might be representing such a person. See Figure 1 for the legislative district boundaries established and followed in the 1972 election.

Because Congress allows the states to apportion the congressional districts from which the members of the United States House of Representatives are chosen, congressional as well as state districts come into the problem of redistricting. After each federal census, the United States Department of Commerce works out the proportion of the 435 house seats for each state on the basis of its population, and in 1950 the number for our state was increased from six to seven. In 1957 and 1959, the state legislature defined the seventh district from which the additional representative was elected. From 1950 to 1956, he was a representative-at-large. The federal district court instructed the present special master for redistricting to redesign the congressional districts by forming the forty-nine legislative districts into seven convenient and contiguous districts. See Figure 2 for the congressional district boundaries now in effect.

Before the matter of redistricting became a federal question, our state Legislative Council had appointed a special committee to study the problem of reapportionment for the state. The committee recommended that the legislature propose a constitutional amendment to establish a reapportionment commission, which would consist of the attorney general, state auditor, lieutenant governor, secretary of state, and a superior court judge. This commission would then be required to redistrict the state at designated intervals if the legislature did not do so. (The committee's recommendation was that it be done every ten years.) If the legislature should propose a constitutional amendment of this kind, and if the voters approve it, then such a reapportionment commission could be compelled by the order of a state court to make a reapportionment of the legislators as required by law. Otherwise, unless the legislature makes an acceptable apportionment, the federal district courts will be responsible for devising a system for doing so, as they have done in the state of Washington.

PROCEDURE FOR PASSING LAWS

The size of the legislature is only one of the problems in connection with its organization. Arguments pro and con in regard to proposed changes for greater efficiency in the form of the legislature and the length of its sessions will have more meaning after we trace the steps involved in the passing of a bill.

Lobbying

The first step in getting a bill passed is presenting it to the legislature for consideration, and, since each bill has to be introduced by a member of the house or senate, it must be a measure which some legislator or committee is willing to sponsor. People who want to have a law passed, therefore, try to persuage a legislator to introduce the desired bill. After it is introduced, they follow its progress through the legislature, using as much influence as possible with the committee that considers it and with the other legislators.

Trying to persuade the legislature to pass a bill has become known as *lobbying*, and we hear much criticism of "high-pressure lobbying." The legislators feel driven almost to distraction sometimes by lobbyists who go to Olympia to try to persuade them to pass certain bills. Sometimes two groups with conflicting interests will be pursuing a legislator—one wanting him to vote for, the other against, a particular measure. When this occurs while he is studying the meaning and effect of hundreds of bills, attending committee meetings at all hours, and attending the legislative sessions themselves, he may wonder if he can live until the close of the session.

On the other hand, the legislators need to know the wishes of the people—those who support and those who oppose a given bill—and, in order to do this, they must hear what people have to say by letter and in person. Technically, such requests are known as *petitions*, and our state constitution guarantees in Article I, Section 4, that "The right of petition and of people peaceably to assemble for the common good shall never be abridged." Consequently, the legislators want to eliminate the harmful type of lobbying and still allow people to express their views to their representatives.

The main concern of the people is that the legislators be aware of the specific individual or group who may be paying a lobbyist to argue for or against a particular bill. If a person pays his own expenses and goes to express

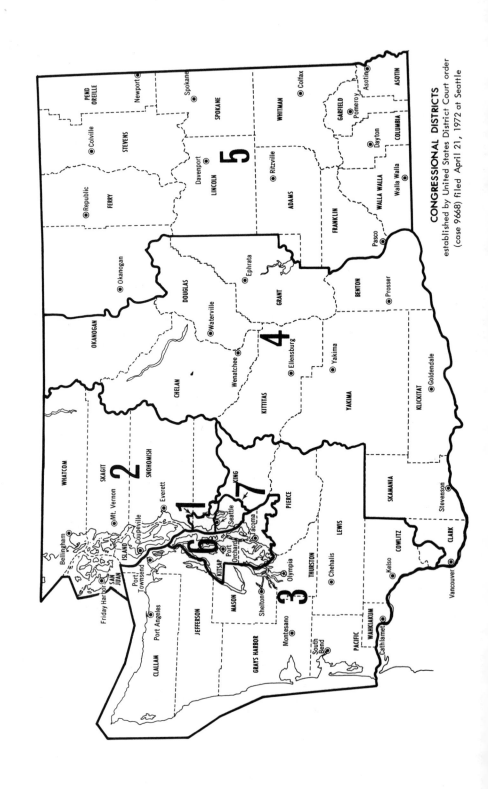

CONGRESSIONAL DISTRICTS
established by United States District Court order
(case 9668) filed April 21, 1972 at Seattle

his desires, he is not likely to represent a special-interest organization or management or labor group. However, if an individual appears to be expressing his own beliefs and needs, but is actually paid by a group to do so, the legislators need to know that this is the case. Consequently, the house of representatives stipulates that all paid lobbyists must register their names and those of their employers. Many members feel that some more stringent ruling is necessary, both to enforce the present provision and to let the legislators and the public know how much the lobbyist is receiving. Bills to this effect have been proposed in several recent sessions of the legislature, and in the 1971 legislature the house passed one requiring a detailed report from every paid lobbyist of his sponsors, the amounts received, and how much and in what way he used the money. However, the senate amended it, the house refused to concur in the amendments, and the bill was not passed. Before a lobbyist, whether or not he is paid, may speak to a committee or to the house as a whole, he must have permission to do so, but this does not prevent lobbyists from making informal contacts with individual legislators nor does it indicate who is paying the hired lobbyists.

In this state any bill may originate in either house.[1] Let us assume that we are following the course of some particular bill and that it originates in the house. The representative who has decided to sponsor it writes out his version of the proposed law and sends it to the bill drafting room. Here persons who are trained in legal phraseology put the ideas of the representative into a form that is clear, accurate, and, presumably, constitutional. They also check to see if the bill conflicts with existing legislation that would need to be repealed if superseded by a new law. They also inform the legislator if the bill duplicates a law already passed.

First Reading of the Bill

From the drafting room, five copies of the bill go to the clerk of the house. On the day after he receives the bill, the clerk reads only the title of the bill to the house, unless a majority of the members present vote to have the entire bill read. After this first reading, the speaker of the house refers it to a standing committee dealing with the general subject of the bill and orders the bill printed. One of the five copies goes to the printer, one to the press, one to the official file, and two to the clerk.

Bill in Committee

As soon as the bill is printed, copies of it are given to the appropriate

1. By agreement, the main appropriations bill is introduced in the house at one session and in the senate at the next.

committee for consideration.[2] Committees in our legislature have become extremely important as the amount of work has increased. At the 1971 session, for example, 931 bills were introduced in the senate during the regular and first special session and 1,134 in the house. It is obvious that if the forty-nine senators tried to discuss each one of these thoroughly, the session could not finish in a year, let alone in the sixty days allowed by the constitution. The ninety-eight representatives would have an even more difficult task. Consequently, small groups of representatives study the bills as committees for the house, and similar groups of senators consider the ones introduced in the senate.

For the 1971 session, there were eighteen standing committees in the senate and sixteen in the house. The largest committee in the senate was ways and means, with thirty-eight members, whereas three had only seven members: labor and industrial insurance, manufacturing and industrial development, and public pensions and social security. In the house, the largest was also the appropriations committee, which is the counterpart of the senate's ways and means committee. The smallest committee in the house was the one for elections and apportionment, with nine members. The 1971 *Legislative Manual* indicates that six committees are the maximum for an individual senator, and most of the senators are on four or five committees. In the house, the maximum was also six committees for a representative, and most of the members were on five committees.

At preliminary meetings of Republican legislators and Democratic legislators, held to make plans for the 1973 session of the legislature, both groups agreed to have sixteen matching house and senate committees, beginning with the 1973 legislative session.[3] If the legislature accepts this plan, having identical committees in the house and senate will make it more feasible to hold joint committee hearings when they are considered desirable.

Custom has made it the practice for the speaker of the house and the president of the senate to give chairmanship of the important committees to members of the political party having the majority in either house; and the members of that party expect the chairmanships to be granted according to the length of time an individual has been a member of the legislature. The house and senate members hold a preliminary meeting, called a *caucus*, before the legislature convenes. The Republicans in the house, for example, meet

2. Bills introduced by a legislative committee go directly from first reading to the second-reading stage.

3. These are named tentatively as: agriculture and consumer protection; commerce and professions; constitutions and elections; financial institutions and insurance; education (common schools); higher education and libraries, judiciary; labor and employment; local government; natural resources and ecology; rules and administration; social and health services; state government; transportation; the committee on parks, tourist, capitol grounds and recreation; and a ways and means committee divided into subcommittees on appropriations and revenue.

together and decide whom they want on the various committees. If they have a majority, they also agree on a speaker and chief clerk. The speaker is regarded as the leader of the majority party in the house. The Democratic members meet for the same purpose, and similar caucuses are held by the senators. Then when the session opens, the party in power can take care of the details of organization quickly, and the speaker and senate president can follow the wishes of their party in assigning members to committee chairmanships. The other places on the committees are distributed among the members of the house or senate so that the two main political parties are represented on the committees, as much as possible, in the same proportion as they are in the house in question.

The committees have the task of analyzing the bills, holding hearings where people may express their opinions of the bill under consideration, calling in experts on a particular subject for advice, doing research on the history of the subject, finding out how similar laws may have worked out in other states, and, in general, making as complete a study as possible of the need for such a law and its probable effects.

It is clear that this would be a big task for a member of one committee, and when he is on five or more, the problem becomes an impossible one. It is complicated, also, by the fact that the legislators are supposed to be in their seats for each day's meetings of the house or senate. Many committee meetings are held at night, but at least one open daytime meeting is required for each bill. Moreover, the trend now is for the committees to have as few executive (closed) sessions as possible, so that finding time for committee meetings is becoming even more difficult. In fact, in the 1972 special session of the 1971 legislature, both houses passed a rule that all regular committee meetings would be open to the public. To try to help, the house and senate now begin work at noon so that the legislators may have the mornings for committee work. The committee chairmen can also get permission from the presiding officer of their house to meet during the legislative sessions. For an important vote, or for any other reason, a majority of the legislators present may demand a *call of the house or senate,* and then the sergeant-at-arms has the authority to bring the absent members back to their seats.

Each house committee is now required to return a bill to the floor within ten days unless the house votes to give it additional time. This rule was enacted in an attempt to prevent bills from "dying in committee." Before this ruling, if the majority of the committee members disapproved of a bill, they could most easily kill it by never letting it get back on the floor of the legislature for action; then, of course, it had no chance of passing. In the senate, a majority of the senators present may call a bill out of committee if it is not reported back after a reasonable time, and the house members, also, may do so by a constitutional majority vote.[4]

When a committee returns a bill to the house or senate, it may make one of several recommendations: that the bill pass just as it is; that it not pass at all; that it pass with certain amendments; or that a substitute bill be passed. If the committee recommends passage of a bill which carries an appropriation of state funds, the presiding officer then refers it to the ways and means committee for its consideration as to the availability of funds. With the approval of the appropriations subcommittee of the ways and means group, the bill is ready for its second reading.

Second Reading of the Bill

The second reading of bills is done in the order in which they appear on the *Calendar* of the house or senate, and the Rules Committee makes up the calendar. For this reason, the Rules Committee is considered probably the most powerful in each house, since it can, by refusing to put a bill on the calendar, prevent its passage. The degree of importance of the Rules Committee is shown by the fact that the speaker of the house and the president of the senate are automatically the chairmen of the respective rules committees. More restrictions are placed on the Rules Committee in the house than in the senate. In the house of representatives, the Rules Committee has to put on the calendar any bill reported back from a standing committee during the first fifteen days of a session carrying a "do pass" recommendation. A constitutional majority vote of the house may call a bill out of the Rules Committee at any time. In the senate a simple majority[5] may do so.

Not only the title, but the entire bill is read at the second reading. If the committee has recommended changes or an entirely new bill, the house or senate members have to consider the various versions, and debate is opened on the bill. At the end of the discussion, the bill, including any amendments, may be defeated, or it may be passed for third reading, in which case it goes back to the Rules Committee to be placed on the calendar for third reading. The third reading cannot occur on the same day as the second reading unless the rules are suspended by vote.

Third Reading of the Bill

On the third reading, the bill is read in full, section by section, and no amendments may be made. When a vote is taken, the vote of each member is recorded by an electric roll-call apparatus, which registers the vote of each

4. A majority of the representatives elected.
5. A majority of those present.

person quickly and avoids the long process of voice vote. It takes a constitutional majority to pass a bill after the third reading, since that is the final vote on a bill before it goes to the second house.

Consideration of Bill by Second House

Once a bill is passed by the house or the senate, it is sent to the other house, and the procedure outlined above begins all over again. The bill will be sent to a committee of the second house corresponding to the committee of the first house to which it was assigned. The second committee may call back for advice the same experts who advised the first committee. This duplication wastes so much time that the two houses in recent years have tried to appoint joint committees in some subjects, particularly for long-range study of a question between legislative sessions. However, if one house has one political party in control and the other house the opposite party, the members object, for the most part, to joint committees because party lines are then blurred in the reports, even when a majority and a minority report are issued, and in campaigning for re-election afterwards, the candidates find it harder to base their statements on a clear-cut division on the issues considered by the joint committees. There is, however, growing pressure from the public to increase the use of joint committees in order to avoid duplicate hearings. The agreement, mentioned above, to have matching committees in the 1973 session is evidence of this. In this instance, however, both houses have a majority in the same party—Democratic.

If the senate is willing to pass a bill only if some changes are made, we have a bill passed in one form by the house and in another by the senate. In this situation, means are taken to see if the two houses can be brought to agreement. To begin with, the bill as passed by the second house is sent back to the first house to find out if the original group will accept the changed form.

Joint Conference Committee

If the original house refuses to accept the changes made by the second house, it may call for a joint conference committee, which consists of three members from each house. If this committee manages to adjust the differences between the two bills, the recommendation is made to both houses. Ordinarily, they accept the compromise bill. If the committee cannot agree on a settlement of the differences as they stand, the two houses may give to it or to a new committee the power of free conference, which permits the committee to disregard the two contradictory bills and to write a new one. It has to be passed by both houses to become a law.

Final Passage of a Bill

Once a bill is passed by both houses, the speaker of the house and the president of the senate then sign the bill, as passed, and it goes to the governor for his approval. If the governor signs the bill, it becomes a law in ninety days after the close of the legislative session unless it is an emergency bill or unless a petition for referendum vote is submitted by the secretary of state. These exceptions will be discussed in the section on initiative and referendum procedure in chapter 6.

If the governor vetoes the whole bill or any part of it, the bill or the vetoed parts are returned to the house in which the bill originated, and two-thirds of the members present have to vote for the bill to pass it over the governor's veto. If the bill is passed by such a vote in the first house, it is sent to the second for a similar vote. If it is also passed there by a two-thirds majority, it becomes a law. If one or both houses do not pass it by a two-thirds vote, it is killed.

We noted in the chapter on the executive branch that the governor in our state does not have the power of pocket veto. Any bill passed during the last five days of the legislative session does not have to be returned to the legislature. After its adjournment, if the governor signs or neglects to sign a bill passed during the last five days, it becomes a law as usual. If the governor vetoes all or part of a bill after the legislature has adjourned, the bill or section does not go into effect, and the legislature has no chance to pass it over his veto or draw up a substitute bill until the next regular or special session. At that time, the secretary of state returns the vetoed bills with the governor's objections to the house where the bill originated.

LENGTH OF LEGISLATIVE SESSION

When the delegates to the state constitutional convention were considering the matter of how often and for how long the state legislature should meet, they were anxious to keep the legislative sessions to a minimum. They were afraid that, if the legislature were allowed to meet as often and as long as it wished, it would pass unnecessary laws and waste the taxpayers' money by staying in session too long. The delegates settled then on a session of sixty days every other year.

The length of time was short even for the business to be transacted in 1889, and although legislators had to work as fast as they could, it was possible then to give fair consideration to the bills introduced. With the speed of industrial and social developments of this century, however, even a minimum of government has become so complex that many legislators feel that sixty days is hardly enough time for an introduction to an adequate session. For several years, the device of stopping the clock on the sixtieth day was used, pretending that the day went on until discussion of essential bills was finished.

After the 1951 legislature had done this, however, a group wanted to circulate a referendum petition to try to have the voters veto a certain law; and they asked the state supreme court to issue a writ of mandamus to force the president of the senate to put the correct date (sixty-first day of the session) on the bill instead of the earlier date, which he had used to pretend that the legislature was still in its sixtieth day. They argued that they were entitled to the extra day in circulating the referendum petition.

The supreme court was able to decide that the petitioners had the proper amount of time for their petition without ruling on the legality of the "stopped clock" procedure. In its decision, however, the court said that the ruse could raise a serious question as to the constitutionality of laws passed after the sixtieth day of a session. Thus, even though the court did not rule on the matter in that particular case, since that time the legislators have not risked bringing the question before the court again. They have adjourned on the sixtieth day, and the governor has then called a special session in order to give the legislators extra time without employing the subterfuge of the stopped clock.

Extra sessions have now become so constant that there is increasing agitation for a constitutional amendment to call the legislature into session each year. In the 1972 special session of the 1971 legislature, a resolution to the effect did pass in the house, but it died in committee in the senate. Other states are finding annual sessions necessary. In 1968 Florida, Idaho, Iowa, and Utah changed from biennial to annual sessions, and Wisconsin deleted from its constitution the provision prohibiting the legislature from meeting oftener than once every two years.

ARGUMENTS FOR AND AGAINST UNICAMERAL LEGISLATURE

The question of time is linked with that of size. A small group could stay in session continuously, if that is desirable, for the same amount of money necessary to keep a large number operating for a short time. Many political scientists believe that, regardless of the length of a session, a larger number of legislators cannot act so wisely and effeciently as a small group. They would favor a small unicameral legislature, similar to the one in Nebraska.[6] Having a small unicameral legislature would avoid the present double discussion of each bill, the duplication of committees with their double hearings that often require some people to go to Olympia twice during a session, rather than

6. As we have seen, Nebraska is the only state that does not have a two-house legislature.

once, and the necessity for limiting the length of a session because of the expense.

Opponents of the one-house legislative system are afraid that bills would be passed too quickly if they were considered by only one group—that they would not have sufficient consideration. They feel that the waste of time and money in having a double discussion of each bill is worthwhile to avoid hasty legislation and, perhaps, a greater number of laws than two houses have time to pass.

The unicameral advocates have made various proposals designed to avoid these evils. They would require that several days, or even weeks, pass between the different readings of a bill so that the group could not rush bills through without a great deal of debate and time for deliberation. It has also been suggested that the legislative session be in two parts. During the first, bills would be proposed and debated to a certain extent. Then the legislators would go home for a month, talk over the proposed laws with their constituents, and study what other states are doing in these matters. Upon returning to the capital for the second half of the session, they would pass the bills which seemed best to them. Even with a bicameral system, California has adopted a divided session of this type.

If a small unicameral legislature were paid sufficiently to make legislation the main occupation of its members, being a member of the legislature would probably require special training and would be considered a full-time profession. This leads to what people call a government by experts. Those who favor such a system point out that our government is such a vital part of our lives that we should have legislators with the best possible ability and training. Those who oppose government by experts are afraid that the legislators will be too much interested in trying out different theories of governmental organization and that their experiments will not be successful. They prefer the present qualifications for the position of legislator in Washington: simply that he be a qualified voter of his legislative district. The opponents of government by experts also believe that a larger number of legislators gives a greater degree of representation to the people. The argument against this is that quality rather than quantity is the important factor.

Many people argue that they would rather have Tom, Dick, and Harry, their neighbors, making laws, which, they think, represent the needs of the average person than a group of professional lawmakers. No one denies that an untrained group makes mistakes and fumbles, but it is true that they will certainly go slowly in making fundamental changes. People differ in their opinions as to whether such an attitude is desirable.

Even if the voters are not willing to try a small unicameral legislature, practically everyone agrees that the present system puts too great a burden on our legislators. Some means have to be found to help them, and it is hoped that the increased use of joint interim committees, mentioned earlier, including the legislative council, will prove to be one such aid. However, the members of these committees find that their work as legislators becomes almost a full-time job, so that the voters are inevitably faced again with the necessity of paying for the quality and amount of service they receive from their legislators and other public officials.

This is true if annual sessions are established since persons of the caliber one wants as legislators ordinarily have to make a decided financial sacrifice in leaving their businesses and professions to spend two months or more in Olympia each year. Even the California system of split sessions does not make the situation easier, inasmuch as the legislators are spending most of the "free" month with their constituents at home. Therefore, voters need to study the whole question of the types of legislative personnel and procedures that are desirable in order that they may be obtained.

RESTRICTIONS ON STATE LEGISLATURE

We have noted that our state constitutional convention delegates were afraid that the legislature would abuse its powers unless many restrictions were placed on it. The restriction on the length of session has already been discussed. Maximum salaries for the legislators as well as for the executive officials were also specified in the constitution for fear that these people would raise their own salaries to an exorbitant sum. This restriction was removed by a constitutional amendment in 1948, and the legislature can now set the compensation for its members. The salary in 1972 was $3,600 per year, plus $40.00 per diem for days in attendance at legislative sessions and ten cents per mile for travel between their homes and Olympia.

During the territorial period, the territorial legislature passed laws for specific people on subjects forbidden to our state legislature by the state constitution. For example, the territorial legislature granted divorces, but the state constitution makes them a matter for court action only. In Article II, Section 28, of the constitution, there is a list of many other subjects on which the legislature may not pass a law for one person or corporation—called a *private* or *special* law. Some of these are: changing a person's name, authorizing the disposal of property belonging to a minor, assessing or collecting taxes, and so forth. This does not mean that the legislature cannot pass any laws on these subjects. The point is that any laws on these matters have to be general ones so that they apply to everyone, not just to one person or firm.

We noted earlier that the 1889 convention delegates were particularly afraid that a corporation might influence the legislature to grant it special privileges. Bribery of legislators by a corporation in any form is forbidden. If a bill concerns any business in which a legislator has a personal interest, he must say so and refrain from voting on it. Moreover, he cannot be a member of Congress or hold any other public office during his own term. If he is elected or appointed to such an office, his seat in the legislature automatically becomes vacant.

Students of government agree that the purpose behind such restrictions is excellent, but they also believe that, when the regulations become too specific, they are in the nature of statutory material, better suited to legislative than to constitutional requirements. Our constitution was meant to last for many years, and the delegates could not foresee the important social and economic changes ahead. A set of specific rules in 1889 for the 1970s would inevitably leave loopholes for the legislature to fill, in any case. The functions which the legislature has given to the Department of Labor and Industries, the Transportation and Utilities Commission, the Department of Ecology, the Department of Social and Health Services, and so forth, are evidence of this. If the time should ever come when the legislature lacked the integrity to resist attempts at its own corruption, a list of rules in the constitution would not help. Occasionally, specific rules may even be a handicap in instituting a broader program of supervision.

When a legislator cannot serve for any reason, the county commissioners of the county from which he was elected (or the joint board if more than one county is included in his district) choose someone of the same political party to fill his place until the next election. The county central committee of his party submits a list of three names from which the commissioners choose one. If the appointment is not made in this way before the legislature is due to convene, the governor appoints a person to take the vacant place for that session. The regular term of office for state representatives is two years and that for senators is four years. Half of the senators are elected every two years so that they cannot all be new at once.[7]

The constitution protects as well as restricts legislators. During a session and for fifteen days beforehand, no process in a civil suit may be served on them, and they cannot be arrested for any crime except treason, felony, or breach of the peace. During legislative debate, no civil or criminal action may be brought against them for anything they may say. These safeguards prevent a legislator from being kept away from a session by a trumped-up charge, and allow him to say what he wants to in debate.

It will be obvious from the discussion of constitutional amendments already passed and of ones under consideration that a number of important changes have been made in our constitution and that more are advocated. We

7. Many political scientists consider the very short term for representatives to be an unfortunate legislative restriction.

now have fifty-eight amendments adopted by the voters. We have seen that a change in the constitution has to be passed by a two-thirds majority of the members of both houses and has to have a majority vote of those voting on the amendment at the next general election. In Oregon, the voters may propose an amendment by initiative action, but our constitution lists only the legislature as the agency to propose constitutional amendments.

As early as 1918 the legislature passed a proposal asking the voters to approve the calling of a constitutional convention to write a new state constitution. In order to call a constitutional convention, two-thirds of the members of both houses of the legislature must vote in favor of the proposal and then in the ensuring election a majority of all the persons casting ballots (whether or not they vote at all on the question of the calling of a constitutional convention) have to favor a constitutional convention. In 1918, 53 percent of the voters voted on the question of the convention, but a majority of them voted against calling one.

Again in recent years, because of the increasingly large number of constitutional amendments, a number of people have felt that the constitution has become unwieldy and that it would be more efficient and satisfactory to call a constitutional convention and submit a rewritten constitution to the voters than to continue the piecemeal changes. In fact, in the 1965 legislative session the house of representatives passed by a vote of 78 to 14 a resolution to present to the voters the question of calling a new state constitutional convention, but it failed in committee in the senate.

One other attempted remedy for the addition of so many individual constitutional amendments has been the proposed "gateway amendment" to the state constitution. At the present time individual articles have to be proposed separately to the voters, and often two or more of these are related and, in a sense, interlocked. This has been particularly true of problems of different types of taxation. If a more general approach could be used in proposing an amendment covering more than a specific issue, this would represent a "gateway" toward a broader revision of the state constitution. So far this, too, has not passed the legislature.

LEGISLATIVE ORGANIZATION

Some of the features of the organization of the legislature have already been mentioned in connection with the choice of the presiding officers. Since the lieutenant governor is president of the senate, he can call the first meeting of that group to order, but someone has to be named to call the first meeting of the house together, since the speaker is elected by the members.

This function is given to the person who served as chief clerk at the previous session. From a certified list of the members given to him by the secretary of state, the clerk calls the roll, and a judge of the state supreme court administers the oath of office. The clerk continues to preside until the members have elected the speaker and chief clerk for the session.

As soon as the speaker is elected, he takes the chair and acts as the presiding officer for the rest of the session. He has considerable authority because he not only appoints the various committees, as we have seen, and serves as chairman of the rules committee, but he decides who is right in a question of procedure (point of order). It is true that the house may object to any of his actions and take a vote on them, but, since he is ordinarily the leader of the majority party, his decisions have more weight than those of a less influential member.

The chief clerk is in charge of the *House Journal,* which contains the minutes of each session of the house. The clerk hires stenographers and clerks to keep a complete record of the house proceedings. He also hires the other employees, such as janitors and guards, but the speaker has to approve all of his appointments. The clerk is not one of the legislators.

The sergeant-at-arms, the third official appointed by the house, has the task of preserving order and of serving any orders given by the house through the speaker. The sergeant admits visitors who have permission to attend sessions and keeps others out, and, as we have seen, if absent members are required for a house session, he is responsible for bringing them in.

General procedures are the same in the senate as in the house, with a few exceptions. The president pro tem, who is elected by the senators, acts as presiding officer of the senate whenever the lieutenant governor is absent, and he has control of the senate chamber and lobby whether he or the lieutenant governor is presiding. The senate also hires a recorder, who is called the secretary of the senate. He has charge of keeping the minutes of the senate meetings. He also appoints the other senate employees with the approval of the senate itself rather than that of the president pro tem. The senate also chooses a sergeant-at-arms, whose function is like that of the house sergeant.

SUGGESTED READINGS

For a discussion of original sources for the laws passed by the legislature and supreme court interpretations of them, see the first paragraph of the Suggested Readings for chapter 3.

The Legislative Council issues minutes of its meetings and texts of bills recommended to the legislature as does the Legislative Budget Committee and various other interim legislative committees. Some of these pertain to the actual working of the legislature; others, to problems of the executive and administrative branches; and still others to specific subjects for legislation. The secretary of state publishes rosters of members of the house and senate, with some biographical data concerning them, and a publication called the *Legislative Manual* is particularly helpful in giving a list of committees, with their individual members, a summary of the rules of the house and senate, a copy of the state constitution, and other useful information. As long as copies of any official publications are available, they may be secured by writing to the issuing agency in Olympia.

If a reader is interested in comparing our governmental procedures with those in other states, besides standard works on state and local government, in general, the *Book of the States* is a convenient source for quick reference.

5. State Judicial Branch

TERRITORIAL COURTS

We have seen that, in our territorial period, there were the territorial supreme court, district courts, a probate court for each county, and justice-of-the-peace courts in election precincts. The judges of the supreme court were appointed by the federal government, and they acted as district court judges also. Since the territory was under the control of the federal government, certain of the district courts were made federal as well as territorial courts. The voters in each county elected their judges of the probate and justice-of-the-peace courts.

STATE COURT SYSTEM

When Washington became a state in 1889, Congress established separate federal district and circuit courts to take care of cases concerning federal questions in the new state, and the state legislature was free to create its own system of state courts. The writers of the state constitution gave our legislature less freedom in establishing our courts than is generally considered desirable. In Article IV of the constitution, each type of state court (except certain inferior courts) is listed with the kinds of cases within its jurisdiction.

The highest court in the state is the state supreme court. Until 1969 the next highest court was the county superior court, and appeals from it had to be made to the state supreme court. However, in 1969 a court of appeals was created as an intermediary appeals court between the county superior courts and the state supreme court. The superior court for each county hears the cases formerly decided by the territorial and probate courts; and the fourth group comprises the courts of justices of the peace in various election precincts, termed *inferior courts.*[1] The constitution permits the legislature to provide other inferior courts. Until 1955, however, the only additional courts created by the legislature were city police courts, which were classified as a type of justice-of-the-peace court to hear cases of violation of city ordinances. The 1955 legislature, however, made city police courts in Class AA counties[2] municipal courts for which the judges are elected by the voters. The 1961 legislature added Class A counties and gave the county commissioners in other counties the privilege of adopting such a plan by majority vote.

Courts of Justices of the Peace

Originally, the term "justice of the peace" referred to a local officer in England who preserved law and order. The title has been kept for the judge of our local courts having jurisdiction over civil and criminal cases which are not serious enough to warrant trial in our superior courts.

The courts of the justices of the peace handle the same kinds of minor civil cases as they did during our territorial period. Samples of these actions are: damage suits; foreclosure of a mortgage or lien; and suits to force a person to fulfill terms of a contract. Until 1952 the maximum amount in controversy in civil cases was $100, but a constitutional amendment passed in that year now allows the legislature to set the maximum at any point between $300 and $1,000. The 1961 legislature made the limit $1,000 for courts of justices who are licensed attorneys, $500 in other justice-of-the-peace courts.

For criminal cases, the courts of justices of the peace now have concurrent jurisdiction with the superior court over all misdemeanors and gross misdemeanors for which the penalty is not greater than $500 or imprisonment in the county or city jail (or both fine and imprisonment). If the legislature wants to assign more serious crimes to the justice courts, it must list each type separately and specifically in a law. Earlier justice court jurisdiction was limited to petty crimes for which the fine was not more than $100. The change was made in an attempt to remove the burden of a great mass of both criminal and civil suits from the superior courts and enable them to settle cases of felonies, grave misdemeanors, and large civil suits more quickly and expeditiously. Samples of crimes listed for the justice courts are: estray laws, larceny, malicious trespass, public nuisance, and suspension or revocation of driver's licenses. The justices of the peace may also act as committing magistrates, conduct preliminary hearings, and have concurrent jurisdiction with the superior courts to keep the peace in their respective counties.

A criminal prosecution in a municipal court is instituted by a complaint,

1. The distinction between a superior and an inferior court will be given later.
2. Counties with population over 500,000.

which must be sworn to before the municipal court judge. If it seems to justify an arrest, the judge signs an arrest warrant, which may be served by a peace officer in any county or city in the state. A jury trial is allowed only for the revocation or suspension of a driver's license or other gross misdemeanor except in Class AA counties. No change of venue was allowed from a municipal court until 1967, when the legislature provided that in actions brought for violation of city ordinances, a change of venue from a police judge could be permitted. A case from a justice court may be taken to the superior court on appeal or writ of review.

The legislature requires that each justice court keep uniform records of each case filed and the proceedings involved. The state supreme court was authorized to prescribe the forms for such records, and the division of municipal corporations of the state auditor's office was instructed to prepare forms for financial accounting by the justice courts.

In 1969 the legislature revised the system for courts of justices of the peace in cities of over 500,000 population. In those cities the municipal court must have three departments, and if the court needs more, the legislative body of the city may create one additional department for each additional 50,000 inhabitants over 500,000. Each department has a municipal judge as its presiding official, and these judges choose one of their number as presiding judge for the city. He assigns the calendars and is responsible for the administration of the courts. The city assumes the cost for the elections of the municipal judges.

This more complicated municipal court is one type of justice of the peace court. In this type of municipal court, the judges appoint a court administrator, with the approval of a majority of the city's legislative body. He supervises the functions of the chief clerk and those of the director of the bureau of traffic violations and performs whatever other duties the presiding judge assigns to him.[3]

The judges of the municipal court also appoint the director of the traffic violations bureau according to the city's civil service rules. He acts under the supervision of the court administrator. The same procedure is followed for the selection of a chief clerk of the municipal court. The municipal courts have concurrent jurisdiction with the superior courts for certain civil and criminal actions. The municipal court judges appoint clerks for such cases involving violations of state law. The clerks have custody of the records of the court, issue process, swear witnesses, receive fines, and keep accurate court records.

The municipal judges also appoint a director of probation services, who supervises the probation officers of the municipal court, and they appoint as

3. The Board of County Commissioners of the county that contains the city decide how many clerks are necessary.

many additional probation officers and bailiffs as are authorized by the legislative body of the city. In this type of municipal court, a trial by a jury of six jurors is allowed in criminal cases involving violations of city ordinances. In other types of cases, the plaintiff or defendant may demand a jury.

For many years the legislature allowed the county commissioners to fix the number of justices of the peace for rural areas and designated the required number for cities of various sizes. In 1961, however, the legislature revised the entire law for courts of the justices of the peace and authorized a system based on optional justice-of-the-peace districts. A justice court districting committee was established for each county, to consist of a judge of the superior court, the prosecuting attorney, a practicing attorney in the county,[4] the judge of an inferior court in the county,[5] the mayors of the first-, second-, and third-class cities in the county, one person to represent the fourth-class cities,[6] the chairman of the county commissioners, and the county auditor.

In Class A counties and any others in which the county commissioners adopt the district plan, this committee divides the county into justice court districts and decides their boundaries, the number of justices of the peace[7] for each, the location of the courts, and the salaries for the part-time justices of the peace. The committee then recommends to the county commissioners that their plan be adopted, and the commissioners, in turn, hold a public hearing on the question before adopting it in its original or in modified form. By a similar procedure, two or more counties may be combined into a justice court district.

The justice court districting committee is limited in the number of justices assigned to a district by the total number of justices of the peace that the 1971 legislature allowed to each county.[8] The limits may be modified for areas which have district courts. In any district that has more than one justice of the peace, if any city or town chooses a person other than a justice of the peace to serve as municipal judge, the board of county commissioners may reduce the number of justices of the peace for the county by one for

4. Chosen by the largest local bar association, if any, or by the county commissioners.
5. Selected by the president of the Washington State Magistrates' Association.
6. Selected by the president of the Association of Washington Cities.
7. Whose name was changed by the 1971 legislature from justice of the peace to district judge for those presiding over courts in a justice court district. A court of justice of the peace in a district is now called a "district court."
8. Adams, 3; Asotin, 1; Benton, 2; Chelan, 1; Clallam, 1; Clark, 4; Columbia, 1; Cowlitz, 2; Douglas, 1; Ferry, 2; Franklin, 1; Garfield, 1; Grant, 1; Grays Harbor, 2; Island, 3; Jefferson, 1; King, 20; Kitsap, 2; Kittitas, 2; Klickitat, 2; Lewis, 1; Lincoln, 2; Mason, 1; Okanogan, 2; Pacific, 3; Pend Oreille, 2; Pierce, 8; San Juan, 1; Skagit, 3; Skamania, 1; Snohomish, 3; Spokane, 8; Stevens, 2; Thurston, 1; Wahkiakum, 2; Walla Walla, 3; Yakima, 6.

each 150,000 persons or fraction. In no case, however, shall the number of justices of the peace in any county be fewer than one for each 100,000 persons nor shall the number of district judges in any district be fewer than one for each 150,000. In turn, the county commissioners may add one full-time justice of the peace in districts having a population of 200,000 or more.

Cities having a population of 20,000 or less may provide for a municipal court to handle violations of city ordinances plus actions pertaining to license penalties. If it does not want a court of this type, it may follow the system provided for larger cities and assign one section of its justice court as the municipal department of the city (or it may be called the municipal court) to consider only matters pertaining to city ordinances. The judge of such a department or court may be called either a municipal judge or a police judge.

The manner of choosing justices of the peace varies with the size of the locality. All rural justices of the peace are elected. The legislative body of any city or town may make the office elective, and it must be elective in cities of 500,000 or more. Municipal judges who are not elected are appointed by the mayor of the city.

When the office is elective, the county auditor assigns a number to each justice position (if there is more than one) within a district, both for rural and for city offices, and a candidate for the office must file for a specific position by its number. If in the primary election, any candidate receives a majority of all votes cast for the position, only his name is printed on the general election ballot, with space left for the voter to write in any other name.

Every justice of the peace must be an attorney, who is licensed to practice in the state or who has already served as an elective justice of the peace, municipal judge, or police judge in the state or who has passed whatever qualifying examinations are provided for the office by the state supreme court in districts under 10,000. In addition, he must be a registered voter of his justice district. In cities of less than 5,000, he need not be an attorney. Justices in cities of more than 20,000 are considered full-time justices and may not engage in private law practice.

The term of office for a justice of the peace is four years, and the county commissioners fill vacancies for rural justices of the peace. The legislative body of a city decides how its vacancies are to be filled. The 1969 legislature made the annual salary of each full-time justice of the peace $20,000 in cities having over 40,000 population. In cities of over 500,000 the city that pays the salary may increase it to an amount not greater than that paid the superior court judges in the county. In cities between 20,000 and 40,000 the justice of the peace receives an annual salary of $18,000. No full-time justice of the peace shall receive any fee for solemnizing civil marriages during courthouse hours or during scheduled sessions of the court.

The first extra session of the 1969 legislature established the rate of pay for part-time district judges.[9] In district courts in which the population of the district is 40,000 or more and the salary for the district judge is more than $9,000, he must serve as a full-time judge. Any justice who is not considered a full-time officer may engage in other occupations, but may not use the office or supplies for his private business or the services of a secretary or other employee paid from public funds. In addition to the salaries, which are set by the county commissioners within the minimum and maximum figures specified by the legislature, the justices of the peace and employees receive reasonable traveling expenses.

If the justice court districting committee approves, one or more justice court commissioners may be appointed by the justices in any justice court district. These officers correspond to the court commissioners for the superior court, who attend to routine matters. In the justice courts, however, they may hear only criminal matters. They have no power to hear or decide civil questions.

The decision of the 1961 legislature to make even part-time justices of the peace salaried officials is regarded by political scientists as a very fine one. Previously, in cities smaller than five thousand, the justices were paid a part of the fees that they collected. Inasmuch as parties in cases before a justice of the peace usually do not pay to have the justice's compensation depend on the amount that he collects. In earlier days, even sheriffs were paid from fees collected for the papers they served, and this practice can lead to their trying to make as many arrests as possible or to put pressure on the prosecuting attorney or other court official to issue unnecessary subpoenas or other documents.

Superior Courts

The superior court in each county hears all cases more serious than those coming under the jurisdiction of courts of justices of the peace. Those for the superior courts cover a large range, from the most serious crimes to civil suits in which the amount of dispute is more than $1,000.[10] They include cases in what is termed *common law, civil law,* and *equity,* words that have various meanings at the present time.

Gradually, in England, the local courts built up the common law from decisions of the courts handed down from one generation to another.

9. Those in districts of fewer than 2,500 persons, not less than $600 nor more than $2,250; more than 2,500, but fewer than 5,000 persons, not less than $600 nor more than $3,375; more than 5,000, but fewer than 10,000 persons, not less than $600 nor more than $5,625; more than 10,000, but fewer than 20,000 persons, not less than $1,200 nor more than $6,750; more than 20,000, but fewer than 30,000 persons, not less than $2,500 nor more than $7,875; more than 30,000, but fewer than 40,000 persons, not less than $3,500 nor more than $9,000.
10. The limit is $500 if the presiding justice of the peace is not a licensed attorney.

Sometimes Parliament passed laws incorporating these decisions, but for the most part the term *common law* was used to refer to court rulings rather than to laws. The phrase also came to mean laws of and for the common people. This body of English law is the basis for our own system of law.

During the Middle Ages, people in England began to feel the need for courts in addition to the courts of common law. For one thing, these courts could not anticipate an action. If someone threatened to tear down a fence on another's property in order to take cattle across fields, for example, the court could do nothing until the fence was actually torn down. Then it could award damages to the victim. In order to prevent actions of this kind from occurring, people began to petition the king to command the person in question not to do the thing threatened. These requests became so numerous that the king could not attend to them himself. Consequently, he asked his officer who corresponded to a modern secretary of state—called the Chancellor—to hear the petitions and make a decision. Such hearings gradually took on the nature of a court called the Court of Chancery and, later, Court of Equity.

In addition to hearing petitions to restrain someone from a particular action, the courts of equity also began to hear cases in which an injustice would be done if the regular common law courts applied the customary penalty for such actions and cases in which the particular situation was not covered by an existing law or precedent. In England there are still separate courts of this kind, and in our country, too, separate courts of equity exist in some states. However, our state does not distinguish between courts of law and courts of equity. The superior court is the one established in the state constitution to hear all civil cases involving damages of more than $1,000, whether or not there is a law or precedent to cover the specific charge. A case in equity has to be a civil case, since there can be no crime which is not defined as such by the legislature or is not punishable under common law. Our legislature has stated, "The provisions of the common law relating to the commission of crime and the punishment thereof, in so far as not inconsistent with the institutions and laws of this state, shall supplement all penal statutes of this state and all persons offending against the same shall be tried in the superior courts of this state."[11] The term *equity* has come to have the general meaning of "equitable," that is, a fair settlement of any dispute. When it is used in that sense, it means simply "general justice."

The term *civil law* in this country is used chiefly to denote "civil" as opposed to "criminal" law. Countless arguments arise between individuals over land claims, foreclosure of mortgages, breach of contracts, claims for damages, and so forth, which must be settled by a court even though they do not constitute actual crimes against an individual or the state. Such civil

11. *Laws of the State of Washington* (1909), p. 902.

actions are usually settled by the payment of damages in one way or another, whereas criminal cases involve a punishment of fines or prison sentences or both.

Originally, however, the term *civil law* was used to refer to the old Roman law, which was written down as a body of rules. A judgs was not free to give a decision on the basis of previous court rulings or on the merits of an individual case; rather, he had to find a similar case in the civil law code and follow the instructions in it. This Roman law was accepted by France, Spain, and the other continental countries, for the most part. It is used in Latin American countries as the basis for their legal system, and in Quebec and Louisiana where French influence is strong.

In our state constitution, the jurisdiction of the superior courts in criminal and civil cases is stated in both general and specific terms. Article IV is devoted to the court system and Section 6 to the powers of the superior court. One group of criminal cases to be heard by the superior court is that of *felonies*—the most serious crimes, such as murder, forgery, arson, and so forth. Another group mentioned consists of all cases of misdemeanor not otherwise provided for. A *misdemeanor* is a crime less serious than a felony, and the only misdemeanors assigned by the legislature to another court are the petty ones mentioned above for the courts of justice of the peace, in which the amount of fine is not over $500.

In the category of civil cases, the constitution gives to the superior court jurisdiction in all cases involving the title or possession of real property plus all other matters of probate, marriage, and divorce. These matters were formerly heard largely by the territorial probate courts. Additional cases heard by the superior court as specified in the constitution are: all cases of equity; any suit involving the legality of a tax or assessment; actions of forcible entry and detainer; proceedings in insolvency; actions to prevent or abate a nuisance; naturalization proceedings; and all other cases not put under the jurisdiction of some other court by the constitution.

In large counties where the legislature allows more than one superior court judge, the judges ordinarily divide the court into various departments, such as civil, criminal, probate, and juvenile. Then a judge may specialize in the type of case for which his experience or preference fits him. In the counties where there is only one superior court judge, however, he has to try all of these kinds of cases.[12]

12. The number of superior court judges now designated by the legislature for the various counties is: King, 26; Spokane, 7; Pierce, 10; Benton and Franklin, jointly, 3; Clallam and Snohomish, 7; Asotin, Columbia, and Garfield, 1; Cowlitz, 2; Klickitat and Skamania, 1; Douglas and Grant, 2; Ferry and Okanogan, 1; Mason and Thurston, 3; Pacific and Wahkiakum, 1; Clark, 4; Pend Oreille and Stevens, 1; Whatcom, 2; Kitsap, 3. Others have one each.

Court Commissioners

The state constitution also provided for the creation of the office of court commissioner within the framework of the county superior court. Court commissioners take care of routine duties for the superior court judge, and, because these sometimes consist in conducting hearings, the commissioner is said to hold *commissioner's court.* Such hearings are mainly concerned with petitions for adoption of children, for dissolving a corporation, or for changing a person's name. The court commissioner may also hold hearings to determine whether or not a person is insane and should be committed to a mental institution, hearings to settle foreclosure proceedings, and other matters of this type.

The superior court judge appoints the court commissioner, whose term of office is at the pleasure of the judge. The court commissioner is paid from the fees he reeives for the papers he issues and services rendered. In larger counties where the volume of business warrants it, the board of county commissioners may authorize a salary for the court commissioner and set the amount. The county commissioners in a justice court district (justice of the peace) may also authorize the appointment of court commissioners for the district court.

When a court hears a case for the first time, that court is said to have *original jurisdiction* on the case, and the superior court has original jurisdiction in the types of cases mentioned above. In this country, every litigant who loses his case, unless it is extremely trivial, has the right to appeal to a higher court. The court which hears cases on appeal is said to have *appellate* jurisdiction. We noted in the chapters on the executive and administrative branches that anyone has the right to appeal to the superior court if he thinks the decision of the head of a department has been unfair in his case. In addition, the superior court has appellate jurisdiction over cases appealed from courts of justices of the peace and city police courts.

Court of Appeals

Until 1969 any case appealed from the superior court had to go to the state cupreme court, the next higher court. However, in that year the legislature created the court of appeals to act as an intermediary appellate court between the superior and the supreme courts.

It has exclusive appellate jurisdiction in most cases appealed from the superior courts—that is, the appeal has to be made from the superior court to the court of appeals rather than directly to the supreme court. However, there are certain exceptions where the state supreme court may still accept an appeal directly from the superior court. Examples are questions of the right of a state official to perform a particular act, a case of "quo warranto," "by what right?"; or prohibition, a refusal to allow a state official to do a particular thing; or a writ of mandamus, commanding a state official to perform some required act. Additional types of cases that may be appealed directly to the supreme court are ones involving the death penalty or cases of such fundamental and urgent issues of broad public import that they require a prompt and ultimate determination. Certain other questions of violation of the state or federal constitution may go directly to the supreme court. In each case, the state supreme court is the agency that decides if the appeal from the superior court must go to the court of appeals or to the supreme court directly. The side that loses a case in the court of appeals may always ask the state supreme court to review the case, but unless the court of appeals overrules a decision of the superior court by less than a unanimous decision, the state supreme court may refuse to consider an appeal from the court of appeals.

The court of appeals has three divisions: one in Seattle, on in Spokane, and one in Tacoma.[13] The chief judge assigns the judges to panels of three, and the judges of the division may sit in other divisions. The court may hold its sessions in Seattle, Everett, Bellingham, Tacoma, Vancouver, Spokane, Yakima, Richland, or Walla Walla, as it may choose.

State Supreme Court

As has been indicated in the preceding paragraphs, if a party to a case wishes to appeal his suit from a superior court to a higher court, he must take it either to the court of appeals or to the state supreme court. The only type of case that may not be appealed from the superior court is a civil case involving less than $200, and even this kind may be heard if the lawsuit involves the legality of a tax or the constitutionality of a state law. The duty of the state supreme court is to decide whether or not the superior court and the court of appeals made a just decision upon the evidence presented to these lower courts.

PROTECTION FOR DEFENDANTS IN COURT CASES

Both the supreme court justices and the superior court judges have original

13. In division 1, there are six judges from three districts: district 1, King County with four judges; district 2 Snohomish County with one judge; district 3, Island, San Juan, Skagit, and Whatcom counties with one judge. In division 2, there are three judges: one from district 1, Pierce County; one from district 2, Clallam, Grays Harbor, Jefferson, Kitsap, Mason, and Thurston counties; one from district 3, Clark, Cowlitz, Lewis, Pacific, Skamania, and Wahkiakum counties. In division 3, three judges: one from district 1, Ferry, Lincoln, Okanogan, Pend Oreille, Spokane, and Stevens counties; one

jurisdiction in issuing various writs. One of these is the writ of *habeas corpus,* a term meaning literally, "have the body." The sense of it is that a person accused of a crime must be produced to determine if there is sufficient evidence to hold him for trial. If anyone is arrested and placed in jail, he or his attorney has the right to ask a judge to issue a writ of habeas corpus. The writ is directed to the sheriff or police officer who has charge of the prisoner, and it orders the officer to bring the prisoner before the proper court and show sufficient reason to hold him for trial. If the judge decides that there is enough evidence against the prisoner to warrant a trial, he may still be held in custody if the offense is one too serious for bail to be granted.

Writs of habeas corpus may also be requested under other circumstances. Sometimes after a person is convicted of a crime by a court, he or his lawyer will ask for a writ of habeas corpus to test the legality of his imprisonment. It is sometimes used to ascertain if an inmate of an insane asylum or other type of custodial institution is being held illegally. It can be requested even against a private citizen if he appears to be holding another person against his will. However, its most common use is to force a preliminary hearing so that the person arrested may know the charge against him and so that the machinery for a trial may be set in motion if the evidence warrants such action.

The writ of habeas corpus is regarded as our greatest safeguard of personal freedom. In a dictatorship (Communist, Fascist, or other kind), it is the first protection to be eliminated. An individual may then be thrown into prison and held there without knowing what the charges are and without any means of demanding a trial in an attempt to prove his innocence. In Article IV, Section 13, our state constitution says, "The privilege of the writ of habeas corpus shall not be suspended, unless in case of rebellion or invasion the public safety requires it." As we saw in an earlier chapter, the governor is the one who decides if conditions have reached such a pass, in which case he can declare martial law. Military courts then replace our civil courts, and, while the latter are inoperative, the use of writs of habeas corpus is suspended.

Our state bill of rights (Article I of the constitution) contains other protections for anyone involved in a criminal or civil lawsuit. For example, he is guaranteed a jury trial in a criminal case, and a person may have a jury trial in a civil case, too, if he wants one. The only modifications are that in a civil case, nine jurors may bring in a verdict, and, in courts of justices of the peace and municipal courts, as we saw earlier, the legislature may allow such courts to set a jury of fewer than twelve persons.

In a criminal prosecution, the accused has the right to reasonable bail, and to an open and speedy trial where he can defend himself, have counsel, and

---

from district 2, Adams, Asotin, Benton, Columbia, Franklin, Garfield, Grant, Walla Walla, and Whitman counties; one from district 3, Chelan, Douglas, Kittitas, Klickitat, and Yakima counties.

meet the witnesses face to face. He cannot be forced to testify against himself or be tried twice for the same offense. If convicted, he cannot be subjected to any punishment except the customary ones prescribed by law. His children cannot be included in a conviction nor his property forfeited to the state, except as it might be seized to pay fines or costs of some kind. No one can be imprisoned for debt unless he is trying to escape.

COURTS OF RECORD

The state supreme court, the court of appeals, and the superior courts are called *courts of record.* Such courts are required to keep accurate minutes of the proceedings in connection with all cases heart by them. When such minutes are attested by the seal of the court, they are then automatically accepted by a higher court in reviewing a case. The decisions in cases in courts of record may also be cited as precedents by judges trying similar cases later. The 1971 legislature specified that each panel of the court of appeals shall decide which of its decisions have enough precedential value to be published opinions of the court. The others are not so considered.

Inferior courts are courts not of record. In our state, they are courts of justices of the peace, including district courts, police courts, and municipal courts. Although they have to keep a docket of their cases, the reports do not have the judicial weight of superior court records, and the justices' decisions do not set a precedent at law.

JUDGES OF SUPREME, APPELLATE, AND SUPERIOR COURTS

When the state constitution was written in 1889, the convention delegates felt that five supreme court judges were sufficient. They gave the state legislature the power to increase the number, however, and there are now nine judges for our state supreme court. The 1971 legislature changed their title from "judge" to "justice." Their term of office is six years, and three are elected at each general election (every two years), so that the entire group never changes at once. If there is a vacancy in the supreme court between elections, the governor appoints someone to act as justice until the next election. The salary of the supreme court justices in 1972 was $27,500 per year. The legislature, as we have seen, set the number of judges of the court of appeals at twelve. They are elected for a term of six years on a staggered basis, and their salary is $25,000 annually. The governor fills vacancies that may occur between elections, as he does also for those of superior court judges, of whom there are now 83. Their term of office is four years, and their salary $22,500 per year.

Justices of the supreme court and judges of the court of appeals and the superior courts cannot serve unless they are entitled to practice law in this state. In addition, the legislature requires that a candidate for the office of judge of the court of appeals must have been admitted to practice law in the state of Washington for not less than five years and have been a resident of his judicial district for not less than one year. All judges and justices run for office on a nonpartisan basis and are not allowed to declare their party affiliation.

Like other state officials, judges of the superior courts, court of appeals, and supreme court take an oath of office, which is filed with the secretary of state. In the oath, a judge swears to support the Constitution of the United States and the constitution of the state of Washington, and to discharge his duties faithfully and impartially to the best of his ability. While a person is serving a term as judge or justice, he may not practice law.

MEANS OF REMOVAL OF COURT OFFICIALS

If a judge of a court of record is not living up to the above requirements, the constitution provides for two different means of removing him: impeachment and legislative removal.

Impeachment

Impeachment is used only for "high crimes or misdemeanors or malfeasance in office," according to Article V, Section 1 of the state constitution, and it may be used against any elective state official including judges of courts of record. The question of starting impeachment proceedings has to be introduced in the house of representatives, and, if a constitutional majority votes in favor of impeachment, the senate then holds an impeachment trial. The senate considers the accusations and defense; a two-thirds majority vote of the elected senators is required to convict the accused. A conviction in an impeachment trial removes the judge from office and prevents him from ever again holding any office of "honor, trust or profit" in the state. It does not carry any criminal sentence, since only the courts may convict an individual of a crime; but, whether he is acquitted or convicted by the senate, he may still be tried for the alleged offense in our regular courts.

Legislative Removal

A judge may be honest and well trained, but be giving poor service because of ill health, insanity, or incompetency. Since impeachment would indicate willful wrongdoing, it would not be applicable, and, even if it were, it would involve personal disgrace, which would be unfair to a well-meaning judge. Consequently, the constitution provides that the legislature may remove a judge of any court of record, the attorney general, or any prosecuting attorney by a joint resolution of three-fourths of the senators and representatives elected. The causes for such removal are "incompetency, corruption, malfeasance, or delinquency in office, or other sufficient cause," as stated in Article IV, Section 9 of the constitution. Before any of these court officials may be removed in this manner, he must be presented with a copy of the charges against him and be given an opportunity to defend himself if he so desires.

Removal of Justices of the Peace by Recall

Since courts of justices of the peace are not courts of record, the justices or district judges are not included among the judges who may be removed by impeachment or legislative removal. Justices of the peace may be removed by a third means of getting officials out of office, however, which involves a popular vote of the people. This system is named the *recall.* [14]

Recall applies to any elected public official except judges of the superior, appellate, and supreme courts. These judges are not included in the recall, because they must be free to make unpopular decisions. Many times a trial will catch the attention of the entire state, or even of the whole United States, and people will become very much excited about it. Even if it is a criminal trial decided by a jury, the judge may influence the outcome in sustaining or overruling objections and in giving instructions to the jury. After such a trial, it might be possible for the people to be so angry at the judge that they could secure enough names on a recall petition to bring the matter to a vote and remove him. To subject judges to such pressures would be unfortunate. Therefore, once the people have elected a judge, they cannot put him out of office until his term expires.

COUNTY COURT OFFICIALS

The superior courts themselves, which are county courts, as well as the courts of the justices of the peace, which are either rural or city courts, are considered part of the state court system. And, since a superior court plus several courts of justices of the peace exists in each county, many county officials are connected with them—county clerk, prosecuting attorney, sheriff, coroner, and probation officer for the superior court, and constables for courts of justices of the peace.

14. Recall procedures will be discussed in chapter 6.

County Clerk

The county clerk acts as secretary for the superior court. We have mentioned that accurate minutes have to be recorded for the proceedings in all court sessions. The clerk is responsible for these, although he does not ordinarily take down the shorthand notes himself. He supervises the court reporters who are hired for this purpose. Once the records are made, it is the duty of the clerk to preserve them carefully. Each court of record has a seal, used to stamp court documents to indicate that they are official, and the clerk is the custodian of the court seal for his county.

The judge of the superior court has the authority to order persons to appear in court, to make decisions in various cases, and to authorize the issuance of many kinds of court papers. The clerk prepares these under his direction and keeps a record of each one. For example, when anyone wishes to bring a civil suit against another person, the clerk issues the papers notifying the defendant to appear in court. Probating estates involves various kinds of affidavits, papers for transfer of property, appointment of administrators, and many other legal forms. Any type of official paper used in any part of the court's work is the responsibility of the clerk, but, since the decisions of a court affect not only the property but also the personal liberty of an individual, the records have to be maintained with the utmost accuracy. The clerk also makes up the list of cases to be heard, called the *court calendar.*

Another of the county clerk's responsibilities is to prepare lists of persons to serve on juries. First, the superior court judges of a county divide it into not fewer than three jury districts, with nearly equal population. Then each city clerk or comptroller who acts as the local registrar of voters sends to the county auditor an annual list of eligible voters. The county auditor adds to these the names for the county seat and rural areas, and places the names from this total list into sections for the various jury districts.

During each July, the superior court judges choose at random names from these jury district lists and certify them to the county clerk as the master list of prospective jurors. Before each session of the superior court, the judges then choose by lot certain precincts within a jury district and take names from them in as nearly equal numbers as possible. This list is called the *venire,* and from it jurors for the cases heard during that session of court are picked. The county clerk or a deputy is blindfolded and draws at random slips containing the names. He always chooses more than the probable number required because some will be unable to serve because of illness or other acceptable cause; the attorneys will challenge some of those who do agree to serve for a particular case; and thus additional people will have to be called. Each person who does serve as juror in a superior court case receives $10.00

per day plus ten cents a mile for distance traveled to and from court. His compensation is paid by the county.

The clerk is required to keep certain records in addition to those for the court, such as a record of the oaths of office and official bonds given by all of the county officials except himself. The county auditor receives the ones for the clerk. The clerk was formerly the only official required to keep a record of marriage certificates, but now the legislature obliges the county auditor to maintain a record, along with the marriage licenses he issues. For details of term of office and other data regarding county officials connected with the court, see chapter 7.

Prosecuting Attorney

The prosecuting attorney acts as an attorney for the county. If any lawsuits are brought against his county or any school district in his county, he defends the county or district in court. If the other county officials need advice on legal matters in connection with their own work, the prosecuting attorney is required to give them his opinion on their questions.

The procedure for bringing criminal charges against an individual is different in our state from that in many states. The older system was that an indictment for a serious criminal offense was brought by a grand jury, which met to consider the evidence against a suspect. However, in this state, a grand jury can be called only at the request of a superior court judge, and it has come to be considered necessary only if there are charges of corruption on the part of public officials or some other condition of general lawlessness.

In this state, when a criminal charge is brought against an individual, the prosecuting attorney examines the evidence. If he thinks a prosecution is warranted, he makes out a statement to that effect, called an *information*. This, in turn, is examined by the superior court judge, who may either refuse to approve it, or may order the clerk to issue a warrant for the arrest of the alleged criminal. After the arrest, the suspect may be released on bail (unless the offense is too serious) until the date set for trial. If the prosecuting attorney later thinks that a criminal prosecution should be dropped, he files a statement to that effect, called a *nolle prosequi*. The judge may override this request, or he may issue a nolle prosequi order himself.

The prosecuting attorney's investigations of evidence sometimes extend beyond crimes committed in his county. For example, when the governor of another state requests our governor to deliver a fugitive who has taken refuge in some county in this state, in most instances the prosecuting attorney of that particular county investigates the case. As we have seen, he then recommends to the governor the action which he thinks should be taken in such interstate rendition cases.

The prosecuting attorney appears in court on behalf of minors and insane or incompetent persons when there are charges against them. He is required to appear in any divorce action in which either husband or wife contests the divorce. He has certain miscellaneous duties, in addition, not a direct part of court hearings. The costs for court action are paid by the county in certain types of cases where the county or state is the plaintiff and loses the suit. The list of expenses is called a *cost bill,* and the prosecuting attorney has to certify to its correctness. He also approves the bonds given by county officials, and he may examine the record of other county officials if there are grounds for suspecting mismanagement or incompetence. We have seen that the governor may ask the prosecuting attorney to investigate any alleged violation of a law.

The prosecuting attorney, like the other county officials, must be a qualified voter of his county. In addition, he must be an attorney, qualified to practice law in this state. If his office becomes vacant between elections, the county commissioners appoint another qualified person to take his place. If he is ill temporarily, the superior court judge may appoint a prosecuting attorney for the time being.

It was pointed out above that legislative removal extends to the attorney general and any other prosecuting attorney as well as to judges of the superior, appellate, and supreme courts. Thus, the legislature may remove a prosecuting attorney from office by a special vote on evidence of incompetence or corruption. Since he is not regarded as a state official, in this sense, however, the legislature cannot impeach him. If the prosecuting attorney is so unpopular with the voters that they wish to have him removed from office, they may do so by the method of recall.

Sheriff

The sheriff is the officer who delivers the papers made out by the clerk. Some of these are warrants of arrest issued on order of the superior court judge or orders to appear in court as a witness or as the defendant in a civil law suit. Such orders are called *subpoenas.* When the court orders property seized for delinquent taxes, the sheriff delivers an order of judgment and sells the property in question if it is real estate. People who hold mortgages or liens on another's property may appeal to the court to foreclose them if they are not redeemed within a certain length of time. The sheriff also serves various foreclosure notices, such as notices of attachment or notices of judgment.

The sheriff is the custodian of any person convicted of a crime by the superior court. He must hold them prisoner in the county jail, if that is the sentence imposed. If the crime is more serious, he must transport the prisoner to the state penitentiary or any other reforming institution to which he has been sentenced. Like all police officers, the sheriff may arrest anyone caught in the act of committing a crime.

If the sheriff's office becomes vacant less than six months before a general election, the county commissioners appoint someone to fill the office for that length of time. If the office becomes vacant earlier than six months before an election, a special election is held to choose another sheriff. If the sheriff is temporarily unable to perform his duties, the coroner acts as sheriff unless the superior court judge wants to appoint someone else for the time being.

Coroner

The coroner's business is to investigate deaths occurring under suspicious circumstances. If a person is found dead and there is any evidence that someone else caused his death, the coroner calls a jury of six persons, four of whom must be present. The coroner may call witnesses, doctors, and other persons who might help in discovering the cause of death. If the jury decides that the deceased was murdered, the testimony is written down and filed with the county clerk. If the jury believes that it knows who the murderer is, the coroner may draw up a warrant for his arrest.

If the body of the dead person is not claimed, the coroner arranges for its burial. Any possessions found on the body are turned over to the legal representative of the deceased, if one appears. If not, the coroner gives the property to the county treasurer and certifies to the county commissioners that he has done so. In counties of more than 250,000, the county commissioners may establish a morgue, and, in that case, the coroner is in charge of it.

If the coroner's office becomes vacant between elections, the county commissioners appoint someone to take his place. In case he is temporarily absent, a justice of the peace may act as a coroner. If the coroner is a lawyer, he is not allowed to practice law while he is serving as coroner. In the smaller counties, Classes IV-IX, a coroner is not elected, but the prosecuting attorney acts as the coroner. Coroners are no longer paid from fees which they collect; they are salaried.

Constable

The justices of the peace need someone to deliver their orders, and the officer who does this is the constable. He does the same type of work for the court of justice of the peace as the sheriff does for the superior court. He has other powers similar to those of a sheriff, such as seizing property when such a judgment is issued by the justice court, ordering a group of more than two people to disperse if they are threatening the peace of the community, and arresting them if they persist.

The legislature allows a justice of the peace to ask the county sheriff to serve a process for him, and justices who are city police judges use the city police. Consequently, the county commissioners may abolish the office of constable if they wish. This practice is due to the fact that in rural areas and in cities of less than 5,000, the constables are still paid from fees that they collect. In larger cities, they receive a salary. For example, in cities ranging between 5,000 and 35,000 population, the constable receives a salary of $720 plus travel expenses. If he is paid by a salary, he cannot retain any fees received, and, as we have seen, this practice is regarded by political scientists as much preferable to a system of payment by fee.

Probation Officers

In counties of over 30,000 population, the superior court judge may appoint one or more probation officers who may be either temporary or permanent. If they are permanent, the county commissioners must approve their appointment. Their term of office is fixed by the court, and the amount of their salary is set by the county commissioners.

These probation officers have the power to arrest anyone violating a law in regard to the care or control of children. When any charges are brought against minors, the court orders the probation officer to investigate the circumstances, and he represents the child at a hearing if there is any question as to his being delinquent. The probation officer is also responsible to the court for the care of the child before and after the trial as directed by the court. The probation officer makes a report to the court of each case investigated by him. These reports are kept until the minor is twenty-one years of age, and then the papers are destroyed. No one is allowed to examine such records except those having a legitimate interest in the case.

Public Defender

The 1969 legislature created the office of public defender to represent accused persons who do not have enough money to hire an attorney. The action came as a result of growing public feeling that since we use public funds to pay a prosecuting attorney to represent the state against an accused person, we should also make some similar provision to enable indigent people to have legal aid in defending themselves.

A single board of county commissioners or the joint boards for two or more contiguous counties may hire a public defender, and the area included is called a "public defender district," whether it is one or more counties. If the governing body of cities within the district wish to join in hiring the defender, he may also serve in the county and municipal courts. He is required to represent without charge any indigent person charged with a crime unless that person in open court rejects his right to be represented by counsel.

The public defender is chosen by a committee consisting of one member of each board of county commissioners, one member of the superior court from each county, and one practicing attorney from each county. The defender must be a qualified attorney licensed to practice in Washington, and his term coincides with that of the prosecuting attorney.

JUDICIAL COUNCIL

As is true of the other branches of our state government, serious problems exist in regard to the organization and functioning of our court system. One of these is the delay in hearing cases. If there is more business than the present number of judges can transact, it may be so long before a case is heard that conditions have changed to the advantage or disadvantage of one of the parties.

The question as to how we should choose our judges is also a difficult one. It is extremely important to have judges who are not only well trained in the law, but who are also qualified by character and temperament for such a task. Under our present system, any resident attorney who is a qualified voter may run for the office. There is no sifting process to try to choose the best possible candidates. Moreover, the fact that a judge has to campaign for office every four or six years (depending on whether he is a supreme or appellate court judge or a judge of a county superior court) means that he has to give some thought to being popular enough for re-election. Such a consideration could conceivably color his attitude in a given court case. Judges in our federal courts are appointed by the President for life and cannot be removed except by impeachment. They are thus as free as possible from pressures from any group. Since the American tradition has been to try to divorce the courts from political influence, objections are immediately raised to having a governor appoint state judges. In New Jersey and Delaware, the state judges are appointed by the governor with the consent of the senate, but in the ten other states where the judges are appointive either the legislature chooses them or the governor does so with the approval of some kind of advisory judicial group. If the average caliber of judges is to be raised, not only is some care in choosing them necessary, but salaries must be high enough to attract superior talent. This problem was mentioned in connection with executive and administrative officials, also.

In a number of states, the legislature has created councils to offer advice on judicial problems, and, although they cannot settle many of the questions

raised, they are of great help in attacking some of them. Washington has been
in the forefront of this movement, having established a judicial council in
1925, two years after the first current one was adopted by Ohio. Our judicial
council has twenty-two members, including judges, attorneys, state legislators, and law school deans.[15]

Court Administrator

One of the recommendations of the judicial council adopted by the 1957
legislature was the creation of the office of court administrator, who is
appointed by the state supreme court from a list of five persons submitted by
the governor. The administrator must be a resident of the state and be under
sixty years of age. His term of office is at the pleasure of the court.

The administrator's duties are to examine the administrative procedures of
the offices of judges and court employees in the state and to make
recommendations through the chief justice to improve them; to scan the
dockets of the superior courts to find out which ones need assistance and
then recommend the transfer of judges to ease the load in such courts; and to
make other studies of the status of the work of the courts in our state.

SUGGESTED READINGS

Original sources for study of our court system are the *Session Laws,* state
constitution, *Supreme Court Reports,* and codes listed in preceding chapters on
government. Secondary sources available in most libraries are *County Government in
Washington State,* ed. Barbara Byers (Olympia: Washington State Association of County
Commissioners, 1957), and Caleb Reinhart's *History of the Supreme Court of the
Territory and State of Washington.* It is also helpful to receive the biennial reports of the
judicial council. Address the Executive Secretary, Judicial Council, Condon Hall,
University of Washington, Seattle, Washington 98105.

15. The judicial council consists of the chief justice of the supreme court and one
other supreme court justice appointed by the chief justice; two judges of the court of
appeals appointed by the three chief judges of the three divisions of the appellate court;
two judges of superior courts appointed by the Superior Court Judges' Association; three
state senators, no more than two of whom are of the same political party, one of whom
is the chairman of the senate judiciary committee and the other two designated by the
chairman; three state representatives chosen in the same manner by the chairman of the
house judiciary committee unless the committee is organized in two sections, in which
case the chirman of each section shall be a member and they designate the third; the
dean of each recognized school of law in the state; five members of the bar, one of
whom is a prosecuting attorney, three of whom are appointed by the chief justice of the
supreme court with the advice and consent of the other justices of the court; two
appointed by the board of governors of the Washington State Bar Association from a list
of nominees submitted by its legislative committee; the attorney general; and two judges
from courts of limited jurisdiction chosen by the Washington State Magistrates'
Association.

6. *Electorate and Citizenry*

INDIVIDUAL RIGHTS

The makers of the state constitution did their best to see that the people of the state of Washington could always have control of their local and state governments. The constitution begins by emphasizing that it is setting up a government of the people. The preamble reads, "We, the People of the State of Washington, Grateful to the Supreme Ruler of the Universe for our Liberties, Do Ordain this Constitution." Section 1 of Article I continues: "All political power is inherent in the people, and governments derive their just powers from the consent of the governed and are established to protect and maintain individual rights."

Many of these individual rights are mentioned in Article I of the constitution, our state bill of rights. The framers of the constitution realized, however, that no group could think of all the needs of individuals which might arise at some time; consequently, they included a statement that the mention of certain rights did not mean that others unmentioned were to be denied.

The ones specifically included are the familiar ones now taken for granted, many of them repetitions of clauses from the Bill of Rights in the United States Constitution. We have grown up accepting them so completely that we do not think about them until we are in a crisis, such as a state of war, and realize how miserable we would be without them; or when, as at the present, we are in a period of social questioning and are asking ourselves if we consider that these rights really do apply to minority groups or others disadvantaged in some way as well as to the economically and socially advantaged.

The state constitution makes the general assertion that "No person shall be deprived of life, liberty or property, without due process of law." In recent cases brought to the United States Supreme Court, it has ruled that in the states having laws allowing capital punishment, the provisions violate the "equal protection" clause of the Fourteenth Amendment, inasmuch as some persons committing a crime calling for the death sentence are executed and some are not. Therefore, at the present time the legislatures of some states, including our own, are debating the question of capital punishment—whether or not it is a necessary deterrent to crime. One suggestion is that if the legislature passes a law specifying capital punishment for some of the most serious crimes, it make the death penalty mandatory for everybody convicted of such a crime. If states pass such a law, or some other version attempting to answer the objections of the United States Supreme Court, each type will undoubtedly be taken again to the Supreme Court to see if it is considered to meet the requirements of the United States Constitution.

One of the most important safeguards for personal dignity and freedom is that no one is allowed to force his way into another's home unless he is specifically authorized to do so by a court. We have freedom of religious worship, and no one can be molested because of his religion. This does not mean, though, that a person, because of his religious beliefs, may do things to harm the peace and safety of the state.

Freedom of speech and writing is also guaranteed. The constitution states that "every person may freely speak, write and publish on all subjects, being responsible for the abuse of that right." This means, for one thing, that if a person publishes lies about another individual he may be prosecuted for slander or libel. For another, in order to guarantee freedom of speech in discussing political questions, the constitution defines treason carefully. "Treason against the state shall consist only in levying war against the state, or adhering to its enemies, or in giving them aid and comfort." The purpose of such a narrow definition is to assure that prosecution for an offense be on the basis of law and not of political prejudice.

Subject to certain limitations, such as a permit system, any individual may carry a gun or other weapon, if he chooses, and he may use it to defend himself or the state. The constitution goes on to say, however, that this permission does not authorize individuals or corporations to employ an armed body of men.

Another right assured to individuals in this state is that of education. The constitution acknowledges that it is the duty of the state to educate all resident children. The legislature is given the right to establish and maintain a school system from elementary schools through colleges. In the section on the state superintendent of public instruction in chapter 2, we discussed the duties of the state Department of Education and the State Board of Education, and in the following chapter we shall consider the county school organization.

A person's property may be taken by the state under certain conditions.

Fines and foreclosures for delinquent taxes have been mentioned. In addition, the state and federal governments may take property if it is needed for public use, making adequate compensation for it. The right to take property for such a purpose is called the *right of eminent domain.*

An example of its use was the condemnation of property behind Grand Coulee Dam. Residents there had to give up their homes because of the lake formed by the dam. People whose property is taken for purposes of this kind have certain protections in the state constitution. They must be paid for the land, and the courts must decide what is a fair price. The legislature is not allowed to take private land for public use if the courts deny that the proposed construction is really for the public good. The only exception consists of land taken by the state for land reclamation and settlement. The constitution states that this is to be automatically considered in the public interest.

One individual or corporation may use the land belonging to another under certain conditions. An irrigation ditch, for example, may be laid across one person's land in order to reach the fields of the individual who is going to use the water. In such cases, the constitution provides that a person may not secure a right of way across another's land until the owner has been paid for the use of the land in question. The court procedure in such instances is similar to that outlined above. There are many other kinds of rights of way, also, some of which we have discussed—such as that for corporations to lay railroad tracks and telegraph and telephone lines across private property or along a public highway. In cases of this kind, a corporation is treated as an individual.

VOTING PROCEDURE

These are some of the basic rights and privileges guaranteed to us by our state constitution, but the privilege which is fundamental to all of these is the right to vote. By voting in our various elections, we not only choose the people who make and enforce our laws, but, in this state, we pass or veto some laws ourselves. In 'fact, voters perform so many governmental functions that they are now regarded by many as a branch of our government, called the *electorate,* along with the executive, legislative, judicial, and administrative branches.

Qualifications for Voting

Recent decisions of the United States Supreme Court in regard to age and residence requirements for eligibility to vote in state elections have made some of the specifications in our state constitution and laws on these subjects unconstitutional, and they are therefore now in the process of being changed to conform to the ruling of the court.

It was mentioned in connection with reapportionment of legislative districts that, until the 1960s, the federal courts refused to consider most aspects of qualifications for voting required by states, either for national or state elections. Such standards were regarded as "political" questions—ones for Congress or the state legislatures to determine, not ones for judicial determination. Age for voting eligibility was one of these questions. Because, traditionally, twenty-one was accepted in this country as the age at which an individual reached maturity, it was the figure ordinarily set in state constitutions as the time when he became old enough to vote. This was true of Washington's state constitution. However, after World War I and, increasingly, after World War II, the argument was advanced that if a man was old enough at eighteen to be drafted into the armed forces, he should also be considered old enough to vote. The fact that television and other mass media of communications had made younger people aware of the issues of state and national political campaigns was also a factor in the demand for an earlier voting eligibility age. Consequently, Congress passed a law specifying that anybody who had reached the age of eighteen was to be allowed to vote in all elections in a state. The law was contested, and the United States Supreme Court ruled that the law was unconstitutional in regard to candidates for local and state offices, but that the Fourteenth Amendment to the United States Constitution gave Congress the right to pass such legislation as far as candidates for the offices of President and Vice President of the United States were concerned.

Congress then proposed to the states a constitutional amendment reducing the required age for voting in all elections to eighteen, and the necessary number of states (thirty-eight) ratified the amendment. Consequently, in the state of Washington eighteen-year-olds voted for local and state officials as well as national ones in the 1972 election.

The matter of woman suffrage has also been one on which individual states were free to make their own decision until the Nineteenth Amendment to the United States Constitution provided that women throughout the United States could not be prohibited from voting by any state on the basis of their sex. This was ratified throughout the country in time for the 1920 election.

The state of Washington, however, was in advance of most of the states in this respect. In fact, we have mentioned earlier that women voted in Washington Territory from 1833 to 1887, when woman suffrage was declared unconstitutional by the territorial supreme court. There are instances recorded of individual women attempting to vote, assuming as a matter of course that they were entitled to do so even before 1883. The delegates to the state constitutional convention in 1889 could not agree on the questions of woman suffrage and prohibition of the sale of alcoholic beverages, and so these issues were submitted to the voters as separate points. Both were defeated, but in 1909 the voters ratified an amendment to the state constitution providing for woman suffrage.

Another recent decision by the United States Supreme Court has made uniform the residence requirements for voting throughout the country and has changed the length of time a person must live in this state to be eligible to vote. The state constitution stipulates one year's residence in the state, ninety days in the county, and thirty days in the city ward or precinct where an individual wishes to vote. In 1966 a state constitutional amendment was adopted by which new residents may vote for president and vice president of the United States after a residence of sixty days, but not for state and local officials. In 1970 three couples in Seattle challenged the one-year residency requirement as unconstitutional on the grounds that it denies equal protection of the laws, the right to travel freely, and the right to sign initiative petitions. The King County Superior Court upheld this contention, and the case was appealed to the state supreme court. However, in the meantime, a case arose in Tennessee on the same issue, and it was appealed to the United States Supreme Court, which ruled that the year's residence requirement in the state was unconstitutional and the ninety-day county stipulation as well. Justice Thurgood Marshall, who wrote the opinion, said, "Thirty days appears to be an ample period of time for the state to complete whatever administrative tasks are necessary to prevent fraud."

Another requirement made in the state constitution was that a voter must be able to read and speak the English language, but the United States Supreme Court has struck out this demand, also.

Certain groups of people are not allowed to vote even though they may fulfill the above requirements. These are: insane persons; idiots; and criminals whose civil rights have not yet been restored. When the constitution was written, Indians who do not pay taxes were also made ineligible to vote. However, rulings of the attorney general in this state emphasized in 1901 that only Indians on reservations where the land is not subject to state taxation might not vote. Then in 1935 the attorney general ruled that even Indians on such reservations pay some kind of tax, such as a personal property tax on automobiles, state tax on gasoline, and sales taxes on food and merchandise. Finally, a similar clause in regard to Indians was declared unconstitutional by the United States Supreme Court in cases from New Mexico and Arizona, where there were the same restrictions. The Court based its ruling on the fact that Congress made Indians American citizens in 1924. Therefore, at the present time, any Indian in this state must be allowed to vote if he fulfills the other requirements, even though the restriction remains in our state constitution. The term *tax* as used in the constitution, however, refers to real and personal property taxes. Therefore, in the interests of consistency and racial equality, many people would like to see the clause removed from our state constitution by amendment.

Permanent Registration System

In order to tell whether or not a person meets these requirements, the constitution specifies that the legislature must set up a system of registration for towns and cities of over 500 population. Those who are properly registered are then permitted to vote. The legislature has included all voters in a permanent registration system, with the county auditor as registrar of voters in any election precinct outside an incorporated town. The clerk or comptroller of an incorporated town or city is its registrar. Deputy registrars may be appointed in libraries or other public offices, and volunteer registrars may be deputized at various times to make certain that everyone may register at convenient places.

The registration books are closed thirty days before election day for change of registration from one county to another, but remain open for an additional fifteen days for transfer of registration from one precinct to another within the county. For the latter type of transfer, the voter may send a signed request to the county auditor or go in person, but a change of address from one county to another requires a new registration. The voter must also sign an authorization for canceling the former registration. If a voter fails to vote for thirty months, he must register anew, as must a woman who changes her name by getting married or any person who has his name changed by law.

Each person registering takes an oath that he will answer truthfully the questions asked him concerning his qualifications for voting. If the registration official is satisfied that the applicant is a United States citizen, has lived in the area the prescribed length of time, and does not come in any of the groups who are not allowed to vote, he asks the registrant to sign his name on two registration forms in a rural precinct and on three in a city precinct. For city voters, one card is kept by the city clerk, one goes to the county auditor, and the third is sent to the secretary of state, who uses his cards to check the signatures on petitions for initiative and referendum measures.

Any precinct officer, committeeman, precinct election officer, or registration officer may challenge the registration of another person on the grounds that he does not actually live at the address claimed. The challenger is subject to perjury penalty if he knowingly makes a false charge. He must make his objections in writing between 1 January and 30 June of each year and file his statement with the county auditor, who notifies the person challenged. He may admit the charge and register correctly, or he may deny it. In the latter case, the county auditor calls the two persons together for a hearing and makes a decision. If a voter's right to vote is challenged by another voter at the polls, he is allowed to vote and the ballot is placed in a sealed envelope until the canvassing board can consider the case and make a decision.

As we saw earlier, the county auditor makes a copy of the list of registered voters within the county from which the superior court judges choose the names of persons to be called for jury duty. In addition, in first-class cities the local registrar of vital statistics[1] sends a monthly report of deaths to the county auditor. For all of the areas in the state outside first-class cities, the state registrar of vital statistics makes such a report to the county auditor of each county. These lists are used for removing names of deceased persons from the registration records in cities, counties, and the office of the secretary of state.

System for Nominating Candidates

There must be some means of presenting to the voters names of candidates from which they may choose their governmental officials. For our national elections, delegates from each political party meet in a national convention and choose two prominent members of their party to run for the offices of President and Vice President of the United States. For many years, the convention system was also used in this country for selection of candidates for local and state officials, but this has now been largely superseded by a primary election for their nomination. In our state, we have a *direct primary* by which we choose candidates for office at a preliminary popular election. Any qualified elector may run for any office except those that require special training—for example, judge or prosecuting attorney. Persons having the qualifications for these special offices may run for them, too, without having to be approved by a political party. Anyone seeking the nomination for an office makes this known by filing what is called a *declaration of candidacy.* If a person wants to run for a state office or for the positions of senator or representative in Congress, he files his declaration with the secretary of state. Candidates for county offices file their declarations with the county auditor, and city candidates file with the city clerk. Except for the nonpartisan offices, they declare their political party affiliation.

Our particular type of direct primary is called the *blanket primary,* and it is different from the type of primary in all other states. In our system, the names of all candidates for each office are listed in one group with the political party supported by each candidate written by the side of his name.

1. Formerly the city clerk.

Each voter then votes for one person from each group. In that way, he may nominate all Republicans, all Democrats, and so forth, or he may nominate a Democrat for one office and a Republican or a member of some other party for another office. For this reason, our system is sometimes referred to as the *wide-open primary*. Voters may also write in the names of people as candidates who have not run for office, but these votes are nearly always scattered among so many people that a *write-in* candidate is hardly ever nominated.

Originally, people had to declare their party affiliation and vote in the primary election only for that party. This type is called a *closed primary*. In many states, a voter does not have to make public to which party he belongs when he goes to vote in a primary election, but, in all except our state, he has to stay within one party in making his nominations. In the ordinary *open* primary, if he should mark some names from one party and some from another, his ballot would be thrown out. We must keep in mind that primary elections are those held to secure nominees for office, not to elect the one person who is actually to hold the office.

Since candidates for city offices run on a nonpartisan ticket in this state, we do not hold city primary elections if not more than two people file declarations of candidacy for each city office. The same arrangement holds for the superintendent of public instruction and officers of first-class school districts except ones having an enrollment of 70,000 or more pupils in Class AA counties. The two names are put directly on the ballot for the general city, school district, and state elections. In the case of justices of the supreme court, judges of the superior court, justices of the peace, directors of first-class school districts, and the state superintendent of public instruction, if one candidate has a majority of all votes cast for the position in the primary, only his name is printed on the general election ballot, with a space for the voter to write in a name, if he wishes.

Our blanket primary system was designed to make the voter as independent as possible of his political party, since he does not have to adhere to its slate even in making nominations. Some people were afraid that such freedom would cause members of one political party to agree to cast a sufficient number of votes for a weak candidate of an opposing party to insure his nomination. Then it would probably be easy to defeat him in the subsequent election. According to studies made on that point, however, there is only one instance where there is any evidence that this happened—in a Seattle mayoralty primary election—and it may not have been the case there. Even if party leaders wanted to organize such a campaign, it would ordinarily be too difficult to control.

Other opponents of the blanket primary contend that it prevents a political party from selecting its candidates. No kind of direct primary system, however, allows party leaders to choose the nominees to represent the party. Direct primaries were instituted to prevent that very thing. Under the usual closed or open primary, any member of a party is free to run for an office for which he is qualified, and, from this group, the entire membership of the party (if everyone votes) makes the selection of the final candidate.

Some form of the convention system seems to be the only means of giving a political party any real control over the selection of its candidates. But that system permits political "bosses" to control the party in many instances, and it is very difficult for the honest, civic-minded members to break their hold because the convention system involves a continuous line of authority from the precinct party elections to the national convention. In the precinct, delegates choose the candidates for local offices and select delegates to attend the county convention. Those delegates in turn select the ones to go to the state convention. At the state convention, delegates for the national convention of the party are chosen. As a result of these procedures, the people who control the selection of delegates at the local level actually have the power to influence the choice of all candidates who run for office under the sponsorship of the political party. It is almost impossible for a member of the party who is in disfavor with the local party leaders to run for office on that party's ticket. On the other hand, as we have seen, in states that have primary elections for the nomination of candidates, any qualified voter may try for nomination for an office under the party of his choice.

It is true that many political scientists think that the trend away from party adherence has gone too far. They argue that much of the strength of the American system of government has come from having two strong, active political parties opposing one another. By taking different stands on public questions, they have given people a chance to crystallize their own thinking and work out at least a partial philosophy of government. Then when one party has put a certain program into effect, the voters have been able to find out what they like and what they do not like about it. These attitudes, in turn, modify the stand taken by both the victorious and the defeated party, and a kind of political evolution thus occurs. If a party adopts a certain platform, however, and then has no way of insuring that the people who run under its name accept these policies, the platform means very little. The only attempt at a safeguard in this respect in our state is a law passed by the 1961 legislature requiring that if a person runs for an office under one political party, he cannot run under another party at the next general election. This, however, does not insure that a candidate will support the platform of his chosen party.

At the present time, local and state political conventions meet to adopt platforms, to plan strategy for election campaigns, and to choose delegates to go to the convention of the next highest unit. The only occasions in this state in which a unit of a political party may name a candidate are the withdrawal of a candidate from an election race or the death or disqualification of a candidate between a primary election and the succeeding general election. For county offices, the county central committee of a party makes the choice; for state offices, the state central committee does so. If a public official dies or is incapacitated for office during his term of office, these committees make nominations for his successor to the proper officials.[2]

Political Party Organization

The organization of each political party begins with a local committeeman for each election precinct. Any member of a party who is a registered voter may run for the office of precinct committeeman by filing a declaration of candidacy with the county auditor by the Friday immediately following the last day for political parties to fill vacancies in the ticket. The names of all candidates for the office of precinct committeeman must appear under the proper party on the ballot for the November election. The one receiving the highest number of votes is declared elected unless he receives less than 10 percent of the number of votes cast for the candidate of his party receiving the greatest number of votes in his precinct. The term of office is two years, beginning at the completion of the official canvass of votes by the county canvassing board of election returns. If there is a vacancy in the office of precinct committeeman, the chairman of the county central committee appoints someone to take his place, except in Class AA counties.

The county central committee of a political party consists of the precinct chairmen within the county, who meet at the county courthouse at 2:00 P.M. the second Saturday in December after each state general election unless the retiring committee gives sufficient notice of a different time and place. At this meeting, the county committee elects a chairman and vice-chairman of opposite sexes, plus a state committeeman and committee woman. These state committeemen and committee women make up the state central committee, which elects its state chairman and vice-chairman of opposite sexes.

When the majority of the precincts in a legislative district are within a Class AA county, the county chairman of each major political party is required to call separate meetings of all elected precinct committeemen to elect a legislative district chairman within forty-five days after a statewide general election. The chairman's term is two years, and he can be removed only by a majority vote of the elected precinct committeemen in his district. If a vacancy occurs in the office of precinct committeeman, the legislative

---

2. For county offices, these are the county commissioners, for the most part, and for state offices, the governor.

district chairman, rather than the county chairman of the particular political party, fills the vacancy.

The state central committee is in charge of arrangements for the state political convention of its party. The state convention elects delegates to the national convention, where presidential nominees are chosen. It also chooses the party delegates to go to the meeting of the Electoral College after a presidential election to cast the official votes by states for President and Vice President of the United States according to the popular vote cast by the voters within their state at the general election.

Some students of government, who would like to strengthen the convention system and retain primaries also, propose that we have candidates for local and state offices from both. They recommend that, at a party convention, the delegates should choose a person as the official party candidate in its unit (county or state) for each office. These candidates would, presumably, support the party's principles and would have the backing of the majority of the party leaders. On the primary ballot, a candidate's name would be marked to indicate that he was the official candidate. In addition, however, any voter would be free, as he is now, to run for any office for which he was qualified and to specify his party. From the names of the official and unofficial candidates, the voter at the primary election would make his choice. If a voter did not approve of the official candidate, he could then still vote for the "man" rather than for the "party." Many people think they would prefer to leave our blanket primary system as it is now, however, for fear that the official nominee would have such an advantage that it would be impossible, under normal circumstances, for an "outsider" to defeat him.

We already have a number of officials who are elected on a nonpartisan basis—state superintendent of public instruction, intermediate school district superintendents, judges of our superior courts and court of appeals, and supreme court justices, city officials, and school directors. It is predicted that, if party adherence is not strengthened, the trend will be toward more and more nonpartisan offices. The question is then, on the state level, at least, what groups would be willing to pay campaign expenses for an individual and how could the beliefs of the candidates be crystallized around meaningful issues.

It is certainly true that, under whatever kind of nominating system we have, if our two-party system is to remain strong and to have the confidence of the public, the ordinary voter will have to stop thinking of politics as corrupt, and he will have to take a more active part in his local party organization. If a sufficient number of public-spirited citizens work hard locally for each party, a larger number of conscientious, able people will be willing to run for all offices.

In this state, new or minor parties are required to hold conventions to nominate their candidates, since they would be at a disadvantage otherwise. Any party which polled less than 10 percent of the total vote cast at the previous general election uses the convention system. After representatives from such a party have met and chosen their candidates, they must file declarations of candidacy with the secretary of state not later than the first Tuesday after the date of the September primaries. The 1955 legislature specified that such a party must have at least 100 registered voters at its convention or ten from each congressional district to be placed on the ballot at the next general election. If a registered voter expects to attend such a convention held at the day of the primary, he may secure an absentee ballot to vote for candidates for nonpartisan offices, but no others.

Election Campaigns

Once the candidates are nominated, each one tries to persuade the voters that he would represent their best choice for the office concerned. With his own money and with that raised on his behalf by his party or by friends, he buys space for advertising in newspapers, time on radio and television programs, and makes as many speeches and personal appearances as he can.

It was stated earlier that it is hard for voters to learn facts about a candidate's training, temperament, and convictions on questions of public policy. In an attempt to get such information to the public, the 1959 legislature authorized the printing of a *Candidates' Pamphlet,* which may be made the second part of the *Voters' Pamphlet* mailed before each general election to each individual place of residence by the secretary of state.[3]

In the *Candidates' Pamphlet,* the candidates themselves write the statements, giving their qualifications for the position and expressing their political views. A fee is charged and the number of words allowed is specified by the legislature. Candidates for the office of United States senator or representative and for governor were required by the 1971 legislature to pay $200 and share not less than two full pages in the *Candidates' Pamphlet.* Candidates for all other state offices that are voted on by all voters in the state pay $100. These candidates share not less than ony full page. The state senators, judges of the court of appeals, and the judges of the superior courts pay $50.00 and share not less than one full page. The state representatives pay $25.00 and share not less than one-half page. Nominees for president and vice president for each political party are allowed one page each (not more than 500 words) free. Their earlier privilege of buying additional pages was revoked. Each political party nominating a presidential candidate may also have one page without charge.[4] No statement may be included for anybody

3. The contents of the *Voters' Pamphlet* will be discussed later in this chapter.
4. The number of words allowed to these various categories of officials by the 1971

who is the sole nominee for a nonpartisan office.

Any candidate who desires to have an article included in the *Candidates'* *Pamphlet* must submit it to the secretary of state at least forty-five days prior to a general election. If the secretary thinks that it contains an objectionable statement, he may refuse to include it. The candidate may then appeal to a board of review consisting of the governor, the attorney general, and the lieutenant governor. A majority decision of this group is final. The secretary of state is required to have the pamphlet printed as soon as possible before the election.

Conduct of Elections

At the close of an election campaign, the voters choose their officials. Our general county and state elections are held in November every other year. The time for such elections is set by the state constitution. We noted that state representatives and half the senators are elected at these regular biennial elections, which are held on the Tuesday after the first Monday in November. State executive officials are elected every four years at the regular election, and these elections coincide with those for presidential candidates. The time of holding city and district elections varied with the size of city and type of district until 1967, when the legislature set the date for city and most district elections, including school districts, on the second Tuesday in November in odd-numbered years. Elections for certain districts, such as officials for port districts, are to be held in November of even-numbered years along with the general state and county elections. Those for public utility districts and others where ownership of property is a requirement for voting have varying dates. This question will be discussed in more detail in the two succeeding chapters on county and city government, respectively.

The term of office for most county officials is four years, and certain of these are elected at the time of the national elections. Most of them, however, are chosen at elections held two years after each national election. Such elections are called *by-elections.*

The state constitutional delegates tried to insure freedom and honesty in voting. In Article I, Section 19 of the state constitution, the statement is made that "All elections shall be free and equal, and no power, civil or military, shall at any time interfere to prevent the free exercise of the right of suffrage." No voter may be arrested while he is voting or on his way to or

---

legislature is: state representatives, 100 words; state senators, superior court judges, appeals court judges, supreme court justices and all other state offices except that of governor, 200 words; governor, 300 words; United States senators and representatives, 300 words.

from the polls for anything except treason, felony, or breach of the peace. All elections are required to be by the older type of paper ballot or by voting machines or punch cards approved by the State Voting Machine Committee. The legislature is instructed in the constitution to provide a system of voting that will give every voter absolute secrecy in preparing and depositing his ballot.

The legislature has put the county election board in charge of all elections in each county except city, town, and school elections in counties of Classes I–IX. In these, the school district clerks are in charge of school elections, and the city clerk is responsible for municipal elections. Originally, the county commissioners made up the election boards, and the commissioners still divide their county into election precincts. The legislature later created an election board, however, to attend to the details of the actual voting. At first, it was established only for counties of Classes A and I, but gradually its jurisdiction has been extended to the types of elections indicated above.

The county election board is composed of the chairman of the board of county commissioners, the county auditor, and the prosecuting attorney. In 1947 the legislature named the county auditor as supervisor of elections, and, in this capacity, he selects suitable places for voting, called polling places. He also appoints the election officials for each election precinct in the county. There must be a judge and an inspector to handle the voting, and these are appointed from the members of the two political parties which polled the highest number of votes for President in the county at the last presidential election. The chairman of the county central committee of each political party makes up the list of persons eligible from his party, and the election supervisor appoints the inspector and one judge from the majority party. One judge is appointed from the minority party. The necessary number of clerks to help with the voting are also appointed, and these are divided as equally as possible between the two leading political parties. The county commissioners set the compensation for the election officials within the limits fixed by law. The county auditor likewise provides ballots, the tally sheets, and the other materials used by the people in voting.

The 1967 legislature provided that any precinct having more than 300 voters must use some type of automation, and experiments are still going on to find which kind of purely automatic device or punch card system is the most feasible and economical. If 300 or more paper ballots are cast in any precinct, the secretary of state, as ex officio chief election officer, reports that fact to the city council, if the precinct is in a first-class city, or to the county commissioners in any other type of precinct. The municipal or county legislative group then divides or combines precincts so that none of them, if possible, contains more than 250 to allow for growth. Precincts using voting machines may have up to 900 registered voters, but there must be a machine for each 300 voters. If there are fewer than 100 registered voters in a precinct, the county auditor or other officer in charge of an election may order that the people in that precinct vote by absentee ballot at the next election.

In addition to the actual voting equipment, whether paper ballots and tally sheets or some kind of machine, the election officials must have the list of registered voters for the precinct. This is sent to the polling place either by the county auditor or by the city clerk, depending on whether the polls are in a rural or town area. When a person comes in to vote, the election clerk looks to see if his name is in the poll book. If it is, the voter signs a poll book, called the county auditor's copy. An election official then copies the voter's name into a second pollbook, called the inspector's copy. It contains carbon paper so that two additional copies may be made. These are given to the county chairman, or someone designated in writing by them, of the two main political parties. Anybody else may have a copy of the pollbook if he is willing to pay for it. After the voter signs the pollbook, he is given a ballot if voting machines are not being used, and he then goes into a cubicle so arranged that no one else can see how he votes. As in the primary election, he may either vote a straight ticket or divide his vote in any proportion among the candidates for the various parties. In addition to voting for the candidates for office, he will usually have initiatives, referenda, or constitutional amendments to vote one. If the precinct uses voting machines, the instructions vary with the type, but the system is one of pulling levers or punching ballot cards, which speeds up the process tremendously.

Once the voter has marked a paper ballot, he folds it and returns it to the clerk, who tears off the number on the ballot or watches the voter do so before putting the ballot in the election box. This number is then kept as a check on the number of ballots deposited, and the person's name is checked on the poll book so that he cannot vote again at that election.

Canvassing the Votes

Until 1955 the same group of precinct officials who conducted the election at the polling places had to stay after the polls closed to count the votes; but the legislature in that year passed a law allowing a second set of inspectors and judges to be appointed for precincts that do not use voting machines. They begin counting votes at 2:00 P.M. Two ballot boxes are provided in order that one may be given to the counting board when it begins work, and the second used until the ballots in the first are counted. They continue to alternate in this manner. To prevent members of the counting board from giving out information as to how the election is going, they are required to work in a private room and may not leave the polling place while the polls are open. A representative of each political party may be present. After the polls are closed, people may watch the counting if they do not touch the ballots or disturb the election officials.

As the election officials count the votes, they record on the tally sheet the number of votes received by each candidate. The ballots themselves are put in an envelope and sealed. These are not opened unless there is a question of the correctness of the count or the legality of the election. The tally sheets and the packet of ballots are sent to the county auditor, who calls the chairman of the Board of County Commissioners and the prosecuting attorney together to help him examine the tally sheets from each precinct to determine the votes for the entire county. This is called *canvassing the votes,* and the legislature refers to the group as the County Canvassing Board of Election Returns. Since the legislature designated the same officials as the County Election Board, however, the latter title is ordinarily used for them for all of their election duties. If two opposing candidates receive precisely the same number of votes, the canvassing group determines the winner by lot.

For the precincts in a county using some kind of voting machine device, the county auditor autorizes counting centers where the ballot cards may be brought for canvassing. The counting centers must be within twenty-five miles of the county seat. The auditor directs one person from each major political party to visit each polling place and pick up the metal boxes, already sealed by precinct election officials. There may be not more than two trips, the first not before 2:00 P.M. and the second after the polls close. A duplicate set of cards is made so that if something happens in transit, another set is available.

If a ballot is damaged so that the machine cannot accept it, a true duplicate copy must be made in the presence of witnesses and substituted. The county auditor keeps the damaged ballots for sixty days. The secretary of state is required to prescribe rules for testing the vote-tallying system before election day. At the test, at least two election officers of different parties have to be present, and the test must be open to the public and the press.

If a person's vote is challenged at a voting-machine polling place, he marks a paper ballot, which is given to the canvassing board. If the challenger appears to state his case, the canvassing board decides whether or not to accept the ballot. If no one appears, the ballot is accepted. For write-in candidates at a primary or general election, the name of the person's political party has to be added on voting machines or ballot cards as well as on paper ballots. Within five days of the official canvass of votes at primary elections, a write-in candidate must make declaration of candidacy and pay the fee. Otherwise, his name cannot be printed on the official ballot at the general election.

After the election board has canvassed the votes, the county auditor makes up an abstract of the votes, showing who has been elected and the number of votes received by each candidate. He sends a certified copy of this to the secretary of state, but the abstract of votes for the elective state officials—the governor, lieutenant governor, secretary of state, and so forth—must be sent separately by registered mail. Until 1967 the successful candidates took office on first day of January following their election. The 1965 legislature, however, changed this to the day on which the proper election official certifies to the election of the individual candidates.

Absentee Ballots

People who have to be away from home at election time or cannot be at the polls because of illness or religious scruple may vote by mail. This procedure is called *absentee voting*. The voter first applies in writing for a certificate from his registration officer (county auditor or city clerk). The registration officer checks his signature against the one on his registration card and, if he is satisfied as to the voter's identity, gives or mails him a certificate allowing him to receive an absentee ballot. Now that *Voters' Pamphlets* are mailed to each home, the 1969 legislature provided that they should contain an application form for absentee ballot as an additional means of enabling people to secure the application forms. One copy of the certificate that the applicant receives from the election official is attached to the voter's permanent registration card; the other is sent to the official having charge of the election (in most instances the county auditor) who makes arrangements for mailing him a ballot.

The ballot, with a sworn statement as to the voter's identity, is returned to the county auditor in one envelope enclosed within another. The inner envelope has no markings on it in order that the voter cannot be identified. The election board removes the outer envelope not later than the election day and opens the inner envelopes on the day when the canvass of absentee votes is made. It may be as early as the day after the election and must be completed by the tenth day after the election. If there is only one candidate for an office, the canvassing board is not required to count absentee votes for that office unless the candidate requests it to do so in writing within sixty days after the election.

Contested Elections

Very often in elections where the vote is close, the losing candidate believes that he would win if the ballots were recounted and a careful check made. The 1961 legislature gave any losing candidate the privilege of having a recount if he is willing to pay for its cost. In addition, an officer of a political party or any group of five or more registered voters who voted on the contested point may demand that the appropriate canvassing board provide for a recount under the same arrangement for payment of costs. If the difference between the vote for two opposing candidates is not more than one-half of 1 percent of the vote for both, the canvassing board is required to order a recount.

The canvassing board notifies the candidates of the time set for the recount (not later than five days after the filing of the application for it), and they as well as the five or more petitioners may be present. The petitioners may see the ballots, which the canvassing board takes from the sealed containers, but only the canvassing board or its representatives may touch them in the counting. If it becomes evident after a recount of certain key precincts that the outcome will not be changed by a recount in others, either the petitioners or the canvassing board may stop the recount at that point.

INITIATIVE, REFERENDUM, AND RECALL PROCEDURES

When the state constitution was written in 1889, the legislature was the only agency given power to make laws. In 1912, however, the constitution was amended to give to the people themselves the power to make or reject laws. Washington was the second state in the Pacific Northwest to adopt this system, Oregon being the first.[5] Lawmaking and vetoing of laws by the electorate are known as the *initiative* and *referendum* power. In an initiative action, the voters of the state decide whether or not they wish to pass a particular law. In a referendum, a law passed by the legislature is referred to the people for their approval or veto.

Allowing the voters to pass or veto laws was a decided change in governmental practice because it was a shift from representative to direct government. In a representative type of government, the people elect representatives who stand in their place to make laws. In direct government, the people themselves make the laws. The latter is considered complete democracy, and our New England town meetings might be considered an older example of the direct system. In our state, we have a combination of the two types.

Arguments For and Against Initiative and Referendum System

People who favor direct government argue that, since the people themselves choose their representatives, they are greater than those

5. Oregon was the third state in the country to accept the principle of direct legislation by the voters, following South Dakota and Utah.

representatives and may take upon themselves the powers delegated to the representatives. They do this to try to make certain that the legislative body does not go against the wishes of the people. Others think that questions of government finance and administration are so complicated that the mass of voters cannot understand them sufficiently to vote intelligently on specific bills. Some people also believe that it is easier for special interest groups to get initiatives passed by the voters than it is to get similar laws passed by the legislature. A corollary of this argument is, also, that legislators tend to avoid making a decision on difficult problems because they can "let the people decide." If the decision proves to be a mistake, the legislature cannot be blamed.

Some safeguards were included in the constitutional amendments specifying the procedures for initiative and referendum measures to protect the people from their own mistakes, and in 1952 the voters passed an amendment adding another safeguard—that the legislature may amend an initiative by a two-thirds vote of the members of both houses.

Steps in Passing Laws by Initiatives

If a group of voters believes that the state needs a law that the legislature has refused to pass or has not considered, they propose it in the form of an initiative petition. The first step in the procedure is that a sponsoring group or individual prepares the text of the proposed law, prints it in a petition form, and circulates copies so that qualified voters may have an opportunity to sign it if they wish. At the present time, the number of qualified voters who sign the petition must equal 8 percent of the number who voted for governor at the last gubernatorial election if the initiative proposal is to appear on the ballot at the next election. When the specified number of voters have signed the petition, it is filed with the secretary of state. It must reach his office not less than four months before a regular election or not less than ten days before the beginning of a regular session of the legislature. The secretary of state then makes a sample check of the list of signatures on the petition against his card file of voters to see that the signatures are those of actual voters.

If the petition is sent to the secretary of state four months before a general election, he includes it in the ballot for that election. In that case, the people vote as to whether or not they favor the proposed law. If the petition reaches the secretary of state ten days before the regular session of the legislature, the secretary of state turns it over to the legislators, who must consider the petition before they take up any other measure except bills appropriating money for the support of the state.

When the legislature receives an initiative bill, it may pass the bill, refer it to the people, refuse to pass it, or take no action. If the legislature votes to accept it, the initiative bill becomes a law like any other, except that the governor may not veto it. The legislators may feel, however, that the people should consider it again. In that case, they pass the initiative bill, but specify that it be referred to the voters. The secretary of state presents it to the voters at the next general election or at a special election if the legislature wishes to have it considered more quickly. If the legislature disapproves of the initiative bill so much that it is rejected completely, the secretary of state must submit it to the people for a vote in the way just described. If the legislature does not act on an initiative bill, the secretary of state must allow the people to vote on it. If the people vote to accept an initiative measure under any of these circumstances, it becomes law thirty days after the election at which it was voted passed, and the legislature must not repeal it for two years and must not amend it except by a two-thirds majority of the legislators. The last redistricting initiative was cited in the chapter on the legislature as one amended by the two-thirds vote. An initiative measure may be repealed by the voters at any regular or special election after it is passed.

Oftentimes when voters are faced with a long ballot, they will vote for the officials in question, but they will not take the trouble to vote on initiatives or constitutional amendments. Consequently, in order to be certain that the majority of a very small number of voters could not put an initiative measure into effect, the constitution requires that at least one-third of those voting on any part of an election must vote on an initiative measure if it is to be valid. A majroity of those voting on the measure have to favor the law proposed by the initiative to pass it.

Steps in Repealing a Law by Referendum

If the people do not like a bill passed by the legislature, they may do away with it through an unfavorable referendum vote. They follow a process similar to that for an initiative. Qualified voters sign a petition calling for an election to pass on the retention of the law. In order for the election to be held, enough qualified voters must sign the petition to equal 4 percent of the number voting for governor at the preceding gubernatorial election. The petition must be filed with the secretary of state not later than ninety days after the adjournment of the legislature. An election is then held in the same manner as that for an initiative. If the required number of signatures is secured for a referendum petition within ninety days, the law in question does not go into effect. It is held in abeyance until the people can vote on it at the next general election, almost two years later. If the people vote then to accept the law, it goes into effect thirty days after the election.

In order to give the people time to secure signatures on a referendum petition, no bill subject to referendum goes into effect until ninety days after the adjournment of the legislature. Bills to which the referendum may not apply are ones "necessary for the immediate preservation of the public peace, health or safety, support of the state government and its existing public institutions." Such bills are called emergency bills and go into effect immediately after their passage unless the legislature has designated in the bill the date on which it is to take effect. If a group of voters believes that an emergency bill is not a legitimate one and tries to challenge it by referendum, the courts have to decide whether or not the bill is subject to referendum.

Voters' Pamphlets

The constitutional amendment that permits the use of the initiative and referendum contains instructions to the legislature to provide machinery for informing the voters as to arguments for and against the passage of initiatives, referenda, and constitutional amendments. The legislature gave to the secretary of state the responsibility for seeing that each registered voter within the state has access to the *Voters' Pamphlet* containing such information. At the present time, he is required to mail a copy to each individual place of residence in the state, and he must provide sufficient additional distribution to give each voter a reasonable opportunity to see the pamphlet.

When the secretary of state receives an initiative or referendum petition with a sufficient number of voters' signatures to place it on the ballot at a general election, he asks the attorney general to prepare a brief statement explaining the law as it presently exists plus the effect which the proposed measure would have. If it is an initiative that has already been presented to the legislature or a referendum on a law passed by the legislature, the attorney general is also required to state how many votes there were for and against it. The attorney general's description goes on the top portion of two facing pages in the *Voters' Pamphlet,* and each one may be read in the office of the secretary of state before it is printed. If anyone feels that the attorney general has not given a fair analysis of the proposed measure, he may ask the superior court of Thurston County to rule on the matter within ten days after the statement reaches the secretary of state. The court may rewrite the descriptions if it wishes, but no appeal may be made from its decision.

Below the statement written by the attorney general, on two facing pages in the *Voters' Pamphlet,* appear arguments for and against the measure. The legislature requires that the president of the senate, the speaker of the house, and the secretary of state appoint two persons known to favor the measure to choose a third individual to make up a committee to write the argument advocating passage of the initiative or referendum. The same group selects two people who choose a third to comprise a committee to write the statement opposing the measure. Each of these committees may name up to five persons to serve as an advisory committee without vote. The secretary of state makes rules for the final dates for filing statements and any other necessary regulations.

In the case of a constitutional amendment or a measure referred to the voters by the legislature instead of by a petition from the voters, the committee that writes the statement favoring the proposal consists of one state senator appointed by the president of the senate and one representative appointed by the speaker of the house who, in turn, choose a third member who may or may not be a legislator. The senator and representative must be known to favor the measure. A similar procedure is used to choose a committee to write the argument opposing the legislation. If no member of the legislature will serve on the committee to write arguments against the measure, the 1971 legislature specified that the committee shall be composed of the secretary of state and the presiding officers of the house and senate, who shall appoint any persons whom they consider qualified.

The legislature appropriates the money to the secretary of state for printing the pamphlets. If the secretary of state finds that a committee's argument contains objectionable language, he may refuse to file it. The committee may then appeal to a board of censors consisting of the governor, the attorney general, and the superintendent of public instruction. The decision of a majority of this group is final.

Until 1971 the secretary of state was required to have the *Voters' Pamphlet* ready to be distributed to the voters at least sixty days before the election at which they are to vote on the measures concerned. In that year, however, the legislature changed this stipulation to "as soon as possible." The secretary of state determines the best size and weight of paper for the pamphlets.

The order in which the measures are placed in the pamphlet is: initiatives, legislative proposals to voters, proposals to the legislature that it has then referred to the voters, initiatives by petition to which the legislature has proposed an alternative, constitutional amendments, and measures recommending a constitutional convention. In addition to giving information about proposed constitutional amendments in the *Voters' Pamphlet,* the secretary of state is required to publish notices of the amendment in every legal newspaper in the state and supplement the notices with radio and television announcements.

The 1971 legislature specified that whenever possible the *Voters' Pamphlet* and the *Candidates' Pamphlet* be combined. In that case, the *Candidates' Pamphlet* appears second in the publication.

Recall Procedure

The voters may dismiss elective officials by a system called *recall.* We have seen that judges of courts of record are the only elective officials who may not be recalled. To dismiss any others, the voters present a petition stating the charges against the official. The number of signatures required varies according to the type of official in question, whether local or state. For example, the number for state officials, officers of first-class cities, school district boards in first-class cities, county officials in counties of Classes I–III is 25 percent; that for state senators, representatives, and officials of all other political subdivisions is 35 percent. A special election is then held, at which time the voters of the affected area vote either to dismiss or to retain the accused official. They also vote on a substitute in case the incumbent is recalled.

SUGGESTED READINGS

In addition to the original sources for a study of our state government listed in preceding chapters, publications concerning election procedures are available upon request from the secretary of state, Olympia. *Voters' Pamphlet* and *Candidates' Pamphlet* have been mentioned. Moreover, there are various maps and charts issued, showing names of elected and certain appointed officials, or giving instructions for voting. Titles and types of these vary, but if one tells the secretary of state that material on election procedures is needed, he will send what is available.

7. County Government

LEGAL STATUS OF COUNTIES

Subdivision of State

In Article XI, Section 1 of the state constitution, the statement is made: "The several counties of the Territory of Washington existing at the time of the adoption of this Constitution are hereby recognized as legal subdivisions of this state." The state supreme court in various cases has upheld that, as a legal subdivision of the state, a county has no inherent powers of its own—only those granted to it by the state legislature or the constitution. The only general statement of autonomy for a county in the constitution is that a county "may make and enforce within its limits all such local police, sanitary and other regulations as are not in conflict with general laws." Even here the "general laws" (laws passed by the state legislature) take precedence, as they do for the basic limits on taxes that counties may levy.

However, in practice, counties have had since 1948 a large amount of leeway in their local government. In that year the voters approved a constitutional amendment giving to the counties the right to choose their type of local government within certain limits set by the legislature. Such freedom in local government is called *home rule.* The larger cities in Washington have had home rule for many years. A second constitutional amendment in 1948 permits a combined county-city government, but none has yet been established.

King County is the only one so far that has adopted a home rule charter for its county. Attempts were made by interested residents of Snohomish, Kitsap, and Cowlitz counties to persuade the voters to adopt a home rule charter for them, but the voters rejected the proposal. In fact, King County turned down the proposal for its charter twice, but accepted it on the third election in 1969.

The main argument of the civic groups favoring the adoption of home rule charters was that county government needs to be streamlined, with fewer elective officials and more appointive ones. In the constitutional amendment authorizing county home rule, the only county officials who are still required to be elected are the prosecuting attorney, the county superintendent of schools,[1] judges of the superior court, and justices of the peace. However, in metropolitan communities, particularly, the feeling was strong that the county legislative body should be larger than the traditional group of three county commissioners.

Both of these changes are represented in the home rule charter adopted by the King County voters. The county council now consists of nine elective members, and a county executive (corresponding to a city manager) is also elected by the voters, but the county assessor is the only other optional official who is still elected. Except for certain main executive and administrative departments specified in the charter, the county council has the authority to create those considered necessary. The county executive appoints the heads of such agencies.

Municipal Corporation

Each county must do a great deal of business for itself if it is to take care of its people efficiently. It must be able to buy and sell property, to make contracts for constructing buildings, to build and repair roads, and to carry out many other acts of a commercial nature. In general, these are the powers granted to any corporation, and, when a corporation is owned and run by the people as a whole, it is called a municipal corporation. We are most familiar with that term in connection with incorporated towns and cities, but it applies in part to counties, also, and the state constitution includes counties in its list of municipal corporations. Later supreme court decisions have also recognized the corporate nature of counties. Consequently, we must define a county of this state as both a legal subdivision of the state and as a municipal corporation.

Recently Congress has added a new relationship with municipal corporations (both counties and cities) by appropriating federal funds directly to these units of local government without allocating the money first to the state to be reapportioned to a county or city. This procedure has made for more diversified connections of municipal corporations with larger areas of government and is designed to give more local control over federal funds made available to counties and cities. The formula for computing the amount is based, roughly, on population, degree of taxation imposed at the local

1. Now intermediate school district superintendent.

level, and relative financial status of each local unit. Thus the element of equalization between poor and wealthy counties is one aspect of the amount of money distributed. Political scientists see this as an important factor, in practice, in the changing status of counties and cities in relation to state governments.

CREATION OF COUNTIES

When the residents of a community feel that they should have a county organization separate from their present one, they first present to the state legislature a petition, which must be signed by a majority of the voters in that area. The legislature considers the petition, and a bill may be proposed for the creation of a new county, giving its boundaries. If such a bill is passed by the legislature, the county is established.

However, minimum population requirements for a new county were set in the constitution, which required, too, that a new county must take over its share of the debts of the parent county. These regulations were included in order to prevent very small communities from securing a county organization. If the population of a county is too small to support a county government easily, the residents suffer. Their rate of taxation is comparatively high, and their roads, schools, and other projects are not so satisfactory as they would be if the community were part of a larger county. People do not like to go a long distance to the county seat, however, as they have to do in a county covering a very large area. A satisfactory medium was attempted then as far as size was concerned. The constitution states that a new county must have a least 2,000 inhabitants and must not reduce its parent county to less than 4,000 in population.

The 1969 legislature also provided for the shift of a part of a county with a small population (not more than 50 registered voters) to another county that is an adjoining one if the change does not reduce the population of the original county to fewer than 4,000. If a majority of registered voters in such a section wish to change, they file a petition with the county commissioners or county council. If the county board approves the request, it orders a special election to be held within ninety days in the section requesting annexation. If three-fifths of those voting favor the move, the results are referred to the county commissioners of the county to which the part will be annexed. If the commissioners of the new county wish to accept the section in question, they may do so and notify the legislature.

Even without any actual annexation by one county of part of another, there are questions about the accuracy of some of the existing lines marking the boundaries of certain counties. The 1967 legislature, consequently, created a temporary County Boundary Advisory Commission to study the county boundary lines in conjunction with the Division of Surveys and Maps in the Department of Natural Resources. The commission was asked to recommend to the 1969 legislature legislation that would make the lines accurate. That group consisted of a representative of the College of Engineering of the University of Washington, a representative of the College of Engineering of Washington State University, and a member of the staff of the Department of Natural Resources.

The 1967 legislature also created a County Boundary Review Board for large counties and an Annexation Review Board for other counties to fix boundaries and keep them accurate for areas annexed by cities within a county.

COUNTY SEAT LOCATION

A temporary seat is named in the bill creating a county, but the voters in a county may put the permanent county seat wherever they choose. Once a county seat is established, it may be moved at any general election if a sufficient number of voters are in favor of the proposed change. The procedure is that a petition is presented to the county commissioners (or other county legislative body) signed by qualified voters in a number equal to at least one-third of all votes cast in the county at the last preceding general election. An election is then held, and to remove the county seat, three-fifths of those voting must favor the same new place.

The question of the location of county seats in Washington has brought on some of our most heated political contests. Each town is anxious to have the county seat in order to increase its business. When people come to the courthouse for any purpose, they are also inclined to do their shopping, banking, and so forth in the county seat. Moreover, the erection and maintenance of the county buildings is a source of income to the local contractors, merchants, and laborers.

The battle between Spokane and Cheney over the possession of the county seat illustrates the height of feeling over the question. In 1879 when Spokane County was created for the second time, the territorial legislature named Spokane Falls, as the town was called then, the temporary county seat. The residents of the county were instructed to choose the permanent location at the following election, and Cheney was determined to win the coveted position. A newspaper, the *Northwest Tribune,* was started there to aid in the battle. The printing press had to be set up under a tree since there was no building for it, and fifteen men on horseback were hired to distribute the papers throughout the county.

Lawsuits in both the probate and district courts followed the election. To begin with, the incumbent county auditor, J. M. Nosler, ran for office against

W. H. Bishop, who claimed, after the election, that the canvassing board had refused to count votes from certain precincts with the result that his opponent was declared the winning candidate for the office and Spokane Falls the continuing temporary county seat. When the suit came before the probate court, Bishop withdrew his complaint about the county seat location and based his case solely on his right to the office of county auditor. Therefore, when the court recounted the votes, it considered only the matter of the number cast for that office, which showed a majority for Bishop, whom the court named auditor.

Cheney supporters then asked the district court to order a recount of the votes for the county seat location, and, when the court complied, the canvassing board found that there were 680 votes for Cheney and 575 for Spokane Falls. The county auditor, as a member of the canvassing board and as custodian of a big proportion of the county records, thereupon ordered the removal of those records to Cheney. Several of those who favored Spokane as the county seat brought another suit in the district court, claiming that the county auditor was in such a hurry to get the records to Cheney that he, along with Cheney supporters, carried them there secretly and illegally during the night of the recount while a big dance diverted the attention of the general public. By the time this suit came to trial in June 1881, all of the county officials had offices in Cheney, and the court found no evidence that Cheney had lost the election. Therefore, the county seat remained at Cheney until 1887, when Spokane had grown to the point that it easily won the county seat location in an election held that year.

TOWNSHIP GOVERNMENT

The state constitution permitted the establishment of township government within a county if the voters wished to have it, and until 1969 two counties in our state—Spokane and Whatcom—had township government.

Townships are subdivisions of counties. In the early days in New England, the voters in each town met regularly in a *town meeting* to take care of the town's business. They voted on all questions of public welfare and elected officers to carry out their wishes. This type of town meeting is still held in many New England towns. In the East and Middle West the next larger unit of local government is called a township. It usually includes more than one town, but is still much smaller than a county. A county will contain many townships.

In the far western states, however, townships were not considered necessary to efficient local government. Towns were separated by greater distances than they were in the East, so that it was often as easy to get to the county seat as to another neighboring town. Our population was smaller, too; and, as a result, the people did not feel the need for an intermediate unit between the county and a town in our state except for the two counties mentioned above.

Originally, a township maintained many of the services on a small scale that the county did on a large one, such as providing township roads and bridges, assessing property, maintaining cemeteries and dog pounds, licensing peddlers and amusement places within its jurisdiction, and enforcing its regulations through a justice-of-the-peace court. Gradually, however, jurisdiction over roads was given to the county or the state as motor vehicles required greater uniformity of type and quality, and the main functions remaining for townships were to establish dog pounds; to make rules concerning the building of fences and the impounding of stray animals; to maintain a cemetery; and to license dogs, peddlers, auctioneers, and places of amusement. These needs have been sufficiently satisfied by city and county activities that the township governmental units in Whatcom and Spokane counties became less and less active until they ceased to function.

When a township is a unit of government, it is called a *civil township.* There is another type called a *congressional township,* which is a division for geographical purposes only. The federal government needed some kind of unit for land measurement so that any piece of land in the country could be identified. For this purpose, counties are divided into units six miles square, which are called *townships.* The township, in turn, is divided into *sections.* We have mentioned the fact that sections 16 and 36 in each township were set aside for school support by the federal government. You will see references to this kind of congressional township in all of our counties, even though there is no township government present.

DISTRICT ORGANIZATION

In this state, there are additional units of local government called districts that are created to perform a particular service. School districts have been mentioned, as well as irrigation, diking, drainage, public utility districts, and so forth. There are over thirty different types. They differ from counties and townships in that the districts are not managed by representatives of the voters in the area; they are organized and run only by the property owners in the district, and the expenses of their operation are met from assessments levied by the district against the property owners and from fees received from the furnishing of services. They are a kind of cooperative enterprise to furnish irrigation, electricity, dikes, drains, soil conservation, and almost any other type of service desired by the majority of property holders in a given section. They are not of uniform size. In fact, several overlapping districts of various kinds may exist in one or more counties.

The procedure for organizing each type of district is specified by the state legislature, and it varies considerably from one type of district to another. In general, however, the property owners in an area send a petition to the county commissioners asking that a district be organized. In certain types of districts, the commissioners supervise the surveys made to determine the cost of the project and if it can be successful in that region. State officials make the surveys for other types. Once a district is established, it elects officers, and the district is run as another municipal corporation. It may levy taxes, but their collection is made part of the regular county tax procedure.

CLASSIFICATION OF COUNTIES

The legislature was allowed to classify the counties on the basis of population as a means of setting fair salaries for county officials, and in 1972 there were twelve classes. The counties, with their population according to the 1970 census and their class according to the 1971 *Legislative Manual*, are as follows:[2]

County	Class	Population
Adams	V	12,014
Asotin	V	13,799
Benton	III	67,540
Chelan	III	41,355
Clallam	IV	34,770
Clark	I	128,454
Columbia	VII	4,439
Cowlitz	III	63,616
Douglas	V	17,787
Ferry	VIII	3,655
Franklin	IV	25,816
Garfield*	VIII	2,911
Grant	III	41,881
Grays Harbor	III	59,553
Island	IV	27,011
Jefferson	VI	10,661
King	AA	1,156,633
Kitsap	II	101,732
Kittitas	IV	25,039
Klickitat	V	12,138

2. The limits for the population of each class are: Class AA, 500,000 or more; Class A, 210-500,000; Class I, 125,000-210,000; Class II, 70,000-125,000; Class III, 40,000-70,000; Class IV, 18,000-40,000; Class V, 12,000-18,000; Class VI, 8,000-12,000; Class VII, 5,000-8,000; Class VIII, 3,300-5,000; Class IX, fewer than 3,300.

County	Class	Population
Lewis	III	45,467
Lincoln	VI	9,572
Mason	IV	20,918
Okanogan	IV	25,867
Pacific	V	15,796
Pend Oreille	VII	6,025
Pierce	A	411,027
San Juan*	IX	3,856
Skagit	III	52,381
Skamania	VII	5,845
Snohomish*	I	265,236
Spokane	A	287,487
Stevens	V	17,405
Thurston*	III	76,894
Wahkiakum	VIII	3,592
Walla Walla	III	42,176
Whatcom	II	81,950
Whitman	IV	37,900
Yakima	I	144,971

*Change of class not made as of 1971.

COUNTY OFFICIALS

When the state constitution was written, the county officials named in Article XI, Section 5 were: "Boards of county commissioners, sheriffs, county clerks, treasurers, prosecuting attorneys." The legislature was authorized to add others, and it created the offices of auditor, assessor, county superintendent of schools (now intermediate school district superintendent), coroner, health officer, county administrator of relief (now inoperative), and optional ones like the agricultural expert, horiticultural inspector, home economics expert, and so on. The superior court judges and justices of the peace, which were established by the constitution, are considered part of the state's judicial system and have been discussed, along with the sheriff, the clerk, and the prosecuting attorney, in chapter 5 on the court system.

Except for King County, as indicated above, which has a somewhat different set of county officials as specified in its home rule charter (aside from the ones that are still mandatory), all of our counties follow the older pattern established by the legislature.

Salaries

Annual salaries for county officials appear in Table 4. Note also in Table 4 that in counties larger than Class III, the prosecuting attorney may not engage in private law practice.

Term of Office

Unless otherwise stated in the section on a county official, the term of office for all county officials is four years. In general, if a vacancy occurs between elections, the Board of County Commissioners appoints someone to fill the office until the next election. Exceptions to this are indicated in the discussion of the individual offices. Except for an office like that of prosecuting attorney, which requires special training, any qualified voter may run for a county office. Certain appointive officials, such as county health officer, agricultural expert, and road engineer, also have to have additional qualifications.

Abolishment of County Offices

Classification of counties by size has been used in the past for many regulations in addition to salary scales, since the problems of counties of approximately the same population are ordinarily similar. However, in recent years the laws permitting counties to add functions, such as maintaining airport facilities, improving environmental quality, and so forth, have been stated in general terms to apply to counties of any size.

One specification still attached to size, however, relates to the combining of certain county offices. In 1925, in counties of Classes VI-IX, the offices of clerk and auditor were combined, as well as the offices of treasurer and assessor. The offices were later separated, however, except for Class IX. No county now has a low enough population to fit into the classification for Class IX, although San Juan County still maintains a Class IX status, having not yet changed to Class VIII where its present population would place it. The only remaining combination of offices is that of prosecuting attorney and coroner in Classes IV-VIII. However, the county commissioners have the authority to hire a coroner for specific investigations, if they wish, or to ask another county official, such as the sheriff, to serve in that capacity temporarily.

Official Oaths and Bonds

The state constitution specifies that the legislature must provide a system of holding county officials responsible for money collected as part of their official duties. The legislature therefore requires an oath of office and official bond from each county official. The amount of money to be given as bond varies with the type of office and amount of fees likely to be collected. For example, the 1971 legislature fixed the minimum amount for county auditor at $10,000 and the maximum for county treasurers in Class A and AA counties at $250,000. The county commissioners or other county legislative body is named as the agency to decide the specific amounts for the county officials in their county except for their own bond, which is set by the legislature. In practice, the counties buy blanket coverage from insurance companies.

The oath of office must be taken and filed in the office of the county auditor and the bond deposited in the office of the county clerk before an elected official can take up his duties. The county clerk's bond is deposited in the county treasurer's office.

Capacities in Which County Officials Act

Since the legislature was given the responsibility of defining the duties of the county officials, the state constitution does not say a great deal about the type of jurisdiction of a county. As we have seen, however, there is a general statement that the counties may make any police and sanitary regulations not in conflict with state laws, and police power extends to any phase of public welfare.

It has been pointed out that counties act both as agents of the state and as municipal corporations. In most cases, we can tell in which capacity a county is acting in a given function. For example, in enforcing the law, holding elections, sponsoring public health and welfare, building or maintaining roads, improving agricultural methods, and recording property titles, the county is acting for the state. As we consider the duties of the various county officials, we shall see how these procedures are carried out.

The function of the county as a corporation is chiefly to provide for county finances and supervise their spending. The legislature defined the powers of the counties in this respect as follows: ". . . to sue and be sued in the manner prescribed by law; to purchase and hold lands within its limits; to make such contracts and to purchase and hold such personal property as may be necessary to its corporate or administrative powers; and to do all other necessary acts in relation to all of the property of the county."[3]

Board of County Commissioners

The group created by the constitution to make the "police and sanitary regulations" for a county is the Board of County Commissioners. In making rules for the county, it corresponds to the state legislature in its law-making capacity for the state. The regulations adopted by the county commissioners are not called laws, however, but ordinances. To make a law, the legislative body has to be a sovereign group, acting in its own right. As we have seen, a county has no inherent right to existence; hence, it exists only at the pleasure of a higher agency, the state legislature. The edicts of the county's governing body are, therefore, called ordinances to make this distinction.[4]

We have seen that, in our state and federal governments, a careful separation is made between legislative, executive, and judicial functions so that each branch stays within its own field except for the specific checks and balances provided for. In a county no such division exists. The county commissioners not only pass ordinances (county laws) and levy taxes, but they also supervise the conduct of the other county officials, and sell or lease county property, make contracts, approve claims, and do various other acts of an executive nature. In meeting as the board of equalization or county board of health, for example, they even act in a quasi-judicial capacity in hearing complaints or arguments and deciding the issue. As part of this function, they have the power to subpoena witnesses, to administer oaths, and to commit for contempt any witness refusing to testify before them or before justices of the peace. Appeals may be taken to the superior court.

The board is required to divide the county into three commissioners' districts, as nearly equal in population as possible. The district boundaries may not be changed oftener than once every four years. A candidate seeks nomination at the primary and election at the general election from the districts in rotation. Only voters in the district nominate, but all voters in the county vote to elect the candidates running from each district.

The Board of County Commissioners is composed of three members, whose term of office is four years. In order to preserve continuity of membership, the legislature makes use of the system of partial renewals. One commissioner is elected at a general election and at the next general election, two years later, two commissioners are elected. If there is a vacancy on the board between elections, the remaining commissioners appoint a third from a list of three persons nominated by the county central committee of the political party to which the previous commissioner belonged. If the two remaining commissioners cannot agree on his successor or, for any reason, do not make an appointment within sixty days after the vacancy occurs, the

---

3. *Laws of the Territory of Washington* (1854-57), p. 329. Law retained by the state legislature.

4. As an aid to securing uniform regulations in matters of public health, building codes, electric wiring, and similar safety measures, the legislature permits the county commissioners to adopt state laws and recognized codes as the standards to be followed in unincorporated areas of the county.

governor makes the appointment from the list of nominees by the county central committee. The appointee must be from the same commissioner's district and the same political party as his predecessor.

It took a state constitutional amendment to clarify the right of the governor to appoint a county commissioner when the two remaining commissioners had not made the appointment within the specified time. In 1958 in the case of *State ex rel Carroll v. Munro,* the state supreme court ruled that the governor could not make such an appointment because the constitution at that time said only that the county commissioners should fill vacancies in county offices. In January 1966 the state attorney general filed a suit in Kitsap County challenging the right of the governor to appoint a county commissioner there. In that instance, a Kitsap county commissioner had resigned, and the remaining two commissioners could not agree on a third. The governor then appointed one in accordance with the provision of the state law mentioned above. To provide for this type of contigency in the future, the legislature in 1967 proposed to the voters a constitutional amendment specifically permitting the governor to fill a vacancy in the office of county commissioner under the circumstances described, and it was ratified by the voters in the 1968 election.

The commissioners are required to meet at the courthouse at least once each quarter, and they may call extra sessions as the county's business demands. In large counties, they are in session almost constantly. The county auditor is the official clerk (secretary) for the board, but the commissioners ordinarily appoint their own secretary, who handles the clerical work except for the official, formal record of their proceedings.

The commissioners represent the county in any of its corporate business. For example, if they find that the county has to sue some person or firm for failure to fulfill a contract, for damages to county property, or for any other reason, the commissioners bring the lawsuit in the name of the county against the person concerned. Likewise, if any person wishes to sue the county, the county commissioners represent the county as defendant. They may also reduce or release a debt to the county if it seems necessary and if none of the commissioners has a personal interest in it. The commissioners also sign contracts, deeds, leases, and so forth in the name of the county. If something happens to a county, township, precinct, or road district official, so that he cannot continue with the office, the county commissioners appoint someone else to take his place until the next election. They have the power, too, to appoint several nonelective county officials, such as the county health officer, the county engineer, and others. We shall discuss the duties of these officials in the sections pertaining to their work. The county commissioners adopt the budget for their county, and in order to keep within the amount of money allotted for a given year, they have the final decision as to the number of deputies or other employees to be hired in the various county offices.

We have seen that the State Department of Highways builds and maintains our state roads. County roads are under the control of the county commissioners, who may levy a tax on real property outside incorporated cities and towns up to whatever maximum amount is set by the legislature. In addition, part of the money collected from the state gasoline tax is spent on county roads, according to formulas established by the legislature. The state director of highways has supervision over the use of these state funds. A county may also secure federal funds for road construction if it can pay approximately half the cost of constructing a road approved by the United States Bureau of Public Roads. Moreover, Congress allows the United States Forest Service to give to counties lying within a national forest 25 percent of the money received from loggers who cut timber there. These receipts are divided between roads and schools. The recent direct federal grants to counties, mentioned earlier, may be used for various projects approved by the county commissioners.

The county commissioners may act as a unit in administering the county's road program or they may divide their county into road districts, ordinarily naming each member of the board as the road commissioner for the road districts in his commissioner's district. The legislature allows the county commissioners to have up to nine road districts, but all counties now operating under the district system have either two or three road districts. Unless the commissioners vote otherwise, at least one road district must be maintained in each commissioner's district. If a county has only two road districts, one county commissioner does not concern himself with road supervision, but sees to the maintenance of the courthouse instead.

The commissioners appoint a county engineer who must be a registered and licensed professional civil engineer. The county engineer and his assistants build and maintain the roads according to the schedule approved by the county commissioners.

The 1961 legislature established a program for a six-year plan for county roads. The county commissioners and the county road engineer must prepare and file with the state director of highways a comprehensive plan and every two years thereafter revise it and compute how much has been realized. The city legislative bodies within the county must make a similar plan.

The 1963 legislature expressed a desire to have county administrative procedures standardized in order to have better coordination, particularly in the fields of roads and social security. It therefore required a biennial report to the governor and legislature from the county commissioners, recommending changes in the present laws or procedures affecting local government. The commissioners use the Washington State Association of Counties as a coordinating agency for these studies, and the affiliate, County

Road Administration Board, makes the biennial reports on roads.

If a county wishes to develop a flood control program that will not affect territory outside the county, the county commissioners may levy a tax of an amount up to one mill for such a purpose. We have seen in chapter 3 that the Department of Ecology has charge of flood control projects for larger areas within the state and that even the federal government is involved in the construction of our biggest dams, which help prevent floods as well as provide water for irrigation and electric power.

We have noted that the various state agencies grant many licenses. The licenses granted by the county commissioners mainly concern salesmen operating outside of an incorporated town. Grocers, auctioneers, ferry operators, and hawkers are mentioned specifically in the *Session Laws,* the compilation of statutes passed by the legislature at each of its sessions. A *hawker* is a salesman who hawks or calls out a description of his wares. We hardly ever hear hawkers now except in cities, where a city ordinance would regulate this type of selling. In fact, a later law was passed referring only to peddlers who get a license from the county treasurer. The old law regarding hawkers, however, still appears in the *Session Laws.* It is an example of a law once used but now obsolete because of a change in people's habits. The county auditor, the technical secretary of the Board of County Commissioners, is listed as the person to present the requests for these licenses to the commissioners for their approval. In practice, the board's own secretary ordinarily handles this type of transaction. The county auditor has an additional responsibility for issuing certain licenses himself, and these will be discussed in the section on the duties of the county auditor.

Some privileges, called franchises, may be granted to an individual or corporation to provide services in which competition is not desirable. Transportation facilities, gas, electricity, and water are some common ones. The legislative body of a city, the county commissioners, or the state legislature may grant certain franchises, depending on the area to be served. One mentioned specifically for county commissioners is the granting of a franchise to use the right-of-way on county roads to install water-works, gas pipes, or other utilities. The county commissioners have the county auditor call a public hearing on the question, and afterward, if such a franchise appears to them to be in the public interest, they may grant it for a period up to fifteen years. They may cancel it if the status of the road is changed.

The county commissioners are required to provide a courthouse and jail for their county. Two or more counties may operate a joint county jail if the boards of county commissioners find such an arrangement more efficient and economical. The county commissioners must provide enough space and equipment for the various county officials in order that they may carry on their work adequately. They levy taxes, but many other officials have a part in the assessment and collection of taxes. Therefore, this subject will be discussed in the section on county finances.

The county commissioners also have some part in the election procedure in that they divide their counties into election precincts. The supervision of elections, however, is now done by the county auditor and the County Election Board, whose duties have already been discussed in connection with election procedure.

There are many miscellaneous activities either permitted or required of the county commissioners. In recent years problems of environmental quality have received increasing attention. For example, the 1967 legislature activated county air pollution control authorities in counties of Classes AA, A, and I, and gave the county commissioners in all other counties permission to create such an authority either by resolution or after a petition by one hundred property owners in the county. The legislature grouped the counties of the state into regional air pollution control authorities under the direction of the Department of Ecology.

The 1967 legislature also required that each board of county commissioners (or joint boards if more than one county acts as a unit) plan a comprehensive system of sewerage and water treatment. In the same session the commissioners were authorized to create a countywide advisory committee on flood control. The 1969 session ordered the establishment in each county of a county disability board to pass on claims for disability by law enforcement officers and fire fighters from their retirement system funds if they are not employed in a city having a disability board. It also allowed the county commissioners (or governing body of a city) in any size county to establish a municipal improvement board to force owners of damaged buildings or ones unfit for human habitation to repair them or tear them down.[5] The governing body creating such a board must also establish an appeals commission to hear complaints against the board's decisions. The 1971 session of the legislature added tourist promotion and parking and business improvement areas as legitimate fields of effort for any county or city. After public hearings, the county commissioners may levy special assessments against the business concerned for such aids to retail trade. The legislature also urges the county commissioners to arrange for an annual county fair either as a single county or in conjunction with others.

One or more of the county commissioners are ex officio members of many county boards, such as the Civil Defense Council, which meets to plan a program of defense for the county in the event of war or any other great disaster, such as a flood, an earthquake, or other natural calamity; the County Board of Health; County Board of Equalization; County Finance Committee; County Election Board; and County Advisory Committee on Public

5. Previously this had been limited to cities in Class AA and A counties.

Assistance.

Officials Concerned with County Finances

Many of the county officials are involved in the same phase of county government. For example, the assessor, treasurer, auditor, and county finance committee, as well as the county commissioners, have important parts in the administration of county finances. The county commissioners must approve all requests for payment of county expenses except those for the courts and districts.

When any county department owes someone money for official services, the head of that department makes out a voucher, showing the name of the claimant, called the *payee,* the type of service done, and the amount of money due him. The county auditor examines these vouchers and satisfies himself that they are legitimate county expenses. He then presents the vouchers to the county commissioners, and, if they approve the voucher, the auditor then makes out warrants in payment, which may be cashed like ordinary checks. The auditor gives the county treasurer a statement of the warrants issued, and, after the warrants are cashed, the banks return the canceled warrants to the treasurer, who enters the transfer of money on his books and returns the canceled warrants to the auditor, who files them.

Even in small counties, the purchase of equipment and supplies is a big job, and in large counties it is stupendous. When each county department makes its own purchases, there is likely to be duplication. Also, large amounts of material can be purchased more cheaply, proportionately, than smaller lots. Consequently, in most counties now, the county commissioners appoint a purchasing agent to do all of the buying for the various county departments, and this is believed to save time and money. The 1961 legislature required Class AA, A, and I counties to have a purchasing department and allowed any others to do so. In any county where the commissioners establish a purchasing department, they must appoint as head a county purchasing agent who has had previous experience in that work. For large purchases, bids are required.

Now that data-processing devices are available to perform accounting services, the 1967 legislature permitted the county commissioners in any county to create a county central services department and appoint a supervisor to install a comprehensive data-processing plan for accounting, record-keeping, and microcopying.

The county commissioners are required to audit the handling of county finances by the various officials. As we have seen, they have a regular routine for checking the auditor's accounts. At each of their quarterly sessions, the commissioners also check the books of the treasurer, who is required by the state constitution to receive all county funds into the county treasury. He gives to the commissioners a certified statement of receipts and disbursements for the preceding quarter, and the commissioners check this against his orders, warrants, and other accounts to see that they are correct. In July, the treasurer makes a yearly report to the county commissioners, who, at that time, compare his books with those of the county auditor. As we saw earlier, the state auditor is also required to make periodic checks of the county financial records.

The County Finance Committee is another group that has a part in the supervision of county finances. The county treasurer needs to deposit the county money in a bank for safekeeping. Moreover, the county can collect interest on its money when it is deposited in a bank or otherwise invested. Consequently, the treasurer selects a bank, makes a contract with it, and takes a bond from the bank covering the money to be deposited. Then the County Finance Committee makes certain that the bank is sound and can live up to its agreements, and approves other investments of county funds allowed by law. The committee consists of the county treasurer, the county auditor, and the chairman of the Board of County Commissioners. The treasurer acts as chairman and the auditor as secretary.

The constitution specifies that the state legislature cannot levy county taxes. It must pass general taxation laws and allow the counties to levy their own taxes in accordance with these laws, including a present option on the part of counties to levy a sales tax of one-half percent. This does not mean that the state cannot collect taxes from the counties. The constitution states that neither counties nor inhabitants of them may be released from state taxes, and, as we have seen, the state Department of Revenue, acting as the state board of equalization, determines how much each county owes the state as its share of state taxes.[6]

Before the taxes can be levied, the county commissioners must know the needs of the various county departments. For this purpose, the head of each county department estimates how much money his unit will need and sends this estimate to the county auditor. The auditor then projects the probable receipts and expenditures for the entire county[7] These figures are made into a preliminary county budget, which goes to the county commissioners. They then hold a public hearing at which any taxpayer may protest the amount allotted to any department, and, after this hearing, the commissioners adopt the budget in its final form by the first Monday in December. They then levy sufficient taxes to cover the budget within the millage limits allowed by law.

6. This money comes largely from the taxes paid by owners of real estate in the county. For the additional sources of revenue from the amount of business done by corporations within a county and other types of taxes, see the section in chapter 3 on the Department of Revenue.

7. Or the county commissioners may have this done by their own budget officer.

If the amount set cannot be raised within those limits, either the budget has to be reduced or arrangements have to be made to borrow money, or to call a special election to see if the voters will agree to raise the levy temporarily.

The county assessor is the official responsible for appraising the value of our real property and, technically, our personal property.[8] The county assessor hires assistants to serve as appraisers. The 1971 legislature encouraged the hiring of trained appraisers as part of its program for securing uniform property evaluation throughout the state. If the appraiser wishes to follow this procedure, he notifies the county commissioners and the state Department of Revenue, each of which designates a representative, who, with the assessor, form a committee to determine the number needed and their salary. The appraisers are then selected from a list prepared by the Department of Personnel after consulting with the Washington State Association of Counties, the Washington State Association of County Assessors, and the Department of Revenue.

In the discussion of the Department of Revenue, we noted that one of its functions is to work out a scale of property values throughout the state so that an assessor in one county will assign a value to a house and lot, for example, which is approximately the same as that given to a similar piece of property in the same type of locality in another county. In an attempt to encourage the retention of "open space" areas—that is, areas left vacant with no buildings on them—the 1971 legislature allowed private individuals to hold such land under an agreement with the county for partial tax release.

Personal property is defined as any possession not attached to the land. Houses and other buildings, consequently, are considered *real property.* Furniture, automobiles, livestock, farm and business equipment, merchandise, and other movable objects are personal property, but the legislature allows a sufficient number of exemptions in these categories for tax purposes that, except for motor vehicles and certain business holdings, personal property taxation is practically nonexistent. The automobile tax, as has been mentioned, is handled as an excise tax through the Department of Motor Vehicles.

In evaluating real property the assessor and his assistants note first the amount and kind of land owned by each person, the size and type of house, the kind of roofing and heating, number of fireplaces, bathrooms, and all of the other features which help determine its value. The assistant appraiser records all of this in a field book, and, from these figures, the amount of assessment is determined.

The complete lists of property for the county are called the assessment rolls, which the county assessor gives to the county commissioners in time for a June meeting. Until 1969 the county commissioners comprised the County

8. Although in this state personal property is almost completely exempt from taxation

Board of Equalization to hear complaints about the assessment placed on specific pieces of property, and they may still form this board at their discretion. However, if they prefer, the legislature now allows the commissioners to appoint additional members to the Board of Equalization or to create a separate board. In either case, the number is to be not less than three nor more than seven. If the commissioners name others to the board, they must be selected for their knowledge of the values of property in the county and they must not hold any elective office or be an employee of any elected official. Their term of office is three years, and they may be removed by a majority vote of the county commissioners.

The County Board of Equalization, with the county assessor as clerk, analyzes the assessment rolls for discrepancies in evaluation of property in the various parts of the county. It may raise or lower the assessment figure for a given piece of property five days after having notified the owner of its intention. Any property owner may protest either the original evaluation of his holdings or any change made by the equalization board. Appeals from the County Board of Equalization are made to the state Department of Revenue, acting as the State Board of Equalization.

After the County Board of Equalization has approved the assessment rolls, the county assessor makes duplicate summaries of the corrected lists. He keeps one copy and sends the other to the state Department of Revenue, which reviews the distribution of corporation taxes among the counties and notifies the counties of the proportion of taxes collected by them that is due the state.

The Department of Revenue sends the corrected assessment lists to the state auditor, who, in the meantime, has received from each county assessor a summary of the taxes paid from tax collections in his county for the preceding year. From this summary, the state auditor can tell if any of the counties still owe the state any taxes from previous years. Such unpaid taxes are called *delinquent* taxes, and a county is allowed seven years in which to send to the state a proportion of the taxes collected in the county. If any county is delinquent in its payment of such taxes to the state for the seventh consecutive year, the state auditor adds this amount to the county's current assessment of state taxes given to him by the Department of Revenue. The state auditor then returns the completed lists to the respective county assessors.

In the meantime, the Board of County Commissioners has made up the county's budget and set the amount of local taxes to be levied in the manner described above. It has also certified to the county assessor the millage rate for other taxing districts in the county. As soon as he receives his equalized

---

except for the sales taxes, and they are a form of excise tax rather than property taxes, as such.

assessment list from the state auditor, the assessor is ready to figure up the total amount of taxes to be raised by applying the millage rate fixed by the commissioners to the assessed valuation of the county. To get the amount of taxes owed by each property owner, he multiplies this percentage figure by the assessment value assigned to each person's holdings. The completed list of the taxes owed by each individual is called the *tax roll*. The assessor turns the tax roll over to the county auditor, who, in turn, gives it to the county treasurer, who is responsible for collecting the taxes.

County Assessor's Miscellaneous Duties

The assessor has several miscellaneous duties in addition to making up the tax rolls. Since he or a deputy assessor visits each family in the county, it is possible for him to obtain statistical information on all of the county's inhabitants. Until the State Census Board was created, he was required to make a census in the middle of each decade (each year that ends in five), and he may still make one at the request of the county commissioners. He makes an assessment for dog licenses in the counties where the county commissioners require them. The assessor also sends to the secretary of state a list of corporations that operate in his county but have their headquarters in some other state. These are known as *foreign corporations.* The assessor gives the state Department of Revenue a list of all corporations whose assessed valuation is over $3,000 so that it can apportion their taxes among the counties in the state.

County Treasurer's Duties

Collecting taxes is one of the county treasurer's most important jobs, although he is concerned in all phases of the county's finances. When he receives the tax rolls from the county auditor, he publishes in the newspaper designated by the commissioners as the county newspaper a notice that taxes are due on and after 15 February. Half of the amount is due before 1 May, and the second half is due before 1 October. If the taxes are not paid by those dates, they are delinquent, and the county demands the payment of interest on the amount owed. The commissioners have considerable leeway in determining how long the county should continue to carry delinquent taxes, but if they decide that the taxes must be collected, the county carries out foreclosure proceedings and seizes the property or as much of it as is required to settle the tax account.

Taxes form a large part of the county's income, but there are other sources of revenue, also. We have seen that the county issues various types of licenses, and the fees for all of these, except those issued for state departments, go into the county treasury. Nearly all of the county officials collect fees for recording documents or issuing papers in connection with their work. These fees, too, are turned over to the county treasurer. The treasurer also receives money from the sale or lease of county property, and fines are another source of county money. The state and federal governments make grants for schools, roads, social security, land use planning, and other aspects of public welfare, and some of this money is divided among the counties. These grants determine, in part, priorities established by the counties for the direction in which their own planning will go. Assessments based on benefits received from road improvements and extermination of peses or weeds are also collected by the county treasurer. He is the custodian of all county funds, regardless of their source.

The treasurer pays money out of the county treasury for county expenses. We have mentioned that the county auditor issues warrants to pay the county expenses after the claims are approved by the Board of County Commissioners, the court, or the directors of a district. The auditor gives to the treasurer a certified record of the warrants issued so that the treasurer knows how many he should pay. If there is not sufficient money in the treasury to redeem all of the warrants issued, they bear interest at a rate agreed upon between the county and the banks concerned.

When cashed warrants are returned to the treasurer by banks, he enters the amounts on his books and returns the canceled warrants to the auditor for filing. According to law, the county treasurer distributes funds to the proper agencies. On the tenth of each month, he gives all city taxes received to the city treasurers, and, after the last day in each month, he sends to the state treasurer the amount of taxes due the state. He reports quarterly to the county commissioenrs, and in July of each year he makes a complete financial report to them.

The treasurer (plus others designated by the county commissioners) issues dog licenses in counties where a county license is required, and he also grants licenses to peddlers outside of incorporated towns. He serves as treasurer for some types of districts in his county. One example is the joint diking and drainage districts; another is the school districts. He is also ex officio tax collector for cities and towns.

Like the other county officials, the county treasurer must take the usual oath of office and give a bond. The bond for the treasurer must be double the amount he is likely to administer during his term of office. This is probably twenty times as large a bond as that required of other county officials. The treasurer, also, may be removed by the county commissioners if a court action is brought against him for misconduct in office. The commissioners appoint a temporary treasurer until the case is tried. If he is cleared of the charge, the treasurer may take up his duties again.

County Auditor's Duties

We have seen that the county auditor takes part in the financial affairs of his county. He approves the tax rolls. He checks each request for payment from county funds, gets the approval of the county commissioners for the payment of each bill requiring their consideration, and writes out a warrant for those to be paid. The auditor and county clerk are required to check the fee books of each county official every month in order to make certain that all fees have been turned over to the county treasurer. Since the auditor is the official clerk of the Board of County Commissioners, he helps with the quarterly and annual check of the treasurer's books.

The county auditor is not responsible, however, for the final check of county books. This is done by examiners appointed by the state auditor, who is responsible for seeing that the county officials in each county are not mismanaging public funds, and who conducts an annual examination of county books.

In addition to his financial duties, the county auditor has many others. He is ex officio recorder for the county. In that capacity, he keeps a record of every deed, mortgage, chattel mortgage, lien, abstract of title, and other papers concerning the ownership of real and personal property. Recording of this kind is done so that anyone may prove that he owns his property. In connection with his registration of property titles, the auditor keeps plat books, which contain diagrams of the plots of land in his county, as a means of identifying any piece of land. If the assessor's appraisal maps are sufficiently detailed, the auditor may use them as current plat books. As registrar of titles, the auditor is also required to keep a register of titles and a numerical and alphabetical index to all papers filed in his office. In large counties, the volume of recording is so great that the auditor keeps a separate department for that purpose with an assistant in charge, but the auditor himself is responsible for the efficiency of both the auditing and recording departments.

In his capacity as clerk of the Board of County Commissioners, the auditor issues licenses for grocers, auctioneers, ferry operators, and hawkers in rural areas. In addition, he is authorized to issue various types of licenses for state officials. The State Department of Motor Vehicles made the county auditors its agents for automobile licenses, and the auditors receive applications for all kinds of vehicle license plates and forward them to the Department of Motor Vehicles. Other agents are also assigned to receive applications for motor vehicle licenses. The state Department of Game also made the auditors its deputies for issuing licenses for hunting and fishing, although other local persons besides the auditors may also be designated as such agents, including proprietors of sports shops and so on.

Even though the State Department of Motor Vehicles is in charge of licensing all types of medical practitioners, the legislature requires that dentists have their licenses recorded in the office of the county auditor of the county in which they practice. Records of marriages are necessary both in connection with probate or divorce actions in our superior courts and with property title registrations in the auditor's office. Until recently, the county auditor issued marriage licenses, and the county clerk recorded the marriage certificates for marriages actually performed. Now, however, the auditor is required to record the marriage certificates, also, and to send a record to the state registrar of vital statistics.

In addition to these chief duties, the auditor has others as ex officio members of many county boards. He is clerk of the County Board of Health, secretary of the County Finance Committee, and a member of the County Election Board. In the last connection, he also has the title of registrar of voters and supervisor of elections.

County Board of Health

The remaining county officials, except for the court officials who have been discussed in chapter 5, are not elected by the voters of the county, but rather are appointed. The county commissioners plus the county auditor as clerk make up the County Board of Health, which appoints the county health officer, who must be a legally qualified physician and have a Master's degree in public health. The board appoints him for a term of two years and sets the amount of his salary. If the County Board of Health fails to appoint a health officer for thirty days after July 1 following a general election, the State Board of Health makes the appointment.

The county health officer is an ex officio member of the County Board of Health and acts as chief executive for the board. The regulations of the Division of Health of the state Department of Social and Health Services have to be observed, and the county board decides on additional steps to be taken to promote more healthful communities within its county. Once these matters are decided, the county health officer is responsible for putting such measures into effect. He has the authority to combat contagious diseases in many ways. He may quarantine anyone who is sick with a contagious disease, and he may order anyone so exposed to be vaccinated. He may also order anyone to disinfect a building or his personal belongings if they have become contaminated or to clean up a garbage dump or anything else which may be a danger to public health. Removing something harmful to the public welfare is called *abating a nuisance.*

We have noted that the State Department of Social and Health Services tries to bring to public attention any improved methods for maintaining health. The county health officer keeps in close touch with the Division of

Health and distributes much information from that office.

In 1967 the legislature authorized the creation of a health district, which could consist of a single county or more than one. The district includes all of the cities in the area except ones of more than 100,000 population, and they may become part of the district, too, if the city and county legislative bodies can agree on division of responsibilities and financial contributions. For them a District Board of Health takes the place of the County Board of Health. The size of the district board varies with the size of the district. For example, in a district comprising one county, the Board of Health consists of not fewer than five members, including the three county commissioners, plus two others selected by the legislative bodies of the cities and towns in the district from their members, based on respective population and financial contributions. In health districts of two or more counties, the composition of the board follows the same pattern except that there are seven members. If a district board is created, it supersedes the county and city or town health boards in the district.

County Agricultural Expert

Each county may have the services of an agricultural expert at the discretion of the county commissioners. They ask the director of the Agricultural Extension Service of Washington State University to choose an agricultural expert for their approval. The commissioners and the state university may make any agreement in regard to his term of office, salary, and so forth.

The agricultural expert, who is usually known locally as the *county agent,* gives instruction and conducts demonstrations in better farming methods for the people of his county. The director of the Extension Service supervises his work, but, in order that the county may have information on his progress, he is required by law to make a monthly report to the county commissioners.

Home Economics Experts

Experts in other fields may be appointed under similar arrangements. Many of the counties now have home economics experts, who help the housewives of the county in learning new canning methods, more efficient care of their homes and families, and similar matters.

Horticultural Inspectors

In chapter 3 we mentioned that inspection of fruit trees was one of the duties of the state Department of Agriculture. There are two types of horticultural inspectors, *inspectors-at-large* and *local inspectors.* The director

Sailboats on Lake Washington. The Lake Washington floating bridge is in the background. (Photo by Washington State Department of Commerce and Economic Development)

of agriculture assigns the inspectors-at-large to duty in one or more counties, and he may move them from one place to another at his discretion. They are paid from state funds. If twenty-five persons who own an orchard or plants of any kind in any county find that they need help in getting rid of plant diseases, they may ask the county commissioners for local inspectors. The county commissioners then request the director of agriculture to appoint one or more local inspectors. These local inspectors work only in that particular county, and they are paid from county funds.

County Horticultural Pest and Disease Board

The 1969 legislature gave the Board of County Commissioners authority to create a County Horticultural Pest and Disease Board, consisting of four members plus the horticultural inspector at large for the horticultural district in which the county is located. The agricultural expert, or somebody appointed by him, is a nonvoting member. The function of the board is to control the spread of horticultural pests and diseases, and it may order landowners to get rid of them or pay for their removal.

County Park and Recreation Board

Another county board having a connection with a phase of public welfare is the County Park and Recreation Board. If the county commissioners wish to have county parks administered by such a board, they appoint seven members who constitute the board.[9] The purpose of the board is to

9. Before 1969 the board consisted of the county superintendent of schools plus six additional members appointed by the county commissioners.

administer county recreational activities and to employ a county park and recreation superintendent to operate parks, playgrounds, or other recreational activities. The 1969 legislature gave the county commissioners the authority to develop open space, park recreation, and community facilities through a county recreational authority and to issue general obligation bonds to pay for the cost if they prefer that approach.

County Civil Service Commission

The 1959 legislature established a County Civil Service Commission in each county, consisting of three members appointed by the county commissioners for six-year terms. Counties of Class IV or lower may combine for the purpose of setting up a civil service commission, in which case the joint boards make the appointment.

Their purpose is to operate a civil service (merit) system for the employment of persons in the county sheriff's office, including deputy sheriffs and all other employees except for the county sheriff himself[10] and certain others, such as one private secretary, a chief criminal deputy, and a chief civil deputy, whom the sheriff might need to choose personally in order to have a small corps of assistants who agreed with his policies. The commission is instructed to establish a classification schedule, to give examinations to determine the capability of applicants for the various positions, and to see that all appointments and promotions are made solely on the basis of merit.

County Libraries

The county commissioenrs have the authority to establish a county library and to maintain additional service to areas outside the county library location by bookmobile, local depositories, or other means. Moreover, two or more counties may join in operating a regional library, and a county or regional library may also contract to furnish books and library services to a city or town. For the relationship of the state library to local libraries, see the sections on the state library organization in chapter 3.

A public library in a county or region is managed by a board of trustees appointed by the county commissioners of the counties affected. The size of the board of trustees varies according to the extent of the area served.

Counties larger than Class VI are required to maintain a county law library for the use of attorneys, judges, and other public officials. Two or more counties may join in a regional law library, but one of adequate size (to be

10. The sheriff is elected by the voters in the standard county commissioner type of county government.

determined by the board of trustees) must be maintained at the courthouse where each superior court is located.

The county board of trustees consists of the chairman of the Board of County Commissioners plus one superior court judge and three attorneys. The 1971 legislature, which provided for regional law libraries, specified that a regional law library board of trustees should consist of one superior court judge, one county commissioner from each county, and one lawyer from each county seat.

Community Mental Health Program Administrative Board

The 1971 legislature permitted the creation of a Community Mental Health Program Administrative Board of not fewer than nine nor more than fifteen members, which must include consumer and minority group representation, to be appointed by the county commissioners. The function of the board is to plan and administer whatever mental health program is maintained in a county.

County Disability Board

The 1969 legislature required that a county disability board be established in each county to pass on claims for disability by law enforcement officers and fire fighters from their retirement system fund for parts of the county not contained in a city having a city disability board. The County Disability Board consists of five members: one from the Board of County Commissioners (or other county legislative group) to be appointed by the body; one member of a city or town legislative body in the county that does not have a city disability board (this member is chosen by a majority of the mayors of such cities and towns within the county); one fire fighter chosen by the fire fighters served, subject to approval by the County Disability Board; one law enforcement officer elected by the law enforcement officers, with the approval of the County Disability Board; and one member from the public at large living in the county but outside a city that has a disability board, appointed by the other four members. The term of office is two years.

County Air Pollution Control Authority

The 1967 legislature created a county air pollution control authority in counties of Classes AA, A, and I and allowed the county commissioners in any other class of county to activate such an authority if, after a public hearing, they think it is wise to do so. If a county does not have its own air pollution authority, it is a part of a regional air pollution control authority.

The governing body of each authority is a board of directors, varying in size with the size of the area covered. For example, in an authority comprising one county, the board consists of two appointees of a city selection committee with one representing the city having the greatest population in the county plus two county commissioners designated by the Board of County Commissioners. The city selection committee for each county consists of the mayors of each incorporated city and town in the county. The board or an individual city without an authority has the power to control the degree of air pollution in its area.

LOCAL SCHOOL ORGANIZATION

Before 1965 the public schools of the state were organized on a state, county, and district basis. Now, however, the county has been virtually eliminated as an administrative unit of the schools, and intermediate school districts have been substituted. An intermediate school district may consist of only part of a county in metropolitan areas or more than one county in rural sections of the state.

In chapter 2 we learned that the State Board of Education sets the general requirements for courses of study and standards to be met by the schools of the state and that the state Department of Education, under the direction of the state superintendent of public instruction, administers these regulations and supervises the work of the schools. The Intermediate School District Board, in turn, adopts rules for the schools of the intermediate district that are not inconsistent with the rules of the State Board of Education and the superintendent of public instruction. It also appoints the intermediate school district superintendent, who puts into effect the regulations adopted by the board. The directors of the individual school districts have charge of the schools in their district and hire the teachers, principals, and local school superintendents.

Intermediate School District Board

The 1971 legislature stated that the purpose of forming intermediate school districts was to develop regional educational service agencies to provide cooperative and informational services to local school districts; make the educational system more readily and efficiently adaptable to the changing economic and educational pattern within the state; provide the pupils within the state with equal educational opportunities; and assist the superintendent of public instruction and the State Board of Education.

The intermediate school district board, which sets the standards (within the limits of the regulations adopted by the State Board of Education), consists of seven members who are elected by the voters of the district. The board may increase its number to nine members if it wishes. The board members are elected at the time of the general school election. Persons wishing to run for the office of board members must file a declaration of candidacy with the county auditor of the county designated as the headquarters county of the intermediate school district at least forty-six days prior to the general school election. The county auditor certifies the names of the candidates to the officials conducting the elections in the board-member districts.

The board fills vacancies in its own group unless there are more than three in a seven-member board or four in a nine-member board. In these cases, the State Board of Education makes appointments to serve until the next general school election when new members are elected to fill the unexpired terms. The term of office is four years, and the members receive an allowance for days spent on intermediate school district business as set by the legislature for state officials. A board member must not be an employee of a school district or a member of the board of directors of a common school district or a member of the State Board of Education. Initially, for the first election of board members in 1969, the State Board of Education set the boundaries for the individual board-member districts. After that, the board itself reviews the boundaries of the board-member districts every ten years (beginning in 1971) to see that they provide equal representation according to population and conform to the boundary changes of the individual school districts within the intermediate school district.

The duties of the Intermediate School District Board are: to appoint and fix the salary of an intermediate school district superintendent; to arrange for one or more teachers' institutes or workshops for in-service training if they believe such meetings to be desirable; to pass on the recommendations of the intermediate school district superintendent on manuals, courses of study, and rules for circulating libraries; to approve the budgets for the district and certify to the Board of County Commissioners the amount needed from county funds, certify to the State Board of Education the estimate of special service funds needed, and certify to the county treasurer the amount due the high school districts, based on reports of attendance and costs received from the individual high school superintendents; to assist the intermediate school district superintendent in selecting personnel and clerical staff; to supervise the common schools of the district; to acquire or dispose of property and enter into contracts necessary to the intermediate school district business; and to fill vacancies existing on the boards of directors of individual school districts within the intermediate school district if there are fewer than a majority of the local district members left to appoint the missing one.

Intermediate School District Superintendent

Once the Intermediate School District Board has adopted the regulations for the schools in the intermediate school district, it is the duty of the intermediate school district superintendent to put them into effect. He is appointed by the intermediate school district board and must have the following qualifications: hold a valid principal's or superintendent's credentials in Washington or meet other criteria set by the State Board of Education for that office. The state board now requires that he must have completed five years of college work and have had at least five years' teaching or educational administration experience in the common schools or office of a county superintendent. His office is nonpartisan.

Some of the specific duties of the intermediate school district superintendent (in addition to those mentioned in the above section) are: to distribute educational materials and forms to the teachers and school directors in his district; to keep a record of contracts held by the teachers in his county and report them to the county auditor; to make a transcript of school district boundaries and furnish a copy to each school district clerk when it is needed; to arrange for institutes or workshops requested by the Intermediate School District Board.

School Districts

Each individual school in a city or rural area has its principal or superintendent (both if it is large enough), depending on its size, and the next larger unit of school administration is the school district. The State Board of Education is the agency that has the final authority to define the boundaries of the school districts. It acts on the recommendation of the County Committee on School District Organization, which consists of a group of from five to nine members elected by the board of school district directors.

The legislature classifies school districts as to size. Those having a population of over 10,000 are first-class districts; others maintaining a fully accredited high school or containing a city of the third or fourth class or an area of one square mile having a population of at least 300 are second class. Any others are third-class districts. Each incorporated city or town comprises one school district, except that two or more may be included in a single school district. If a school district has an average daily attendance of fewer than five pupils or has not maintained the minimum terms of school, the intermediate school district superintendent is to report this to the County Committee on School District Organization, which shall consider recommending the dissolution of the school district and its annexation to some other district.

Boards of Directors of School Districts

Within each school district, a board of directors has charge of the management of the individual elementary and high schools and, until 1967, community (junior) colleges. The board of directors is elected by the voters of the district. The 1971 legislature enacted the following regulations as to the size of the board: third-class districts, three directors, one to be elected for a term of two years and two for a term of four eyars; second-class districts, five directors, two to be elected for a term of two years and three for a term of four years, the election to be either at large or by director districts; first-class districts, five directors, two for a term of two years and three for four years, the election to be either at large or by director districts. However, in counties of Class AA or A containing a city of the first class, two directors are elected for a term of three years and three for a term of six years. Other exceptions are that in districts of the first class that have been formed from more than one former first-class districts, except for those having six-year terms, five directors are elected, either at large or by director districts, two for two years and three for four years. If a first-class district has an enrollment of 70,000 pupils or more in class AA counties, seven directors are elected by director districts, two for two-year terms, two for four-year terms, and three for six-year terms. All school district elections are held on the second Tuesday in November in odd-numbered years. The term of office of all school district officers begins on the date when the canvassing board certifies that the winning candidates have been elected.

Except for school districts of the first class in Class AA counties having an enrollment of 70,000 pupils or more, if no more than two people have filed declarations of candidacy for each office, their names are not included in the primary election ballot, only on the general election ballot. The same regulation holds for the state superintendent of public instruction.

The county committee on school district organization divides into five school directors' districts all first- and second-class districts except those containing a city of over 7,000, which may choose at a special election whether or not it wants to be so divided. For the school districts not divided into school directors' districts, the directors are elected at large. In a district with directors' districts, if five directors are to be elected, the voters of the entire district choose one director from each director's district. If only three directors are elected, they are chosen at large.

The board of directors selects the teachers in its district and fixes the amount of their salary. In second- and third-class districts, the contract which they make with a teacher has to be approved by the intermediate school district superintendent. The Board of School District Directors may dismiss a teacher for sufficient cause, provided that he is given a proper hearing. The teacher may appeal from the board to the county superintendent and from him to the state superintendent of public instruction or to the superior court, depending on the type of charge. If a school has more than one teacher, the directors appoint a principal, and, if the district has more than one building, they appoint a superintendent for the district.

In addition to employing the teachers for its district, the Board of School District Directors helps to enforce the rules laid down by the state superintendent of public instruction and by the State Board of Education. It adopts policies for the selection of textbooks with the advice of the instructional materials committee and the curriculum development committee. In districts that have only elementary schools, the intermediate district school superintendent correlates the adoptions for the elementary schools with those of the high school districts so that the texts in the lower grade fit into the design for the upper ones. In some districts the directors buy supplies and textbooks, which are lent to the pupils; in others, students are required to buy part or all of their schoolbooks. The 1971 legislature amended the law that allows the boards of school district directors to suspend or expel students, requiring the board to adopt and make available to each pupil and parent "reasonable written rules regarding pupil conduct, discipline and rights." The rules must be consistent with the law and with rules of the superintendent of public instruction or the State Board of Education. They must include substantive and procedural due process guarantees as prescribed by the State Board of Education. Under these circumstances, the district directors may suspend, expel, or discipline pupils.

The board may provide transportation for children who live too far away from school to get there by themselves. It has the authority to buy or lease real property for the district at the mandate of the people in the district. and it may sell school property within certain limits set by the legislature. The board is also in charge of supplying furniture and other school equipment and of seeing that the buildings are properly heated, lighted, and ventilated. The 1971 legislature stipulated that each board should join with boards of directors of other school districts in buying supplies, equipment, and services by establishing a joint purchasing agency. The agency may also include private schools in its joint purchases of supplies, equipment, and services, as long as the private schools pay their proportionate share of the costs involved and prepare the required budget forms. Each board is required to provide every school in its district with a United States flag.

PROPOSED CHANGES IN COUNTY ADMINISTRATION

After a study of our state and county offices, it is obvious in the fields of public welfare, finance, elections, public health, roads, education, and, to a limited extent, agriculture that state officials and boards have their counterparts in each county. In most instances, these county officials are supervised to some extent by the state officers. The county commissioners form the liaison group between the state and local officials, and in most fields they have considerable leeway in conforming to decisions of the state officials. The commissioners also exercise some supervision over the county officials. Students of government have pointed out that such divided authority over county officials makes for inefficiency and sometimes confusion and that it would be more efficient to have counties acting purely as subdivisions of the state. The inhabitants of a given area, however, like to feel that they have control of their local government. We have seen how, during the territorial period, the people resented the "long distance" control of the territory from Washington, D.C., and, to a certain extent, many people feel the same way about the management of local affairs from Olympia. So, wherever uniformity is not essential, the voters seem to prefer to keep considerable division of authority, even if it is more costly and cumbersome. It is too early to tell what the addition of direct relations between counties and the federal government will do to the county-state relationship.

However, in counties which contain a big city, a third conflicting jurisdiction appears—the city government. In a county like King, for example, the government of its main city, Seattle, overshadows that of the county. There is not only the question of ironing out differences of opinion between state and county officials over their respective jurisdictions, but also between county and city agencies. Moreover, the problem of supervising the work of county officials in a large county is a huge task, and it is harder for a group (the Board of County Commissioners) to act as an executive in this respect than for one individual to do so. Therefore, political scientists have proposed that, even if we continue to maintain county autonomy in various fields, we could increase the efficiency of county administration greatly by allowing the Board of County Commissioners to continue to act as the county legislature, but create an office of county executive to supervise the work of the county officials and to see that the county ordinances are carried out. This is the form of government recently adopted by King County,[11] and students of local government are watching its progress with interest. A further proposal, as we have seen, is to combine the county and city governments in places where a city dominates the county and have one legislative body and one county-city manager as the supervisor.

If a manager (whether he be county or city or both) has to supervise elective officials, his task is more difficult than if they are appointive. We saw how this is true with the governor's supervision of the work of the other state executive officials. Many political scientists, therefore, advocate the short ballot for local as well as state government, and, as has been pointed out, King County in its new charter has followed this principle as well.

At the 1965 Institute for County Commissioners, Ed Munro, county

11. The nine-member legislative body is called the county council.

commissioner for King County, discussed some of the problems of a county that contains a large city. He feels that the county itself should have the power to provide sewers, water, fire protection, libraries, and other services for the city as well as the county. Such functions are now performed for the cities, ordinarily, by sewer districts, water districts, and so on, called junior taxing districts because they have the power to make assessments within their district for the specific service rendered. He says that if the county could supply these needs "the county could properly plan and develop necessary urban facilities along with actual growth, instead of waiting till things get bad enough that junior taxing districts are formed to solve the problem."

He continues:

I'm convinced that, in the long run, there's only going to be one government at the local level. In the old days when you got to the city limits you were in farm land. Today when you get to a city limits you're in the same grid pattern of streets, and you have the same demand for urban services. Your problems are statewide, and your government should be areawide, too. The first step should be to consolidate government within counties. There is no reason why, if the problems are areawide, more than one government should administer the areas.

In King County we have over 200 taxing districts, and this is insanity. We've got fire districts in King County that are so rich they've got better fire equipment than New York City, and they could put out a fire in the Empire State Building—but the whole district hasn't got a three-story house in it! But they've got the money and the law says they can spend it, so they do spend it. When we think of the demand for services that we are being requested to supply, and to think that money is being used in that fashion, it's just nonsense. And that is why you just have to have overall control of that budget. The money that is coming in has to be distributed according to need. It can't be distributed on some set formula. But because it all too often is, we as county commissioners have inadequate income to finance the services required of us.

County government is divided internally, as well as in the external sense of sharing power with other jurisdictions. I don't think that three men with equal powers, having administrative or executive powers, legislative powers, and quasi-judicial powers, should be wearing all of these hats. I don't think this is right. I think there has got to be a separation of these powers. You have to have one executive, and you have to have a legislative body to control him. That was the basic function of a legislature, historically. The reason it was set up was to control the power of the chief executive. There has to be a single executive and I think he ought to be elected, because I'm of the opinion that any man who is ruling us should not be free from our being able to decide whether he should stay there or not. Now we stumble around a lot, but we've still got the best government in the world because it's responsive, and government has to be responsive as well as responsible.

In order to solve a vital problem we've always been confronted with, which is cooperation between units of government, we have formed in my part of the state the Puget Sound Governmental Conference, which is a free association of the counties of King, Pierce, Kitsap, and Snohomish, and the cities of Seattle, Everett, Bremerton, and Tacoma. It is not a legal entity, but we sit around a table and we agree on policy matters relating to our region. We've now embarked on the greatest transportation study in the history of this state. The impetus for this came right out of the

Governmental Conference. We've had a joint jail study for our area, and also an open space study. We've gotten some laws through that will allow King County to go in with the other counties and the cities in building a joint jail to take care of all the prisoners, and we're actually moving in this direction. The procedure involved in this leads me to another suggestion: Get acquainted with your legislator, and talk to him before he goes to Olympia and before he runs for office. Government has to move, and it has to operate, and these are some of the ways to see that it does.[12]

It has been pointed out that, as government services have increased, local and state taxes have mounted to the point where legislators are urged by many groups to curb public expenditures. Yet, when they attempt to reduce spending by abolishing governmental services, they discover that it is extremely difficult to find an agency sufficiently unpopular that people are willing to give it up. Moreover, as we have seen, increased salaries are necessary for many public offices if first-rate candidates are to be secured. More efficient organization of our state and local agencies appears to be one partial solution for our dilemma. If the voters are unwilling to bear increasing government costs and yet do not approve recommendations for streamlining county and city governments or for reorganizing the state executive and administrative agencies, then the voters will have to study these problems seriously enough to propose other remedies.

Citizens of urban and rural areas, regardless of the type of local government, must give serious attention to such problems as providing adequate transportation without raising the air pollution level, assuring traffic control, preventing the deterioration of the "inner city" as residents and businesses move to the suburbs, maintaining environmental quality as well as increasing recreation areas, educating both students and adults not only in conventional learning but in awareness of their possibilities in service to society. The 1961 legislature provided that a county or city may join with one or more other counties or cities or private organizations to form a regional planning commission to propose the best policies for future regulation of the physical growth of an area and its industrial development. It may plan the utilization of natural resources, conservation, recreation, transportation, sewage disposal, public buildings, housing, slum clearance, and so on.

12. *Proceedings of the Institute for County Commissioners, Pullman, Washington, March 9-10, 1965,* ed. George A. Condon and Paul R. Meyer (Pullman: Division of Governmental Studies and Services, Washington State University; Olympia: Washington State Association of County Commissioners, 1965).

SUGGESTED READINGS

In chapter 5, *County Government in Washington State,* edited by Barbara Byers, was recommended as a reference for the county officials connected with the superior court. The remainder of the book is equally helpful for other aspects of county government.

In addition, the county auditor's annual report for one's own county and, perhaps, neighboring counties gives very useful statistical information concerning receipts, expenditures, types of districts, names of local officials, and so forth, for the county concerned. Copies for recent years may be secured upon request from the county auditor's office in a given county.

The Washington State Association of Counties, whose headquarters are in Olympia, issues very useful bulletins on various aspects of current county problems. Any that are available may be obtained upon request. The latest edition of the Washington Research Council's *Handbook* (Olympia) gives helpful information on county government.

TABLE IV
SALARIES OF COUNTY OFFICIALS (1973)*

Classification of County	County Commissioners	Auditor	Clerk	Treasurer	Sheriff	Assessor	Prosecuting Attorney	Coroner
AA	$18,000	$18,000	$18,000	$18,000	$18,000	$19,000	$27,500	$18,000
A	$17,700	$16,000	$16,000	$16,000	$17,700	$16,000	$22,500	$15,000
I	$16,000	$14,500	$14,500	$14,500	$16,000	$14,500	$22,500	$ 8,000
II	$13,500	$13,500	$13,500	$13,500	$13,500	$13,500	$21,500	$ 5,000
III	$12,500	$12,500	$12,500	$12,500	$12,500	$12,500	$21,500	$ 3,600
IV	$10,000	$11,000	$11,000	$11,000	$11,000	$11,000	$15,000 in county with state univ.; $13,000 in one without	pros. atty acts
V	$ 8,500	$ 9,100	$ 9,100	$ 9,100	$ 9,200	$ 9,100	$12,000	pros. atty. acts
VI	$ 6,400	$ 9,100	$ 9,100	$ 9,100	$10,200	$ 9,100	$ 9,000	pros. atty. acts
VII	$ 5,950	$ 8,300	$ 8,300	$ 8,300	$ 9,500	$ 8,300	$ 9,000	pros. atty. acts
VIII	$ 5,950	$ 8,300	$ 8,300	$ 8,300	$ 9,500	$ 8,300	$ 9,000	pros. atty acts
IX	$ 5,500	$ 7,450	auditor acts	$ 7,450	$ 8,500	treas. acts	$ 9,000	pros. atty acts

* The intermediate school district superintendent is no longer considered a county official because he is employed by the Intermediate Board of School District Directors, which may represent a section of one county or an area comprising more than one county.

8. City Government

CLASSIFICATION OF CITIES

The type of government for a city in this state is largely determined by its size, although in recent years the legislature has given all cities an increasing number of choices. The classes established by the legislature are: I, cities over 20,000 population; II, 10,000-20,000 population; III, 1,500-10,000 population; IV, incorporated towns of 300-1,500 population.

CITY HOME RULE

The state constitution provides that any city having a population of more than 20,000 has *home rule;* that is, it may choose its own type of city government. The 1965 legislature extended this privilege to Class II cities. Consequently, any city of 10,000 or more population now has home rule.

The procedure stipulated for choosing its type of city government under home rule is that the existing city council, or other legislative group, calls a city election to choose a committee of fifteen qualified voters and freeholders (property owners). This committee meets within ten days after the election and drafts a charter for the city government. The constitution specifies that the charter must conform to our state constitution and to the laws passed by our legislature.

After the committee has drawn up a proposed charter, it is published in two newspapers. Thirty days afterward, an election is held so that the people may vote to accept or reject the new city government. If the voters approve of the charter, it is put into effect.

TYPES OF CITY GOVERNMENT

Until 1967 cities of the third and fourth classes had to follow the pattern of organization laid down for each class by the state legislature, and unless second-class cities had drafted a charter for a special type of government under their home-rule privilege they too were bound by specific legislative regulations. However, in 1967 the legislature authorized any city larger than 300 population to organize a code city government, and this form allows considerable flexibility. If a city is already operating under a home-rule charter, or wishes to establish one, and adopts the code city organization, it is called a charter code city. If it does not have a charter, but chooses the code city arrangement, it is known as a noncharter code city. Although there are some differences in the regulations applying to each, the system for both type of code cities is essentially the same.

Even before the legislature established the code city type of government, second-, third-, and fourth-class cities had a choice in their type of government. Any incorporated city or town may have the mayor-council or council-manager form of government (the latter having a mayor, council, and city manager); and any city of over 2,000 population may also choose the commission type of city government. The regulations for these apply only to cities not under a home-rule charter. A first- or second-class city may have a home-rule government called mayor-council, commission, or council-manager, but the provisions do not have to follow the outline for that type of city as specified by the legislature. By 1972 no city had adopted the code city type of government, and no second-class city had fashioned its own charter; therefore, the second-class cities listed below are governed by the regular provisions for second-class cities.

TYPES OF CITY GOVERNMENT IN FIRST- OR SECOND-CLASS CITIES
First-Class Cities (over 20,000)

Mayor-Council	Commission	Council-Manager
Aberdeen	Bremerton	Richland
(mayor + 12 councilmen)	(3 commissioners)	(mayor + 6 councilmen)
Bellingham	Everett	Spokane
(mayor + 7 councilmen)	(3 commissioners)	(mayor + 6 councilmen)
Seattle		Tacoma
(mayor + 9 councilmen)		(mayor + 8 councilmen)
		Vancouver
		(mayor + 6 councilmen)
		Yakima
		(mayor + 6 councilmen)

Second-Class Cities (10,000-20,000)

Mayor-Council	Commission	Council-Manager
Hoquiam		Mercer Island (City)
(mayor + 12 councilmen)		(seven councilmen)
Renton		Port Angeles
(mayor + 12 councilmen)		(seven councilmen)

Fifty-nine third-class cities use the mayor-council government, seven use the commission form, and seventeen the council-manager form. Also, fourteen of the third-class cities having the mayor-manager form. Also, fourteen of the third-class cities having the mayor-council form have a city supervisor, who performs some of the types of administrative duties assigned to a city manager in cities under the council-manager form of government. All of the 173 units incorporated as fourth-class towns have the mayor-council type of government except East Redmond, which has the council-manager form. Waitsburg still operates under its territorial charter. Under state law, it would classify as a fourth-class town.

When an unincorporated town wishes to become incorporated, the people present a petition to the county commissioners, who provide for an election at which the people vote on the question. If the vote is favorable, they choose their type of government within the limits mentioned above.

If a city wishes to annex outlying areas, its legislative body may file a resolution to that effect with the county commissioners. If residents of such localities want to become a part of the city, they, too, may file a petition with the county commissioners. In either case, the commissioners arrange for a review board consisting of school directors and representatives of the city and county, plus the director of the state Department of Commerce and Economic Development. If the board recommends annexation, the county commissioners arrange for a special election. If the area proposed for annexation is less than ten acres and $200,000 in assessed valuation, a review board is not required. This step, recommended by the Legislative Council, now allows cities to initiate annexation proceedings instead of being dependent on county action.

MAYOR-COUNCIL TYPE OF GOVERNMENT

In the mayor-council type of city government, the offices vary with the class of city. The first-class cities indicate in their charter what officials they wish.

Second-class cities elect a mayor, clerk, treasurer, police judge, and twelve councilmen. The term of office of the police judge is two years; that of the others, four years. The mayor appoints a police chief, street commissioners, attorney, and whatever other officials the council authorizes.

Third-class cities elect a mayor, seven councilmen, a clerk, treasurer, and attorney. The council may make the offices of city clerk, attorney, and treasurer appointive by the mayor with the confirmation by a majority vote of the council. One councilman-at-large serves for two years; the other officials, as well as six councilmen, have four-year terms. The mayor appoints the police chief, police judge, street superintendent, health officer, and any others whom the council designates. Full- or part-time engineers may be authorized or contracts made with engineering firms. The 1969 legislature provided that the offices of the treasurer and clerk may be combined.

In four-class towns, the voters elect a mayor, five councilmen, and a treasurer unless the council wishes to combine the treasurer's office with that of clerk, an appointive office. The term of office for the councilmen is two years; for the others, four years. The mayor appoints a clerk, marshal, police justice, and others established by the ordinance. In third- and fourth-class cities, the mayor has a vote only if there is a tie in the vote of the council.

City Clerk

The clerk acts as secretary for the city council. He keeps minutes of the meetings, a record of the ordinances passed, and all other papers pertaining to the council's business. He likewise acts as the city auditor. You will recall that the county auditor is the official clerk of the Board of County Commissioners and presents claims for payment to the board for approval. A similar procedure is used in cities in that whenever the city owes money to someone for services or for materials purchased, the city clerk presents a bill to the city council. If the council approves the bill, the clerk makes out a warrant in payment, which is honored by the city treasurer.

The only exception to this procedure is that the 1967 legislature established the office of budget director for cities of over 300,000. He is appointed by the mayor outside civil service rules and is subject to confirmation by a majority of the members of the city council. The city budget director prepares the budget for the approval of the city legislative body.

In addition to secretarial and fiscal duries, the city clerk acts as the registrar of voters for his city. We have mentioned that the county auditor is the registrar of voters for all election precincts outside of incorporated cities. In an incorporated city, the city clerk keeps the registration books, and each voter must be properly registered before he can vote. The city clerk also issues any licenses granted by the city council. All of these duties parallel those of the county auditor for his county.

City Treasurer

Second-, third-, and fourth-class cities have in the past elected a treasurer for each city and may still do so. However, the 1969 legislature provided that the city council of third-class cities may allow the city treasurer to be appointed rather than elected. If it decides to make the office appointive, the mayor, with the approval of the council, makes the appointment. We have noted that the offices of treasurer and clerk may be combined in third-class cities.

The city treasurer has charge of all money collected by the city. We have mentioned that the county treasurer turns over to the city treasurers once each month the city's share of the taxes collected. In addition to this money, there are fees collected for the various city licenses, water payments, fines from the police court, assessments for street paving, and payments made for other city services. When the city treasurer receives warrants from the city clerk or other authorized officials, he pays them from the city treasury. He keeps an accurate account of the money received and disbursed and makes a financial report each month to the city council.

City Police Court

It was pointed out in chapter 5 that the city police courts in all cities under 500,000 population are presided over by justices of the peace, who are elected by the voters in second-class cities and in those having a commission form of government. In other cities, they are appointed by the mayor or city manager. In cities of 500,000 the city police judge is called judge of the municipal court and is elected by the people. A vacancy in the office of municipal judge is filled by the mayor, subject to confirmation by the city's legislative body. If the city council creates the office of city attorney, the mayor appoints him. The methods of choosing the chief of police or marshal, as he is called in four-class cities, have been described above.

The city police court is established primarily to deal with violations of city ordinances. The court may impose fines up to $300 in first-class cities and up to $100 in the other classes of cities. The police court may also inflict jail sentences up to ninety days in first-class cities and up to thirty days in the other classes.

The violations appearing most often before our police courts are traffic violations, drunken or disorderly conduct, and other disturbances threatening the safety of individuals or the peace and quiet of a neighborhood. Civil suits not covered by a city ordinance are tried by the police court only if they are brought on a *change of venue*[1] from some other court of a justice of the peace. Any decision of the police court judge may be appealed to the superior court if one of the parties to the suit so wishes. The judge makes the decisions himself in all cases involving violation of city ordinances, since no jury is allowed in such trials.

The chief of police in second- and third-class cities and the marshal in

1. A court order allowing a case to be moved from a court in one locality to a similar court elsewhere because of probable prejudice or high feeling against the defendant in the first area.

fourth-class cities correspond to the county sheriff. They have the power to serve all warrants of arrest issued to them by the police judge, and they can arrest any person caught in the violation of a city ordinance or for any public offense. They do not serve papers for civil cases except ones specifically provided for by law.

City Attorney

The city attorney corresponds to the county prosecuting attorney. He advises the city officials on legal matters and represents the city in police court. He prosecutes all violations of city ordinances. In fourth-class cities, if there is no city attorney provided for by ordinance, the marshal performs the duties of the city attorney. City attorneys in third-class cities are appointed by the mayor. The marshal is ex officio tax and license collector.

Optional Offices

In addition to these city officials, a street commissioner is appointed by the mayor in second-class cities. His duty is to supervise the maintenance of city streets. Also, in second- and third-class cities, if a public library is established, there must be five trustees appointed to manage it. If third-class cities maintain a public park, three commissioners must be appointed to take charge of it. Other city offices are left to the discretion of the city council.

A city engineer, harbor master, poundkeeper, city jailer, chief of the fire department, street superintendent, and health officer are mentioned in our state laws as approved city offices if the city council wishes to create them. The councilmen are not limited to these, however. They may establish any city office deemed necessary to carry on the work of a city.

COMMISSION FORM OF GOVERNMENT

The commission form of city government operates in a similar manner to the mayor-council type just discussed. The state legislature feels, however, that it is not suitable for very small towns and has limited its use to cities whose population is over 2,000. The maximum population limit for the commission form is 30,000. However, this figure would represent a first-class city, which could choose its own form of commission government if it wished.

Under a commission form of city government, a mayor, a commissioner of finance and accounting, and a commissioner of streets and public improvements are elected every three years. The mayor acts as the head of the department of public safety. These officials form the city commission, which passes all ordinances and administers the city's business in the same manner as the city council in the mayor-council type of government. The mayor acts as president of the commission, but he has no veto power, and the vote of two members of the commission is sufficient to pass an ordinance. The commission appoints all other members of the city government except the police judge, who is elected.

Initiative and Referendum Procedure

The voters of the city can propose ordinances or repeal ones already passed through a system of city initiative and referendum. Under a commission form of government, if a group of voters within the city believe that a certain ordinance should be passed, they sign a petition, which may include a request that the matter be submitted to the city voters if the commission does not pass it. The petition must be signed by 25 percent of the people who voted for all mayor candidates in the last city election. The city commission considers the petition, and if it does not pass, the commission calls a special election, unless a general election will occur within ninety days. At this election, the city electors vote on the proposed ordinance, and a simple majority decides the issue. An ordinance passed in this manner cannot be repealed or amended except by a similar vote of the people.

Any ordinance passed by the commission does not go into effect for thirty days unless it involves the immediate preservation of the public peace, health, or safety. The period of thirty days is provided so that the voters will have an opportunity to repeal the ordinance if they wish to. The procedure for the referendum is similar to that for the initiative. A petition for repeal signed by at least 25 percent of the voters in the last city election must be presented to the commission within thirty days after the ordinance is passed. If the commission does not repeal the ordinance, it must present the matter to the people in an election and let them decide whether or not the ordinance shall be put into effect.

COUNCIL-MANAGER FORM OF GOVERNMENT

In the council-manager type of municipal government, a council is elected, the number of councilmen depending on the size of the city. One of 2,000 or fewer inhabitants elects five council members; one over 2,000 residents elects seven council members. The term of office for all councilmen is four years, and vacancies between elections are filled by the remaining councilmen. As is true for the commission type of government, the legislature specifies 30,000 population as the maximum for the council-manager form, but a city of that size is a first-class city and may choose its own version of a council-manager type if it wishes.

The council chooses a chairman from its members, who serves as mayor. His duties in this capacity are simply to preside at council meetings and represent the city for ceremonial purposes. In a public emergency the council may place him in charge of the police, responsible for maintaining law and order. The council passes ordinances for the city and appoints a city manager, who is the chief executive and administrative officer for the city. The council may remove a manager by majority vote.

The 1965 legislature listed the powers and duties of a city manager as follows: to have general supervision over the administration of city affairs; to appoint and remove at any time all department heads and employees except members of the council unless the council requires the mayor to appoint advisory boards, including the city planning commission. The manager is required to attend all meetings of the council and to see that their ordinances are faithfully executed. He is to recommend to the council measures for adoption and to keep the council advised of the financial condition of the city. Part of his financial duties consists in making a tentative budget for the approval of the council.

CODE CITY GOVERNMENT

Any city with at least 3,000 inhabitants may adopt the most recent type of city government specified by the legislature—that of a code city.

The procedure for organizing in this fashion is similar to that for choosing another kind of city government. A petition for the code city form must be signed by 10 percent of the voters, based on the votes cast in the last general state election in the proposed area. The county auditor verifies the boundary description, the number of signatures, and the number of inhabitants and transmits the petition, if it is valid, to the county commissioners who hold a hearing, after a proper publication notice. If they approve the proposal, they establish the boundaries and call for an election at which the people vote on the establishment of that type of government and also choose the officers for the proposed government.[2] A majority vote is sufficient to validate the change of government. If a city already has a home-rule charter, the percentage of the voters signing the petition has to be 10 percent, like that of the others, but if 50 percent sign the petition, the city's legislative body then announces, without an election, that the change to a charter code city has been made, subject to referendum.

The main feature of the code type of city government is that classes of cities are eliminated. There are still variations in procedures between small

2. The candidates are required to file the usual declarations of candidacy.

and large cities, such as that mentioned above for a petition in a city large enough to have a home-rule charter. However, in the main, the regulations are the same for all of the cities within a certain type of government: mayor-council, commission, or council-manager. Code cities may provide for initiative and referendum procedures, and elective officials may be recalled. If there is a planning board, a board of adjustment must be created to hear appeals. From it, such appeals go to the superior court.

Mayor-Council Type of Government for Code Cities

The mayor-council noncharter code cities having fewer than 2,500 inhabitants have five members in the council, elected on a nonpartisan basis; cities with more than 2,500 population have seven. Charter code cities may have any uneven number in the council not to exceed eleven. The mayor is elected in both types. A city clerk and chief law enforcement officer are required and are appointed by the council. Legal counsel may be secured either by appointment of a part-time or full-time city attorney or by contract for particular tasks. The council sets the salaries of all city officials with the exception of the appointed police judge or municipal judge, whose compensation must be within the limits set by the legislature. The mayor and councilmen serve for four-year terms and are elected from the city at large unless the legislative body provides for election by wards. If there is a vacancy in the office of mayor or city council, the remaining council members make the appointment. If they fail to do so for thirty days, the mayor makes the appointment.

The mayor appoints and may remove any of the appointive officers and employees subject to any applicable civil service regulations, except that an appointive police judge or municipal judge may be removed only on conviction of misconduct or for mentally or physically incapacitating disability. If qualifications for appointive offices have not been established by ordinance or charter, the council may pass upon the appointments by the mayor.

The mayor is the chief executive and administrative officer. He sees that the laws are enforced, supervises the city administration, approves the bonds given by city officials, brings legal proceedings to force the fulfillment of contracts with the approval of the council, presides at council meetings (but has a vote only in case of a tie), and vetos ordinances passed by the council, although a majority plus one of the council may override his veto.

Commission Type of Government for Code Cities

The 1967 legislature made no changes for charter and noncharter code cities from the earlier form established for the commission type of city government. For the details of its operation, see the section on commission form of city government.

Council-Manager Type of Government for Code Cities

In the council-manager type of government for code cities, the councilmen are the only elective officials (nonpartisan) in a city unless an elective police judge is required by law for its particular size. The council then appoints a city manager, who is the chief executive officer and head of the administrative branch of the city government. In cities smaller than 2,500 inhabitants, the council consists of five members; in larger cities, there are seven. In charter code cities, there may be an uneven number of councilmen, not to exceed eleven. The provisions in regard to term of office, filling of vacancies, and so forth are the same as those for the mayor-council form of government described above.

At the first meeting after biennial elections, the council chooses a mayor from its members. He presides at council meetings, but retains his right to vote as a council member. He is also recognized as the head for ceremonial purposes and by the governor in case of declaration of martial law. He has no regular administrative duties except that in the case of such an emergency, he commands the police and enforces order whether or not the governor has declared martial law.

The council may create whatever departments and jobs it wishes, but the appointive officers must include a city clerk and chief of police or other law enforcement officer. The city manager may dismiss any appointees, subject to civil service provisions, except the municipal judge, and there is no appeal from the city manager's decision. In a noncharter code city, the city manager appoints the municipal judge, who may be called police judge, but he must be a justice of the peace or attorney licensed to practice in Washington.[3] The term for the municipal judge is four years, concurrent with the term of a justice of the peace.

A charter code city may make the office of municipal judge elective, the person to have the same qualifications as those for the noncharter code city. An appointive municipal judge may be removed only on conviction of misconduct or malfeasance or physical or mental disability, as is true for the other types of city government. Any code city of 20,000 or more may provide for the election or appointment of an additional municipal judge, with the purpose of making one judge primarily responsible for traffic violations.

3. Except that in cities under 5,000 population, the council may allow a person to serve who is neither a justice of the peace or a licensed attorney.

Besides his powers as a justice of the peace, which are to prosecute for violation of criminal laws of the state within the city and handle civil cases coming on change of venue from another justice of the peace within the city, the municipal judge has exclusive jurisdiction over offenses against city ordinances. He has the power to issue all warrants and process necessary. No jury is allowed for trials in his court, but the parties may appeal to the superior court.

The clerk or comptroller of each code city is designated as registrar of voters except for the one in the county seat, where the county auditor has his office.

POWERS OF A CITY

The mayor and the council members, or the commissioners, form the governing body of the city. They have the same type of ordinance-making power for their city that the county commissioners have for their county, and the city commissioners, like the county commissioners, have executive as well as legislative powers. In the mayor-council and council-manager forms, however, the mayor and the manager, respectively, act as the executive for the city. The mayor has actual veto power over ordinances passed by the city council in noncharter cities, but the manager does not.

It is interesting to note the shift in the placing of executive responsibility in the evolution of our city government throughout the country. The mayor-council form was generally in use before 1900, but during that time the mayor had very little power. He was a kind of figurehead to represent the city at festivals, official dinners, and similar functions. The council was also very large, often over one hundred, sometimes divided into two houses in imitation of Congress and state legislatures. The administrative officials were either chosen by the council or appointed by some kind of board so that the mayor had very little control over them. The council was too large to act effectively as the city's executive. As a result, city governments in many places became very corrupt, and people demanded a reform. Consequently, the mayor was given veto power and the right to appoint the city's employees who were not elected by the voters. The size of the council was reduced to a workable figure. This change represented the turning from a *weak mayor* to a *strong mayor* type of city government.

People found this arrangement much more satisfactory, but there continued to be a demand for greater centralization of authority so that one person could be held responsible for a specific phase of a city's needs. This movement led to the establishment of a commission form of government in which even fewer city legislators were elected and each one was responsible for certain functions. In our state this is exemplified by the titles of our three commissioners—commissioner of public safety, commissioner of finance and accounting, and commissioner of streets and public improvements.

Under this system, the mayor's powers were again weakened so that before long citizens were urging again the creation of some kind of strong city executive. This time, the proposal was to elect a council (or commission) as usual, but then to allow the city to appoint a *manager,* who would be trained in problems of city administration, to act as an executive for the city. The council would then set policies and control the one who was to put them into effect, since he would be responsible to the group as an appointee rather than to the voters as an elective official. The city-manager plan, or council-manager, as it is called by our legislature, is considered by most students of government at the present time to have the best possibilities for an efficient city government. The success of any system depends, however, on the voters' care in electing their officials and in studying the problems of their governmental units.

In order that a city may transact its business, the state legislature has included cities specifically in the list of municipal corporations with the same powers as those given to counties as municipal corporations. A city can sue and be sued. It can buy, sell, or lease property and do all the other acts necessary for the management of the city's property and money.

Specific powers of cities to provide services are mentioned in the state laws. For example, a city has the right of eminent domain, by which it can take private property for city purposes through ordinary court procedure and after paying fair compensation. When a city or other government unit uses the right of eminent domain, it is said to "condemn" the property it takes. If the city government decides that a business or residential area is the best site for a public playground, swimming pool, or other city project, it can bring a suit in the county superior court to acquire the property (if the owners are unwilling to sell). The judge holds hearings, and, unless there is some reason for denying the city's request, he appoints appraisers to determine the value of the property so that the city will pay the owners the amount stipulated.

The city can punish violation of ordinances by fines and certain imprisonments. A city may license hotels, shows, taverns, saloons, dance halls, and other places of entertainment in order to maintain good order. It may also license various kinds of business firms as a means of producing revenue. It may establish a city police system and regulate liquor traffic. A city may control the speed of vehicles within its limits except for state arterials and provide off-street parking. It may establish and regulate a pedestrian mall in the city and forbid cars to enter. A city that has an airport may vest authority for its construction and operation in a city board already in existence or in a municipal airport commission to consist of at least five resident taxpayers to be appointed by the city's governing body. A city may maintain a fire department, a system for sewage disposal, parks, and libraries. It may establish a board to health and hospitals. It may abate nuisances and control certain trades—slaughterhouses, laundries, and so on. It may provide a city water supply and a system of street cleaning. It may maintain a stockpound and keeper for stray animals. It may build bridges and wharves; it may build and improve streets and sidewalks, although property owners along such streets pay assessments to cover part of the cost. The council or commission sets the amount of salary to be received by all city officials and employees within limits set by law. Such powers are the ones listed, for the most part, for second-class cities, but, in general, the same ones apply to cities of all classes.

If commercial ambulance service is not easily available to third-class cities, they may provide such services either directly or by contract with another municipal corporation. One specific authorization for fourth-class towns is that they may provide off-street parking and may acquire property for this purpose.

In the preceding chapter on county government, it was pointed out that the problems of preventing the deterioration of living conditions in the heart of a big city is a very grave one and that one solution proposes combining county and city government in metropolitan areas. Planning groups, on a combined county–city level, like the voluntary one mentioned in connection with the Puget Sound counties and cities and like various official ones created by the legislature from time to time, have the purpose of analyzing such problems. They try to foresee which programs will tend to eliminate unemployment, control pollution of the environment and provide comfortable and attractive housing, recreational areas, and health facilities for the "inner city" areas that are losing their more affluent residents to the suburbs. The Association of Washington Cities is one organization sponsoring such studies.

In the preceding chapter, it was mentioned that the recent allocation by Congress of federal funds directly to cities and counties, without the intermediate step of distribution to local government units by a state agency, is an attempt to encourage local officials and citizen groups to provide solutions to these problems. The cities' share of the federal funds goes to them individually and is not controlled by the county in which the city is situated.

DISINCORPORATION PROCEDURE

Sometimes the population of a town may decline until the residents find it difficult to maintain their city government. Moreover, even though the population of a small town may remain constant, the people may decide that the advantages of a city government are not worth the expense and trouble in that particular town. The state legislature has provided a means for such towns to dissolve their incorporation. Any city of the third or fourth class having a population of less than 4,000 may disband its city government.

The procedure is that a majority of the registered voters of the city present a petition for disincorporation to the city council. A special election is held, and if the majority favor dissolving the corporation, the city government then ceases to function. The town remains unincorporated until it votes to become incorporated again. The county is the local unit of government for unincorporated towns.

Sometimes a small incorporated town may dwindle in population, or interest in local government may lag until elections are not held. If this happens for two successive years, or if the city officials fail to qualify for office for two successive years, the town may be disincorporated without an election. The procedure is that the Division of Municipal Corporations of the state auditor's office petitions the superior court in the county where the town is located to issue an order disincorporating the town, and the superior court sets the date for a hearing on the question. Any property owner or qualified voter of the town may appear at the hearing and file a written objection to the granting of the petition. If it appears to the court that the city government has not functioned for two successive years, it orders the town disincorporated.

SUGGESTED READINGS

In addition to the *Session Laws* and other official documents mentioned in preceding chapters, there are various reports available on cities in our state. For example, the secretary of state, Olympia, issues a publication called *Officials of Washington Cities,* and the current edition may be secured upon request from his office. The Association of Washington Cities, whose headquarters are at the University of Washington, Seattle, 98105, publishes various bulletins that give data on activities and problems of cities in general.

The Research Council's *Handbook,* published by the Washington State Research Council in Olympia and referred to in connection with sources for material on county government, is very helpful, too, for questions on city government.

Often the League of Women Voters or other civic organizations publish surveys of local communities, which ordinarily include a study of the city council.

If the summary of the proceedings of the local city council is followed in the town's newspaper over a period of time, a clearer picture of the type of city organization present and the problems facing it may be attained.

Index

Absentee voting, 242, 247
Accountancy, Board of, 125, 137
Accounts: licensing of, 125
Adams County: justices of the peace in, 213; in appeals court district, 220; classification of, 260
Adjutant general, 128
Administration, State Department of General. *See* General Administration, State Department of
Administration, state director of general, 104, 129
Administrative Board, State, 134-35, 137
Administrative branch: definition of, 27, 29; composition and function of, 70-135
Administrative code, 71
Administrator, court, 212, 230
Administrator for interstate rendition compact, 35
Administrators (of estates). *See* Probate cases
Aeronautics Commission, Washington State, 122, 137
Aging, Washington State Council on, 107, 137
Agricultural experts, county: appointment of, 80-81, 262; creation of office, 261; function of, 277
Agricultural Extension Service: aid to farmers by, 63, 80-81, 277
Agricultural lands (state), 55-56, 62-63, 94
Agriculture: regulations concerning, 72; conservation in, 72-81

Agriculture, State Department of: function of, 72-81, 277; sanitation program, 102
Agriculture, state director of: powers and duties of, 73, 76-79; part in pollution control, 77, 85; member of Administrative Board, 134; how chosen, 136; appointments by, 278
Agriculture, U. S. Department of, 73, 74, 77
Agriculture, U. S. secretary of, 62
Agriculture Experiment Station, State, 72
Air: pollution of, 72, 81, 86-87, 268, 280
Air Pollution Control Authority, Board of Directors of County, 200, 280
Air Pollution Control Board: abolished, 81; history of, 85
Air Quality Section, 61
Alabama: governmental procedures in, 38
Alaska, 30
Alcoholism: program to counteract, 102
Aliens: regulations concerning, 22
Aluminum reduction plants: control of pollution from, 85
Amendments, state constitution: part of secretary of state in, 43; abolishment of office of county superintendent of schools, 53, 252; power to amend initiatives, 191; removal of maximum salary restriction, 205; proposed, 206-7; affecting jurisdiction of courts, 211; woman suffrage, 234-35; voting

205, 221; of city officials, 214; of county officials, 218, 221, 224-25, 262

Salaries, Governor's Advisory Committee on, 182

Salmon: conservation of, 88-92

Sanitarians, Washington State Board of Registered, 126, 183

Sanitation requirements: for processing plants, 78; for bedding, 103

San Juan County: taxes in, 131; justices of the peace in, 213; superior court judges in, 217; in appeals court district, 219; classification of, 261, 262

School District Directors, Board of: primary election regulations for, 42; connection with Board of Education, 52-53; nonpartisan, 238, 241; function of, 281-85

School District Organization, County Committee on, 83, 284

School districts, intermediate, 52-53, 281-83

School districts, organization of: local, 52-53; youth programs in, 95; aid to recreation in, 96; prosecuting attorney as court defender of, 225; elections in, 242, 244; organization of, 283-85

School Emergency Construction Commission, 116, 183

School for the blind, 107

School for the deaf, 107

School Land Commission, State, 25

School lands: control of, 16, 54; constitutional convention debate on, 22-23

Schools: in Washington Territory, 8-9, 12; land grants for, 16, 52; role of superintendent of public instruction in public, 50-54; relationship of State Board of Education to, 51-52; taxes for, 52, 274; youth camps for, 94; aid from U. S. Forest Service to, 266; local organization of, 281-85

Sciences, Examining Committee in Basic, 126, 183

Scotland, 17

Seal: state, 40, 41; court, 224

Sealer of weights and measures, state, 25, 79

Search warrants, 88, 90

Seattle, Wash.: historic sites in, 94, central area in, 101; Fircrest School in, 107; Skid Road projects, 112; federal district court in, 188; court of appeals division in, 219; court case on voting eligibility in, 235; use of blanket primary in, 238; proposed county-city government for, 286-88

Seattle *Post-Intelligencer,* 20

Secretary of senate, 208

Secretary of state: how chosen, 27; executive official, 27-28; emergency order filed with, 33; general powers and duties, 35, 41-43, 208; as successor to governor, 39, 40; recording of state documents, 41-42; duties relating to elections, 42-43, 236-37, 242; early role as insurance commissioner, 65; to be on proposed Reapportionment Commission, 194; role in procedures for initiatives, referenda, and recall, 249-51; procedures for *Voters' Pamphlets* of, 251-52; keeps lists of corporations, 273

Secretary of Washington Territory, 5-6, 9

Sedro Wooley, Wash., 106

Seed Potato Commission, Washington State, 80, 178

Seeds: regulations for sale of, 72-73, 76

Segregation: court decisions on, 15

Selah, Wash., 107

Selective logging, 58-59

Senate (state): size of, 19; confirmation of governor's appointments, 70, 73, 81, 88, 98, 124, 125, 128, 129, 130, 134; apportionment of, 188-95; organization of, 207-8; tries impeachment charges, 222

Senate (U. S.): approves appointment of territorial officials, 5; size of, 188

Senators (state): on Oceanographic Commission, 95; constituency of, 188-89; term of office, 206; part in legislative removal, 223; election for, 242-43

Senators (U. S.): seating of, 14-15; vacancies of office of, 32; constituency of, 188-89; declarations of candidacy for, 237; statements in *Candidates' Pamphlets* by, 242

Sequim Bay State Park, 94

Sergeant-at-arms (state legislature), 208